The Ralph Engel Collection
bequeathed by
Ralph Engel, Professor of English
Scholars Program
1969 - 1975

MARCEL PROUST

Reviews and Estimates in English

MARCEL PROUST

Reviews and Estimates in English

Compiled by

GLADYS DUDLEY LINDNER

STANFORD UNIVERSITY PRESS
Stanford University, California

STANFORD UNIVERSITY PRESS
STANFORD UNIVERSITY, CALIFORNIA

THE BAKER AND TAYLOR COMPANY
55 FIFTH AVENUE, NEW YORK

PRINTED AND BOUND IN THE UNITED STATES
OF AMERICA BY STANFORD UNIVERSITY PRESS

Lovingly dedicated
to
CLARENCE RICHARD LINDNER
with gratitude for
his rare understanding
and faith

FOREWORD

A NEW BOOK on Marcel Proust may seem at first, in these troubled times of ours, an altogether useless and untimely venture. The artificial, strange world depicted in Proust's works has been forever swept away in the tidal wave of the French disaster. Further, the delicate shades of emotion, the pointed subtleties of thought which he analyzed with delightful cleverness seem to have been all but crushed out of existence under the impact of the tremendous brute forces which are, even now, pounding at our once familiar, human universe with cataclysmal violence.

Yet, out of the modern chaos, a new universe will undoubtedly, some day, come into being. We are all trying anxiously to discern in the midst of today's ephemeral, confused shapes the first clear delineation of what will be the world of tomorrow. Will that world be a cold, efficient, soulless machine? Will it be able to retain some of the charm, some of the rare spiritual qualities which, in spite of countless absurdities and injustices, formed in the world of yesterday a priceless hidden treasure? The answer will depend, to a very large extent, upon our own attitude. If we can keep and transmit intact the best of what the past centuries had to offer, we may hope to see, instead of a superorganization of robots, the unfolding of a rich, powerful, and truly human harmony.

Viewed in this light, Mrs. Lindner's book assumes a more than ordinary importance. Proust evidently appeared to his generation as having something of permanent value to offer. The modern Anglo-Saxon world, in particular, in the higher aspects of its literature and art, has been profoundly affected by his influence. Yet certain elements of Proust's thought are not easily assimilable, either in England or in America, by an average cultivated mind. For a quarter of a century, critics have endeavored to bring within the reach of the Anglo-Saxon reader what he can effectively absorb of the multifarious, provocative suggestions of the great French novelist.

Mrs. Lindner presents in her book a striking and remarkably intelligent picture of these endeavors. She has chosen with great skill and tact the most illustrative and at the same time the most penetrating criticism of Proust published in the English-speaking countries during the last twenty-five years. That she left out entirely the otherwise not negligible German critics calls for no apology in view of her set program and purpose.

The program of her book is twofold. On the one hand, she enables us to follow step by step, as it were, the slow but definite progress made in this country since 1922 in the ever deeper understanding of the intricacies of Proust's thought. On the other hand, we find ourselves thus insensibly initiated—better than by any single study, however scholarly and complete—into the unbelievably complex and rich contribution that Proust was able to make to our culture.

Maurice Barrès, though himself one of the most perspicacious among Proust's early acquaintances, once confessed that when he first met "le petit Marcel" he could see in him nothing but a "gentil compagnon." Yet, a few years later, the epochmaking development of Proust's work revealed beyond dispute to Maurice Barrès, and to all, that Marcel was one of the intellectual giants of our age. Similarly, whatever may be our firsthand knowledge of *A la Recherche du Temps perdu,* Mrs. Lindner's book will help us to realize that Proust had still more facets to his personality than we probably ever suspected and, above all, that he had for his time, perhaps for all times, a truly portentous message.

Georges Lemaitre

Stanford University, California

COMPILER'S PREFACE

In a truly Proustian way did my interest in Proust begin—through insomnia. A physician had told me how to ease my wakeful hours; not to worry if I could not sleep, he said, but to do some constructive work or engage in an absorbing study. The quiet of the deep night was conducive to contemplative reading. But I found that books were ending by the time I had become most deeply engrossed. A dear friend was inspired. He gave me *Remembrance of Things Past* in Scott-Moncrieff's marvelous translation. "This," he said, "will put off the ending for a long, long time." It did! For five years. Not really; for the end is not yet. I have read, and I am rereading, and always something new comes forth.

I was enchanted from the very beginning. Not tedious to me were the famous pages on sleep; from my own experience I knew what Proust was writing about. And almost immediately I discovered that quality which E. M. Forster celebrates: "how amazingly does Proust describe not only the working of his characters, but the personal equipment of the reader, so that he keeps stopping with a gasp to say 'Oh, how did he find that out about me. I didn't even know it myself until he informed me, but it is so.' "

Clive Bell exposes the prime weakness of the Proustian: "Have I friend or acquaintance whom I have not implicated in long, presumably tedious conversations about Proust and his ways?" And I? How many must I have bored that way, those especially to whom the name meant little.

I have made some converts, too—a mutual pleasure. Witness the plight of Mr. Aldous Huxley, who for some twenty minutes listened so attentively to my rhapsody of *Remembrance*. Hours later, to my real distress, I recalled that in his novel, *Eyeless in Gaza,* he had written vitriolically of Proust and in my rage I had thrown his book into a corner. When, contritely, I told all this to Mr. W. R. Hearst, he smiled and said: "You were fortunate to find in Mr. Huxley an intellectual gentleman who permitted you to differ from his opinion."

When I was not reading Proust, I wanted to read about him. I collected everything I could find. And then I decided to put together, in one book, such of those things said of his work as might show the reaction it occasioned on minds in England and the United States. For it seemed to me that there could be few bookshelves that did not have room for one thin volume of all that the Anglo-American critics had said about Proust. That was a naïve notion. What promised, at first, to be the "all" for that "thin" volume grew to be a long shelf's worth in itself. So, to meet the limitations of a reasonable book, I have been forced to condense, or rather to extract, most of the essays brought together here. So much that might interest the true Proustian could not be included. But my bibliography will aid toward finding the full texts of the original material. Some may not be available quickly but, given time, booksellers can find them—can even bring them from England in this wartime as they did for me.

I am deeply indebted to many English and American authors and publishers. Regardless of the problems occasioned by the war, those in England have most helpfully responded to my requests for copyright privileges and I have many gracious letters; such as that which Mr. F. L. Lucas wrote to my lawyer: "Tell Mrs. Lindner my fee, if she could send them, would be a couple of destroyers; but as she can not, please ask her to accept the gift as a small token of appreciation of all that your country is doing for mine and for the hard-pressed cause of decency on earth." I note with interest the lawyer's reply to this amazing letter: "Fortunately the President announced, as your letter arrived, the transfer of an additional twenty destroyers to Britain. Some anthropomorphic god must have been looking over your shoulder as you granted Mrs. Lindner's request."

To Georges E. Lemaitre, well-recognized authority on Proust and French literature generally, I am deeply grateful, for his introduction to this volume and for his many kindnesses during its preparation.

I have felt that Proust and his critics foresaw the conditions now existing in France; but I cannot subscribe to the statement made by the poet Alfred Noyes, who said of the fall of France that Marcel Proust was "enough in himself to cause it."

Marcel Proust! Even in the name there is music. And, as I read again and again, I am as Swann listening to the music of Vinteuil—each time familiar, each time a new experience, each time a little more understanding of the symphony entitled *Remembrance of Things Past.*

G. D. L.

CONTENTS

Contents

Contents

MARCEL PROUST

Reviews and Estimates in English

1. *M. Marcel Proust—A New Sensibility**

J. Middleton Murry

The most apparent phases in the evolution of literature are marked by a twofold change—in the intelligence and in the sensibility that find expression in it. The writers of a new period seem to know and to feel more than the writers of the period before them; and these separate developments are bound together in the mesh of a continual interaction. They feel more because they know more. A man who has absorbed the aimless principle of Natural Selection develops a new nerve of sensibility which perceives, isolates, and emphasises the aimless quality in all experience. Similarly, a man who has assimilated the Freudian psychology will respond with a new awareness to every manifestation of the sex impulse in the life before his eyes. Every atom of new knowledge that is really apprehended and digested by the mind serves, if not positively to enlarge, at least to rearrange the mechanism of the sensibility . . . .

But these precisely epoch-making changes in the intelligence and the sensibility, though they mark the historical advance of

* *Quarterly Review,* July 1922.

one period upon another, and serve to distinguish phases of the general consciousness and of the literature in which the general consciousness is reflected, do not necessarily mark an advance in the quality of the literature itself. The changed sensibility will respond to many elements in experience which have hitherto passed unnoticed; it will emphasise, and may easily overemphasise them. It will be induced to fasten upon a new truth of fact—as, for example, the ubiquity of the sex impulse under the strangest disguises—and to neglect old truths of fact which are not less true because they are familiar—as, for example, that the disguises which the sex impulse is compelled to assume are one of the essentials of civilisation. So that when we leave the historical or evolutionary aspect of literature for literature itself, the significance of a change in the general intelligence and sensibility becomes dependent upon the degree of comprehensiveness that has been reached after the change. An extension of the sensibility has in itself no literary value; and, even when the alchemy of art has intervened, the complete expression of a new emotion will be far less significant than the complete expression of a comprehensive attitude to life, into which the new perceptions have been absorbed. . . . .

Whatever may have been our final judgment on the strange novel of M. Marcel Proust . . . . the persistent element in all our changing opinions was that it marked the arrival of a new sensibility. We were being made aware in new ways, induced to perceive existence in new relations. We seemed to be drawn by a strong and novel enchantment to follow the writer down the long and misty avenues of his consciousness to the discovery of a forgotten childhood. And it was not as though his compelling us to enter into and share the process of his self-exploration was accidental; it was most deliberate. Whatever might be his underlying purpose, M. Proust was not in the least like an artist who in making a sketch should leave all his tentative and abandoned lines upon the paper. . . . .

It is better to admit that on a canvas so large a strict subordination of every part to the literary purpose of the whole is not to be expected. We are conscious that a single sensibility pervades all the parts, even though the power of projecting it so completely as in the episodes of the musical evening and the death of the grandmother is intermittent. And this sensibility is our chief concern. The underlying motive which animates, or the law which governs it, is that which appears so plainly in the first volume—the dependence of memory and mental life as a whole upon association. . . . . This psychological fact at once governs the conduct of the narrative itself, in so far as it is presented in terms of a single consciousness, and determines the conduct of various characters who appear in it. More than this, the act of penetrating through some present circumstance to a fragment of past experience, which it seems to hold strangely concealed behind it, is represented as a consummation of personality. To enter into complete possession of the past by means of such circumstances is to possess oneself wholly; they are, as M. Proust says, the door that opens upon "la vraie vie." This conviction of the writer can be interpreted in two ways, according as we regard the whole narrative as the history of the consciousness of a writer or as the development of an extreme but none the less typical modern mind. In one of the few indications of his own plan, M. Proust seems to declare that his aim is to describe the evolution of a literary sensibility. . . . .

The description of his vain endeavour to seize the significance of three strange-familiar trees seen while driving in Mme. de Villeparisis' carriage at Balbec suggests a larger scope to this activity of the mind . . . .

It suggests that at the end we shall find the writer, deliberately and with all the resources of his will, concentrating upon that very sensation of reminiscence, the *malaise* at night in bed, with which *A la Recherche du Temps Perdu* opens. Such a doubling of the consciousness upon itself would make a fittingly subtle finale to the subtlest of all psychological fictions, and present us at the last with a book which would be in essentials the story of its own creation. But for the moment it is sufficient to regard the writer's conviction of the supreme importance of these acts of penetration as dictated by the knowledge of his own vocation, as a declaration that the "vraie vie" is that to which the writer has access, and rather as a deliberate placing of the literary consciousness at the summit of the mental hierarchy than an assertion that complete possession of the self by this means is the highest moral end, the most perfect *ascesis,* for all human beings.

What M. Proust undoubtedly does, however, is to represent this process of association as dominant in the mental lives of all men who can be said to live at all. A writer's exclusive preoccupation with it is only a completer realisation of a tendency which distinguishes the higher grades of consciousness. It determines, for instance, Swann's attitude to Odette, and his decision to marry her really rests upon it. In more general terms, M. Proust regards the life of man as a perpetual effort to penetrate an unknown—the mind of the woman he loves, the friend he admires, the society with which he is acquainted. This desire is, indeed, the very condition of love. . . . . But this desire to penetrate the unknown of others is never satisfied. . . . . This recurrent theme of perpetual disillusion, of impotent encounter with the unknown, may be called the philosophical background of the book; and from this angle we might regard it as a philosophical justification of the art of writing, presented through the history of a consciousness. For, as the growing man turns away from the continual disillusion which is the only result of his attempt to penetrate the reality beyond himself, he more clearly sees that the only reality he can hope to master is his own experience. . . . .

This concealed motive it is which differentiates M. Proust's book from all that have gone before. The metaphysician might call it the history of a solipsist. But such a definition would be as misleading as all other attempts to find a philosophical definition for a particular work of literature. For, though M. Proust is in a sense applying a theory to experience, he is doing so by the strikingly novel method of describing the process by which the theory was gradually and inevitably formed in the consciousness which applies it. If, therefore, M. Proust's book ends, as we believe it will end, in its own beginning, ... it will be the first book in the world that has been the psychological history of its own creation, and a philosophical justification of its own necessity. It will belong essentially to a new order of literature. And that is what we already vaguely feel as we read it. It is something more than a book in an unfamiliar language, more than a fiction of greater psychological subtlety than we are accustomed to. For better or worse, it marks the emergence of a new kind, the arrival of a new sensibility.

This is its uncommon significance. To find an approximate parallel in the history of modern literature we should probably have to go back to Rousseau . . . . the only work of literature with which *A la Recherche du Temps Perdu* could profitably be compared is the *Confessions* of Jean-Jacques. There is a real likeness between the driving impulses at work in these books; and a careful comparison might enable us to determine the more important differences between the new sensibility of the 18th, and the new sensibility of the 20th century. At all events a century of science has passed between. M. Proust is not preoccupied with finding God, but with finding "la vraie vie" though a previous quotation shows that, whereas Rousseau always identified them, he sometimes does so. But, more evidently still, a century of psychology, of astronomical physics, of the biology of Natural Selection has intervened. The last shreds of anthropocentrism have been worn away. Where Rousseau felt his own isolation, and was tormented by the discrepancy between his dream and the reality, and could not reconcile himself to his isolation or his torment, M. Proust can reconcile himself. He accepts these conditions; he formulates them as an actual law of human existence; and the acceptance has been incorporated into the very mechanism of his sensibility. He discerns in the world that which he feels in himself; he is a Rousseau to whom all the hidden causes of his perplexity have been made plain.

And the detailed knowledge of a century of science is at his fingers' ends to help him refine and express his sensibility. How many times does he use the simile of a camera to make more apparent the working of two planes of consciousness! . . . .

But, in endeavouring to analyse the singular impression which M. Proust's work makes upon us and to isolate the elements which produce the effect of novelty, in trying to investigate and assess its deeply-rooted originality, we are in danger of neglecting the more immediately accessible qualities of a book which exhibits at least as many beauties as it conceals. . . . .

It is something much more than a dark narrative with frequent gleams of beauty; it is a book with at least one of the qualities of permanence, an animating soul. It is maintained by a high and subtle purpose, informed by a view of life as a whole; and, because this secret fire glows steadily within it, we feel the radiance through the most forbidding pages long before we are able to detect its source. One consequence of this is that, though M. Proust's language is sometimes alembicated to a point of grotesqueness, he has style; we might more exactly apply to him a phrase which he himself has aptly used of a great predecessor, Stendhal, and say that his work has "la grande ossature du style," a thing of infinitely more importance than limpidity or beauty in the detail of expression. M. Proust's style, in this larger meaning, is as new and profoundly original as is the sensibility to which it owes its being.

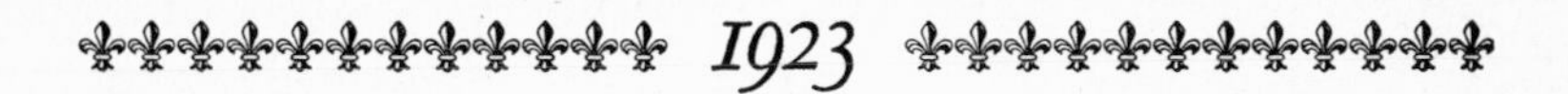

2. *A Portrait**

STEPHEN HUDSON

IN TRYING to represent the personality of . . . . Proust . . . . I find myself driven back to the frequently used but unilluminating word unique for want of a better expression. This uniqueness consisted less, I think, in his obvious possession to an outstanding degree of gifts and charms than in his use of them. Others probably have been and are as wise, witty, cultured, sympathetic, have possessed or possess his conversational powers, his charm of manner, his graciousness. But no one I have ever known combined in his own person so many attractive qualities and could bring them into play so spontaneously. Yet, while his use of these powers resulted in his eliciting the utmost fruitfulness from social inter-

* From *Marcel Proust—An English Tribute,* T. Seltzer, London, 1923.

The death of Marcel Proust in Paris on November 18, 1922, inspired many articles of tribute, notably in England and France. In France, these were collected by the editor of *Nouvelle Revue Française.* In England, C. K. Scott-Moncrieff, translator of all but the last volume of *Remembrance of Things Past,* collected and published twenty critical essays under the title, *Marcel Proust—An English Tribute.*

Where, in the various texts quoted here, the titles of *Remembrance of Things Past* and its component works occur in the original French, I have used Mr. Scott-Moncrieff's English equivalents. The other French passages have been translated for me by Miss Ginevra Weyand.

course, there was an impalpable objectivity about him, an aloofness felt rather than observed. It was as though the personality revealed at the particular moment was but one of many, while the dominant consciousness lay behind them, preserving its complete inviolability. It was, I believe, in the depth and capacity of this ultimate consciousness that his uniqueness lay, as it is there that the source of his creative power and sensibility is to be found.

It seems to me that the essential element of this ultimate ego in Proust was goodness. This goodness had nothing ethical in it, must not be confounded with righteousness; and yet, seeking another word to define its nature, purity is the only one that occurs to me. There was in him the fundamental simplicity which was typified by Dostoevsky in Myshkin, and out of it grew the intellectual integrity which governed and informed his philosophy.

He possessed that rarest gift of touching everyday people, things, and concerns with gold, imparting to them a vital and abiding interest. Anything and everything served as a starting-point, nothing was too minute to kindle idea and provoke suggestive utterance. He could do this because he was himself the most interesting of men, and because Life was one long exciting adventure to him wherein nothing was trivial or negligible. It was not that loving beauty he desired nothing else, and was seeking an aesthetic disguise for the ugly, the sordid, or the base. On the contrary, he recognised that these also are of the stuff of which humanity is made, and that truth and beauty are as often as not masked by their opposites. In him extremes were not only reconciled but united. Supremely conscious and utterly unegotistical, one may look in vain in his work for a trace of vanity, of self-glorification, or even self-justification. He is intensely concerned with his own consciousness, he is never concerned with himself. I can think of no conversation in any of his books in which he takes other than a minor part, and of very few in which he takes any part at all. He is wholly taken up with the thing in itself, whatever it may be, regarding his consciousness as an instrument of revelation apart from himself. And as he shows himself in his books, so he was in life.

In reply to a letter in which, expressing my disappointment at not seeing him on a certain occasion, I went on to say that, much as I loved his books, I would rather see and hear him talk than read them, he wrote me:

> Between that which a person says and that which, through meditation, he extracts from the depths where the naked spirit hidden in veils dwells, there is a world of difference. It is true that there are a few individuals who are better than their books, but that is because their books are not *books*. I believe that Ruskin, who now and then spoke sensibly, expressed fairly well a part at least of what I mean. . . . . If you do not read my book, it is not my fault; it is the fault of the book, for if it were really a great book it would immediately bring harmony among scattered spirits and peace to troubled hearts.[1]

His immersion in the subject of conversation or inquiry was complete; nothing else existed until he had got to the bottom of it. But his world was echoless; the voice never repeated itself, and banality could not enter in, because neither formula nor classification existed for him. Just as in his eyes one particular water-lily in the Vivonne was different from any other water-lily, so each fresh experience was an isolated unit complete in itself and unlike all other units in the world of his consciousness. His mind, so far from being overlaid by obliterating layers of experience, was as a virgin soil which by some magic renews itself after each fresh crop has been harvested.

[1] "Entre ce qu'une personne dit et ce qu'elle extrait par la méditation des profondeurs où l'esprit nu gît, couvert de voiles, il y a un monde. Il est vrai qu'il y a des gens supérieurs à leurs livres mais c'est que leurs livres ne sont pas des *Livres*. Il me semble que Ruskin, qui disait de temps en temps des choses sensées, a assez bien exprimé une partie au moins de cela. ... Si vous ne lisez pas mon livre ce n'est pas ma faute; c'est la faute de mon livre, car s'il était vraiment un beau livre il ferait aussitôt l'unité dans les esprits épars et rendrait le calme aux cœurs troubles."

This power of mental renewal pervades and gives a peculiar freshness to all that he has written. It is in essence a youthful quality which was very marked in his personality. He was penetrated with boyish eagerness and curiosity, asked endless questions, wanted always to know more. What had you heard, what did you think, what did you say or do, whatever *it* was and whoever *they* were. And there was no denying him this or anything he wanted; he must always have his way—he always did have it, till the end of his life. And the great comfort to those who loved him is that till the last he was a glorious spoilt child. . . . .

. . . . Céleste, who devoted her life to his service for many years and was with him to the last, ... wrote of him: "Monsieur resembled no one. He was incomparable—composed of two parts—mind and heart—and what heart!"[2]

Knowing the intensity of his interest in and sympathy with humble lives, the suggestion of snobbishness in connexion with such a man is ridiculous. Proust, like all great artists, needed access to all human types. It is one of the drawbacks of our modern civilisation that the opportunities for varied social intercourse are limited and beset with conventional prejudices. No man went further than he did to surmount these. He knew people of the "monde" as he knew others. . . . .

His friends were in fact of all classes, but his friendship was accorded only on his own terms, and a condition of it was the capacity to bear hearing the truth. His friends knew themselves the better for knowing him, for he was impatient of the slightest insincerity or disingenuousness and could not tolerate pretence. Lies tired him. In a letter he alluded thus to one whom we both knew well:

> The thing I hold against him is that he lies. He made my acquaintance thanks to a lie and has hardly stopped since. He always manages

[2] "Monsieur ne ressemblait à personne. C'était un être incomparable—composé de deux choses, intelligence et cœur—et quel cœur!"

to spoil his qualities with these little lies, which he believes add to his assets—little lies, sometimes enormous ones.[3]

Proust's insistence on truthfulness and sincerity caused him more than once to renounce lifelong associations. His sensibility was so delicate that a gesture or a note in the voice revealed to him a motive, perhaps slight and passing, of evasion or pretence. He was exacting about sincerity only. In other respects his tolerance was so wide that a hard truth from his lips, so far from wounding, stimulated. To his friends, he was frankness itself, and spoke his mind without reserve. I once asked him to tell me if there were not someone, some friend of his, to whom I could talk about him. There was so much I wanted to know, and on the all too rare occasions when he was well enough to see me there was never time. In answer to this he wrote me:

> If you want to put a question to someone who understands me, it's quite simple, just ask me. I have no friend who understands me completely . . . . I know all about myself and will gladly tell you all; it is useless therefore to point out to you some ill-informed friend who, through lack of knowledge, would lose his claim to being a friend, if he answered you.[4]

Thus in his words we reach the final conclusion that, even if Proust's friends had the power of expressing all that they feel about him, they would still be "mal-informés" and would have to return to him for that deeper knowledge which only he could impart. As to this, there is his further assurance that his work is the best part of himself. Providentially, he was spared until that work was done and "Fin" on the last page was written by his own hand.

[3] "Ce que je lui reproche, c'est d'être un menteur. Il a fait ma connaissance à la faveur d'un mensonge et depuis n'a guère cessé. Il trouve toujours le moyen de gâter ses qualités par ces petits mensonges qu'il croit l'avantager—tout petits et quelquefois énormes."

[4] "Si vous désirez poser quelque interrogation à une personne qui me comprenne, c'est bien simple, adressez-vous à moi. D'ami qui me connaisse entièrement je n'en ai pas. ... Je sais tout sur moi et vous dirai volontiers tout; il est donc inutile de vous désigner quelque ami mal informé et qui dans la faible mesure de sa compétence cesserait de mériter le nom d'ami s'il vous répondait."

3. *The Prophet of Despair**

Francis Birrell

It is the privilege of those known as the world's greatest artists to create the illusion of dragging the reader through the whole mechanism of life. . . . . Such was . . . . the gift of Shakespeare, ... Balzac, ... [and] Tolstoy, whom Proust in some ways so much resembles. Such is the gift of Proust in his astonishing pseudo-autobiography, *Remembrance of Things Past.*

. . . . Proust was eminently fertile, and, within the limits imposed by his own delicate health, he could go on indefinitely, so profound and so all-embracing was his interest in human beings and human emotions. But he was fertile in a new way. Not for him was the uncritical spate of nineteenth-century verbiage. His intellectual integrity, of which M. C. Dubos has written so well in his *Approximations,* always compelled him to check and ponder every move upon the chessboard of life, every comment on human feelings. For Proust is the latest great prophet of sensibility, and it is bearing this in mind that we can trace the intellectual stock of which he comes. . . . .

The new sentimental movement, developed to such a pitch of perfection by the author of *Clarissa Harlowe,* was one of enormous value to life and art. But inevitably it was pushed much too far, and the novels of the *école larmoyante* are now well-nigh intolerable, even when written by men of genius like Rousseau. . . . .

Rousseau had one great pupil, a great name in the history of the French novel, Stendhal. . . . . Nourished on Shakespeare, Rousseau, and de Tracy, Stendhal became one of the

* From *Marcel Proust—An English Tribute.*

first completely modern men. . . . . Proust is in turn the intellectual child of Stendhal, and has bespattered *Remembrance of Things Past* with expressions of admiration for his master. In truth, he has taken over not only the methods but the philosophy of his teacher. It will be remembered that Stendhal insists in his analysis of *L'Amour-Passion* that crystallisation can only be effected after doubt has been experienced. So, for Proust, love, the *mal sacré* as he calls it, can only be called into being by jealousy, *le plus affreux des supplices.* We want nothing till we have been cheated out of getting it; whence it follows that we can get nothing till we have ceased to want it, and in any case, once obtained, it would *ipso facto* cease to be desirable. Hence Man, ... is doomed by the nature of his being to unsatisfied desire and restless misery, till Proust becomes, as I have called him above, the prophet of despair . . . . happiness in love is by nature impossible, as it demands an impossible spiritual relationship. . . . .

Proust, having . . . . reduced all human society to misery, builds upon the ruins his philosophy of salvation: Only by much suffering shall we enter into the Kingdom of Heaven. . . . .

The enormous wealth of the author's gifts tends to bury the structure under the superb splendour of the ornament. For Proust combines, to a degree never before realised in literature, the qualities of the aesthete and the scientist. It is the quality which first strikes the reader who does not notice, in the aesthetic rapture communicated by perfect style, that all pleasures are made pegs for disillusion. Human beauty, the beauty of buildings, of the sea, of the sky, the beauty of transmitted qualities in families and in the country-side, the beauty of history, of good breeding, of self-assurance—few people have felt these things as Proust. For him the soft place-names of France are implicit with memories too deep for tears.

. . . . pause for a moment to consider one of the most important aspects of Proust's aesthetic impulse, which is expressed in the title *Remembrance of Things Past.* This is more than the expression of a desire to write an autobiography, to recapitulate one's own vanishing experience. It is an endeavour to reconstruct the whole of the past, on which the present is merely a not particularly valuable comment. . . . .

. . . . so wide-minded is this lyric poet who can speak with the voice of Claudel and of Fustel de Coulanges, that he is perhaps the coldest analyst who has ever devoted his attention to fiction. His knife cuts down into the very souls of his patients, as he calls into play all the resources of his wit, animosities, sympathy, and intelligence. He is a master of all the smaller nuances of social relations, of all the half-whispered subterranean emotions that bind Society together while Society barely dreams of their existence.

It is also worth remark that Proust is the first author to treat sexual inversion as a current and ordinary phenomenon, which he describes neither in the vein of tedious panegyric adopted by certain decadent writers, nor yet with the air of a showman displaying to an agitated tourist abysses of unfathomable horror. Treating this important social phenomenon as neither more nor less important than it is, he has derived from it new material for his study of social relations, and has greatly enriched and complicated the texture of his plot. His extreme honesty meets nowhere with more triumphant rewards. It is by the splendid use of so much unusual knowledge that Proust gains his greatest victories as a pure novelist. Royalty, actresses, bourgeois, servants, peasants, men, women, and children—they all have the genuine third dimension and seem to the reader more real than his own friends. . . . . To read *Remembrance of Things Past* is to live in the world, at any rate in Proust's world—a world more sensitive, variegated, and interesting than our own.

. . . . Proust, it seems to me, had the extremely rare faculty of seeing his characters objectively and subjectively at the same moment. He can project himself so far into the mind of the persons he is describing that he seems to know more about them than they can ever know themselves, ... Proust, though the most objective, is also the most personal of writers. As we get accustomed to the long, tortuous sentences, the huge elaboration of conscientious metaphor, the continual refining on what cannot be further refined, we insensibly become listeners to a long and brilliant conversation by the wisest and wittiest of men. For Proust, as much as any man, has grafted the mellowness and also the exacerbation of experience on to the untiring inquisitiveness of youth. . . . .

This is not the moment to pretend to estimate impartially his exact place and achievement in letters. For the present we can only feel his death, almost personally, so much has he woven himself into the hearts of his readers, and apply to him in all sincerity the words Diderot used of his predecessor in time: "The more beautiful a person's soul, the more exquisite and pure his taste, the more he knows nature, the more he loves truth, the more he will appreciate Proust's works."[1]

4. *A Sensitive Petronius**

RALPH WRIGHT

. . . . SOMEONE HAS SAID that the difference between a play and a novel is that while watching a play you have the privileges of a most intimate friend, but while reading a novel the privileges of God.

[1] "Plus on a l'âme belle, plus on a le goût exquis et pur, plus on connaît la nature, plus on aime la vérité, plus on estime les ouvrages de Proust."

* From *Marcel Proust—An English Tribute.*

. . . . Whatever is valuable in the advances that the novel has made during its latest period is valuable just in so far as it is the result of an insistence, with Rousseau, on being interested in the intricacies of human feeling, and an equal insistence, with Voltaire, in refusing to sentimentalise them. That these are the only lines on which the novelist can advance no one would dream of asserting. But it is more particularly because Marcel Proust seems here to stand head and shoulders above his generation, and not on account of his many other merits as an artist, that he has such a passionate, if still comparatively small, following today.

He is, perhaps, if we return to that definition of the difference between a novel and a play, more of the essential novelist than any man has ever been. His aim is by a hundred different methods to make you know his chief characters, not as if you were meeting them every day, but as if you yourself had for the moment actually been living in their skins and inhabiting their minds. . . . . The man who knows himself is not common, and to know Proust's characters as you know yourself may be only a small advance in knowledge. So every motive of importance, every reaction to whatever stimulus they receive, is analysed and explained until your feeling will probably be, not only how well you know this being, who is in so many respects unlike you, but how far more clearly you have seen into the obscure motives of your own most distressing and ridiculous actions, how far more understandable is an attitude to life or to your neighbours that you yourself have almost unconsciously, and perhaps in mere self-protection, adopted. . . . . It is along these lines that Marcel Proust has adventured farther than any other man.

And here, of course, he has great advantages. Proust, unlike so many of the great creative artists, started late in life the work by which he will be judged. He is mature as few great men have been mature, cultured as still fewer have been cultured. Wide reading is far from common among great artists. The driving force necessary to the accomplishment of any work of art is seldom found in alliance with wide culture; that, more often than not, is to be found among the world's half-failures. Neither Shakespeare, nor Molière, nor Fielding, nor Richardson, nor Balzac, nor Dickens, nor Dostoevsky, nor Ibsen was a widely cultured man. . . . .

. . . . But Proust, like Montaigne and like Racine, besides having an extreme sensitiveness to all forms of beauty and ugliness, happiness and misery, that he has met in his social existence, has also read widely in the works of other sensitive men, has compared their impressions with each other and with his own, has learnt from their successes and failures; he is armed with more than his natural equipment, has more eyes to see through than his own. Actually his books are filled from end to end with criticisms of music, of painting, of literature, not in the way that is unfortunately familiar in this country, as unassimilated chunks in the main stream of the narrative, but as expressions of the opinions of different characters.

This is not the only, nor indeed the chief, advantage that a wide experience in other arts, and other men's art, has given him. What is of more importance is the attitude that springs from it of seeing historically the age and society in which he lives. Nothing for him stands still, not even today; and, because he realises that today itself will tomorrow be only part of the stream of the past, he can view it with the same calmly passionate interest as that which we bring to the discoveries at Luxor.

. . . . One charge against Proust seems to be that he deals more than is necessary with what are called "unpleasant" subjects and people; another is clearly, though not usually put into so few words, that he is a snob. As regards the first charge, it is true that Proust, like most French writers, is apt to claim with Terence, *Humani nihil a me alienum puto;* to urge that he is ever coarse, that he is ever anything, in fact, but extremely discriminating in his touch, is, as a matter of fact, absurd. But the other charge is more valuable because, while mistaken, it does emphasise a side of Proust's interests in life which is of some considerable significance. . . . . But to call this interest snobbery is, surely, a sign of rather careless reading. It is to assume that the *naïveté* of the young man's first adoration of the old families of France, long before he had learnt to know them, is, in fact, the attitude of Proust himself. . . . .

As a fact, of course, what these complainants have missed is the use to which this aristocratic circle has been put in the life-history of the hero. . . . . If there is one theme that is being insistently played throughout the whole work, ... it is that theme of sadness that no ideal state is attainable in this world, not so much because we cannot climb, nor even because the ideal becomes illusion on attainment, but because the object to which we attach our ideal is, of necessity, not seen as it really is, but always as we long for it to be. This, with its complement that the mere fact of not being able to possess may lead to desire even when the object in itself does not seem very desirable, is at the very heart of Proust's philosophy.

This worship of his hero's for aristocracy is only an incident in this continual theme. It is in essence exactly the same as all his other deceptions.

. . . . There are some unforgettable pages on the Jews. There is even that little world of the hotel servants that has plainly interested Proust almost as much as any of the larger worlds he has spent so much care in describing. . . . . Never, with the exceptions of Saint-Simon and Tolstoy, has any author succeeded so well in giving the atmosphere of a particular house or a particular party; never has any one analysed so closely the behaviour of people in small homogeneous masses.

. . . . He was supremely sensitive and continually surprised by beauty. But, unlike most sensitive people, he neither railed at mankind, nor shut himself up, nor built for himself a palace of escape from reality in his own theorising about the meaning of it all. He set himself to observe and to note his observations.

In many ways Anatole France's description of him as the ingenuous Petronius of our times is extremely intelligent. And our times are in many ways extremely like the days in which Petronius wrote. There is an aristocracy that has lost its *raison d'être,* and a continual flow of new plutocrats without traditions, without taste, without any object in life beyond spending to the best of their power of self-advertisement. The faith in the old social order has gone, and nothing new has arisen to take its place. Where we differ entirely from that age is in self-consciousness. And that, too, is where a modern Petronius must differ from the old one. For better in some ways and for worse in others, we are far more complex than we have ever been; our motives are at once more mixed and more clearly scrutinised. And a writer who can satisfactorily cram this age within the pages of a book must not only be extremely intelligent and extremely observant, but must also have forged for himself a style capable of expressing the finest shades of feeling; he must refuse the easy simplifications both of the moralist and the maker of plots; he must be infinitely sensitive and infinitely truthful. That Marcel Proust personifies this ideal no one would completely claim. But he does, at least to some people, seem to have approached it more nearly than any other writer of our time.

5. *The "Little Proust"**

LOGAN PEARSALL SMITH

TO THOSE OF US who are readers and assiduous re-readers of Proust's enormous novel, it is a curious experience to turn back to his earliest publication, to the book written by the precocious boy, whose social successes are described at such length in *Remembrance of Things Past.* This first book, *Les Plaisirs et les jours* . . . . [was] written, the author tells us, between his twentieth and his twenty-third year; the style is somewhat sententious, immature and precocious: it is the writing of a boy—but, one sees at once, of a boy of genius. For here, not only in their bud, but in their first exquisite flowering, we find all the great qualities of Proust's later work . . . . Indeed, most of the themes, and often the very situations, of the later work, are not only adumbrated, but happily rendered in this boyish volume . . . . And here, too, we find something which, to my mind, is of even greater interest, and about which, as Proust's other critics have hardly mentioned it, a few words may not be out of place.

When the little Proust plunged into the full stream of his Parisian experiences, he was, we are told by one of his friends, already, from his early studies, steeped in the philosophy of Plato; and although his feverish days were filled with love-affairs and worldly successes, and he drained to its dregs, as we say, the enchanting cup of life, all that he felt and saw seems but to have confirmed in that precocious youth the lesson which Plato had already taught him—the lesson, namely, that the true meaning of life is never to be found in immediate ex-

* Logan Pearsall Smith's article, written originally for *The New Statesman,* appeared in *Marcel Proust: An English Tribute* in 1923. Here we quote, by permission, from the revision in *Reperusals and Recollections,* Harcourt, Brace and Company, Inc., 1937.

perience; that there is another reality which can be envisaged only by the mind, and, as it were, created by the intellect—a deeper and more ultimate reality, in the presence of which life no longer seems contingent, mediocre, mortal. Certainly in that great battle between the Giants and the Gods, which Plato describes, the battle in which the Giants affirm that only those things are real which can be touched and handled, while the Gods defend themselves from above out of an unseen world, "mightily contending" that true essence consists in intelligible ideas,—in this eternal warfare Proust is found fighting as conspicuously as Shelley on the side of the Gods. Hope for him, as for Shelley,

> creates
> From its own wreck the thing it contemplates;

and it is this attitude towards life, this creative contemplation of experience, which to my mind gives its deeper significance to Proust's work, and lends an importance and depth of meaning to the youthful and rather shabby love-affairs, the fashionable worldlinesses which form so large a part of his subject-matter. Proust's ultimate "intention" in writing his great novel, the intention which gives a form to this immense work, was made clear at last by the publication of the final volume. . . . .

That there is something irremediably wrong in the present moment; that the true reality is the creation of desire and memory, and is most present in hope, in recollection and absence, but never in immediate experience; that we kill our souls by living, and that it is in solitude, in illness, or at the approach of death that we most truly possess them—it is on these themes, which are repeated with deeper harmonies and richer modulations throughout his later work, that the young Proust harps in this overture to the masterpiece which was to come. Surely, one thinks, a book of such exquisite promise and youthful achievement, heralded as it was to the world by Anatole France's preface, and talked of, no doubt, in the Paris salons, must have produced a remarkable impression on people so cultivated as the Parisians, so alert to discover and appreciate literary merit. However, as we know, it produced no such impression; no one seems to have had the slightest notion of its importance, or to have guessed that a new genius had appeared, a bright star of morning had arisen. . . . .

When we read the lives of the great artists of the past, we are apt to be amazed at the indifference of their contemporaries to their early achievements; we cannot believe that we, too, in the same circumstances, would have been so undiscerning. But here, happening in our own days, is an obvious instance of this contemporary blindness; and as I read the little Proust's first volume, and see spread so clearly before me, as in the light of a beautiful dawn, the world of his creation, I try to make myself believe that if the noontide of his genius had never illuminated that world, and made it familiar to me, that if Proust had never lived to write *Swann* and the *Guermantes,* I, too, should be as blind as were his friends to its beauty and merits. I tell myself this, and yet with the book before me, I cannot believe it. But then I remind myself of what I already know very well, that new dawns in art are apt to appear on just the horizons toward which we are not looking, and over landscapes of which we have as yet not the slightest knowledge; and that it is only afterwards, when the master's whole *œuvre* is familiar to us, that we can see the real merits of his early attempts, and read back into them the meaning and value of his complete and acknowledged achievement. The moral of all this (and it is pleasant to end, if possible, one's reflections with a moral)—the moral is that we do not know, we cannot know, what those tiresome persons, our younger contemporaries, are really up to, and what shadows they already cast before them; that we must "look to the end," as the old saying has it; and that in the first attempts of other youths who, like the little Proust, were endowed with genius, but whose gifts,

nique of his work a new formula, in its style a new prose rhythm, and in the spirit of it an alert and original intelligence, will always look on Gilberte as one of his most fortunate successes.

8. *Proust's Women**

CATHERINE CARSWELL

. . . . IT IS IN . . . . his . . . . treatment of . . . . women that we perceive how rigorously Proust applies his artistic method. He never seeks to transcend his own personality. In him, the observer, the whole of creation lives and moves and has its being. Men are creatures made in his own image. He can faithfully follow his own emotions, and "by his belief" can conscientiously endow his men with souls. But women are in a different case. He has no inner guide to assure him that they are anything more than the phantoms they seem. Strictly speaking, this should imply no more than a negative attitude. In fact, however, Proust goes further. Because he has no grounds for belief he passes into unbelief. In his philosophy *esse est percipi,* therefore, the souls of women for him have no existence. Herein it is likely that he has borne out the avowed experience of most men. Whether or no, he certainly has expressed the truth of his own experience with a purity that few, even among great writers, can rival. . . . .

* From *Marcel Proust—An English Tribute.*

9. *The Best Record**

REGINALD TURNER

ONE OF MY feelings whenever I read Marcel Proust is regret that Henry James is not alive to enjoy him, as he would have done immensely and amazedly, though, judging from the letters of that great master of the art of writing fiction, no doubt he would not have given him his unqualified approval. But he would have recognised him as working at his own level, while not in his own groove. Yet, for all that Proust is the author of practically only one book, big though that book is, in that one book he has spread his nets wider, and sunk them deeper, than did Henry James in the sum of all his novels. One wonders if such mastery has ever been obtained so suddenly and so completely; indeed, the sureness of touch seems a little less certain in the last published volumes than in the earlier ones. We had revealed to us from the beginning a new way of writing fiction, or rather of describing life. It had never so been done before. Let us pray that he will have no disciples—one can foresee the horror of them; but influence he must have.

My own interest begins with the second volume of *Swann,* though my admiration begins with the first sentence of the first; and my advice to new readers would be to take up any volume after *Swann*—to start in the middle—when I am sure they will insist on knowing everything the author has to say about his characters from the beginning. You become soaked in the lives of these people as a sponge becomes soaked with water. In the process you live your own life over again and . . . . tread the same ground.

* From *Marcel Proust—An English Tribute.*

Proust has no "story" to tell. He sets down life as it was lived by certain people at a certain period: Parisian society from the middle of the Dreyfus case to the present day. . . . . Life recorded with matchless insight or remembrance. We need not compare, but how pale is *Jean Christophe* beside these pages! . . . .

The more we study the great writers of all ages, and the more we observe for ourselves, the more we realise that the world never alters; we can only ring the changes on the same material. Harmony and discord, beauty and ugliness! It is like a gramophone disc. The records vary, the melodies, the arrangements, make their individual effect, but the substance is the same. The Masters make their records on an unchanging surface. Marcel Proust's is a magnificent record; perhaps the most brilliant ever achieved. It requires only that we bring to it a sympathetic and sharp-pointed needle. . . . .

*10. A Foot-Note**

CLIVE BELL

THOUGH in England almost every one, who has read and understood, admires the works of Marcel Proust, it is not so in France. There, not to go beyond my own experience, I have met plenty of writers, and good ones too, who cannot away with them. Even that essay on the style of Flaubert, which I had supposed would be universally reckoned a masterpiece, I have heard described by a friend of mine, a charming poet and admired dramatist, as childish. Now, when I hear such a one, and others whom I respect, dis-

* From *Marcel Proust—An English Tribute.*

paraging Proust, I do not fly into a passion; I seek the cause, instead. And I find it—though the discovery, should they ever come to hear of it, would a good deal shock some of my French friends and surprise perhaps a few of my English—in Politics.

The French themselves seem hardly to realise how sharp and deep their political divisions are become. Yet when we remember that during the last forty years politics have been able to make of that gentle Latin scepticism, which gave us Montaigne, Bayle, and Voltaire, and still gives us M. Anatole France, something as narrow and bitter almost as Calvinism; when we hear of such pretty place-names as (say) St. Symphorien being changed into (say) Émile Combesville; we ought not to be surprised if literature even gets splashed a little in the dirty dog-fight. Because Marcel Proust is supposed to have chosen as the subject of his epic the *faubourg St. Germain,* it is assumed that he admired and believed in it. Was not *L'Action Française* amongst the first to hail his rising genius? Is he not half a Jew and therefore wholly a renegade? He is a black reactionary and an enemy of light. He is not a good man, so how can he be a good writer? We are back again in a very familiar world of criticism; only the English critics can prove that he was good, after all.

. . . . When some one quotes a saying by Dr. Johnson or the Duke of Wellington we need not verify by the book; their characters are so vivid to us, and they speak so much in character, that their phrases have the ring of familiar voices. It is the same with Madame de Guermantes. How many authors have achieved this miracle? Shakespeare, of course, who achieved all miracles, can distinguish even his minor characters. . . . .

One word more: a translation may do very well, but we can have no English Proust. No Englishman, I mean, writing in English, would be allowed to publish in England so complete a picture of life. Wherefore as a novel- and play-writing nation we have lost pride of place, and cannot hope to regain it till we have set our laws in order. An artist must be possessed by his subject; but the English novelist who is inspired by his sense of contemporary life is not allowed to express that by which he is possessed. Fielding, Jane Austen, Thackeray, Dickens, Meredith, James, and Hardy, English novelists who took contemporary life for their province, all had something to say which may have shocked or hurt but which the age did not prohibit. They were, therefore, as free to express the best that was in them as Balzac, Zola, or Proust. But today our subtlest and most active minds, affected maybe, consciously or unconsciously, by modern psychological discoveries, are concerned, so far as they are concerned with life at all, with certain aspects of it, with certain relations, of which they may not treat freely. . . . . Proust moves in a world unknown almost to the intellectual slums, or to those intellectual lower middle classes from which are drawn too many of our magistrates, judges, and legislators. These lag behind, and impose their veto on the sincere treatment of English manners by a first-rate English artist. And perhaps the best tribute which English admirers of Proust could pay his memory would be to agitate for the repeal of those absurd and barbarous laws which make an English *Remembrance of Things Past* impossible.

*11. The Spell of Proust**

ETHEL COLBURN MAYNE

THE MAGIC RING which Marcel Proust drew, almost literally, round his readers—since it is in the circle of "le temps perdu" which is to become "le temps

* From *Marcel Proust—An English Tribute.*

retrouvé" that he sets us and himself—seemed early in the incantation to betray a break whereby we might escape, did we so wish, from his compulsion. For, enthralled as we had been by *Swann,* there was a sensible relaxing of the spell with the *Blossoming Girls*. . . . . We heard, and we responded to, the cry: "Those flappers are so tedious!"—and as Albertine grew more and more significant, *we* grew more sceptical, and told ourselves that we could step outside the ring at any moment we might choose. But somehow, that emancipative moment never came . . . . —there always was a reason why we could not break away. And finally, we realised that we were wrong, and that the spell had but become more absolute, in both the shades of meaning in that word. For now that some of the more normal baits for interest were laid aside, we could perceive that here was sorcery in its pure state—the thing itself, stripped of all seeming. Now we could not so easily, or easily at all, "say why" when the profane inquired of us what the magic was—why, reading Proust, we were so interested. We were *not* so interested; we could scarcely say, or even think, that we were "interested" any more.

The miracle had happened. We were spellbound, for good and all, within the magic ring. . . . . This was because we now could feel more deeply the extent of what the wizard meant to do with us. We were not passively to stand within the circle. We were, with him, to pace it mystically round, while time ran back to fetch the Age of Gold. *Le temps passé* would be transmuted, imperceptibly, into *le temps retrouvé,* and our aid was necessary to the necromancer's full success. . . . .

This is the proof, to me, of Marcel Proust's (as one might think, indisputable; yet by a few disputed) genius. . . . . In the great elegiac glories of the death of Bergotte (not yet published in book-form), and of that *grand'mère* who is the *motif,* as it were, in the symphonic composition of the unnamed central figure's personality, Proust sounded chords which lay till then beyond the compass of his readers' hearing, but were then revealed to sense that shall not lose them while it yet survives.

But over all this virtuosity there rules a mightier gift—the master-gift of insight. Proust, one could say, "knows everything," in the restricted meaning of the words. No bent, no twist, of modern thought escapes him; . . . .

If there were nothing else than Charlus in the books, Proust must be given pride of place among the masters. . . . . More than a master, one would say, a writer cannot be. Yet in the image here suggested of the magic circle, there is possibly the one thing more that causes Proustians to divide their reading lives into the time before and after they have read these books. No spell had yet been worked on us of potency like this; for though we are pent within the ring, we move within it too—the world revolves, for us, as in a crystal held beneath our gaze by one who, moving with us, will reveal the secret hidden not there only but in our own dim sense, when at the last *le temps perdu* shall have become *le temps retrouvé.*

*12. A New Psychometry**

A. B. Walkley

To JUDGE from the newspapers, there have been tremendous "crises" in public affairs during the last few days: the triumph of Fascismo in Italy, the Lausanne Conference, the English elections. . . . . But one announcement in *The Times* of last Monday week shocked many of us with a sudden, absurdly indignant bewilderment, like a

* From *Marcel Proust—An English Tribute.* This is included in *More Prejudice* by Mr. Walkley, published in 1923.

foul blow: I mean the death of Marcel Proust. It is not only absurd but impious to be indignant with the decrees of Fate. . . . . But, on the death of an author, there is this peculiar consolation that never fails: his work lives absolutely unaffected by his death. . . . .

It has been said that Proust will go down to posterity as the author of one book. This is only true in a literal sense. For the many volumes of *Remembrance* that already crowd the shelves are several "books" in one. It is not a "story," but a panorama of many stories. Indeed, who reads Proust for the "story"? His book is really a picture of the modern world and the modern spirit, and that is its peculiar fascination for us. There are "morbid" elements in it, to be sure, ... and it is not for nothing that *The Times* has compared him to Petronius Arbiter. But one of the advantages of this hyperaesthesia is a heightened sensibility for *everything,* the perception and accurate notation of innumerable details in thought and feeling that escape a normal observer.

Take, for instance, the account of the famous author "Bergotte." Proust, little more than a child, but already his ardent reader, meets him at luncheon. And, first, the boy's imagined author, a "languishing old man," has to give place to the reality, much younger, a little man with a chin-tuft and a nose like a snail-shell. Then comes an elaborate description of his spoken diction, pronunciation, etc., and an attempt to reconcile these with the peculiarities of his written style. . . . .

It is, further, explained how this man of genius came to pay court to his intellectual inferiors with an eye on the Academy, and how, while his own private morals were bad, the moral tone of his books was of the loftiest. . . . .

Nor is the portrait finished yet. Bergotte was at bottom a man who really loved only certain images and to compose and paint them in words. Had he had to defend himself before a tribunal, in spite of himself he would have chosen his words, not for their effect on the judge, but in view of images which the judge would certainly never have perceived.

It is this extraordinarily minute "psychometry" that is the peculiar mark of Proust's work. . . . .

. . . . Since Henry Bernstein first mentioned Proust's name to me in the year before the war I have returned again and again for a tit-bit to that feast. Proust is dead; but we can still go on enjoying his work. In that sense the cry of the child in Maeterlinck's *Oiseau Bleu* is true enough: "There is no death."

*13. Proust and the Modern Consciousness**

J. MIDDLETON MURRY

FOR ENGLISHMEN Marcel Proust has already become one of the great figures of modern literature. The feeling is common to many of his readers that in some way his work marks an epoch. What kind of epoch it is harder to say. Is he an end, or a beginning? And, again, yet another question insinuates itself continually as we pass slowly through his long volumes. What precisely—if answers to such questions can be made precise—was his own intention as a writer? . . . .

. . . . Marcel Proust's book may be fairly said to bristle with difficulties. Its obvious theme, its surface intention, as we perceive it in the brilliant opening pages of *Swann's Way,* is the presentation by an adult man of his memories of childhood. We feel, though with peculiar qualifications to which we must return, that we are on the threshold of a spiritual autobiography; we are to be the enchanted witnesses of the unfolding and

* From *Marcel Proust—An English Tribute.*

growth of a strangely sensitive consciousness. But no sooner are we attuned to the subtleties of this investigation and have accustomed ourselves to Proust's breathless, tiptoe following of the faint and evanescent threads of association . . . . than the thread is abruptly snapped. We do not complain at the moment, for the episode *Swann in Love* is the highest sustained achievement of Proust as a prose-writer. Perhaps the devouring passion of love—"Venus herself clinging to her prey"[1]—the smouldering, torturing flame of unsatisfied passion which by law of its own nature can never be satisfied, has never been so subtly and so steadily anatomised before. Perhaps it has been more wonderfully presented, but never more wonderfully analysed.

It is not surprising that in the fascination of this intolerable and unwonted history, in which every psychological subtlety of the author is properly and beautifully dominated by the tragic theme, we forget that this is not at all the thing we went out to see. The boy whose history we have been following could not have known of Swann's discomfiture before he was a man. . . . . In other words, the angle of presentation has abruptly changed. Into a narrative concerned, as we imagine, solely with what a boy knew and felt, and how he knew and felt it, is suddenly thrust an episode of which he could have known nothing at all.

. . . . The contrast, the building up of the character of Swann, as it were, from two sides at once, was the quite sufficient motive of the book. But, so understood, it was Swann's book, not the boy's.

But the next volumes brought us back to the boy's history . . . . the key to the story as a whole might be found in the earlier emphasis upon the manner in which the author went in search of the past. At the beginning of *Swann's Way* he had been at pains to give us not merely his results but his method

[1] Vénus toute entière à sa proie attachée.

also. . . . . There is, for example, the beautiful account of his mysterious excitement at a sight of the spires and towers of Martinville church . . . . Then the sudden sight of a tiny clump of trees seen while he is driving with the Marquise de Villeparisis makes him feel that they are stretching out imploring arms towards him in a mute appeal. If he can divine what they have to tell him (they seem to say) he will touch the secret of "la vraie vie" of life indeed. And then the writer warns us that the story of his search to make this secret his own is to come, and that this premonition of a task to be accomplished was to haunt him throughout his life.

At this moment Marcel Proust came nearest, we may believe, to revealing to the reader the hidden soul of his own book. . . . .

. . . . What he was to discover, when the demand that he should surrender himself to his moments of vision became urgent and finally irresistible, was the history of what he was. Proust . . . . was much more than a sentimental autobiographer of genius; he was a man trying to maintain his soul alive. . . . . The explanation, we believe, is that in spite of his great gifts, Proust was a writer *malgré lui;* he composed against the grain. We mean that had it been only for the sake of the satisfaction of literary creation, he probably would not have written at all. It was only when writing presented itself to him as the only available means for getting down to the bedrock of his own personality, as the only instrument by which his *fin-de-siècle* soul . . . . could probe to something solid to live by, that he seriously took up the pen. It was the lance with which he rode after the Grail—"la vraie vie." . . . .

So . . . . we return to our first question. Proust marks an epoch. What kind of epoch? Is it an end or a beginning? . . . . Proust is both an end and a beginning. More an end than a beginning, perhaps, if we have regard to the technique and texture of his work. In the art of literature itself he opens up no new way. And, in the deeper sense, he indicates a need more than he satisfies it. The modern mind, looking into the astonishing mirror which Proust holds up to it, will not see in it the gleam of something to live by; but it will see, if it knows how to look, an acknowledgement of that necessity and a burning desire to satisfy it. By so much Marcel Proust marks a beginning also. It is the flame of this desire which smoulders always through his book, and at times breaks out; it is this . . . . which gives it, in the true sense, style.

14. *Proust's Way**

VIOLET HUNT

. . . . PROUST? What is Proust? This is the cry of the Carping Uninitiated among us. To such persons, constitutionally unwilling to be instructed, one replies that Proust is a fashion—a disease—and that a Proustian, so-called, is an Opium-Eater. But, to those who know him and love him, he is a wise and cunning Prospero whose wand is style, and Combray an enchanted island—Ferdinand, not much Miranda, but Caliban, drunken sailors and all.

The Opium Trance, indeed, offers some parallel. Dr. Hochst tells us that the wily subconsciousness . . . . is able to invoke and maintain an attitude of benign stupor towards the universe, holding it, as it were, at arm's length, able to subsist in tranquil abstraction from chill and hateful circumstance. And one can easily imagine some triply disillusioned soul, rebuffed of love and ambition and the fount of life itself, entering on a course of the Master, content to live, ... through terms of

* From *Marcel Proust—An English Tribute.*

months or even years, till the stupor, benign in character, ends at last in the ordinary manner, the patient dying, still *en plein Proust,* with, perhaps, a volume or two unread . . . .

The normal, healthy person, still active, still complying with life, finds it more than soothing to commit himself to this peaceable, effluent mind-flow, a current of thought that has, like life, its eddies, its *transes,* but persists, ... in its appointed borders and so gains something of the peace of resignation that Renan speaks of: "There is nothing so sweet as the renouncement of joy, nothing so pleasant as the enchantment of disenchantment."[1]

. . . . [Proust's] style is the magician's wand without whose composed and certain wielding we should never have allowed him to lead us, like willing children, through the mazes, winding, twisting, but always planned and in order, of his mind—or Swann's. . . . .

*15. M. Vinteuil's Sonata**

DYNELEY HUSSEY

["THE LITTLE PHRASE," a vital theme throughout Swann's stock, is the subject of Mr. Hussey's study, which ends with:] I can only point to the exquisite sensibility of these passages, where music is brought to the touchstone of life, and human experience, in its turn, is elucidated in terms of music. Indeed, this "Proust" shows himself preternaturally sensitive . . . . to musical sounds . . . .

[1] "Il n'y a rien de suave comme le renoncement de la joie, rien de doux comme l'enchantement du désenchantement."

* From *Marcel Proust—An English Tribute.*

*16. The Little Phrase**

W. J. TURNER

MY ONLY EXCUSE for contributing anything to this collection is that it provides an opportunity to give some information. Readers may want to know whether the Sonata to which Proust refers in *Swann's Way* as being played at Mme. de Sainte-Euverte's party was wholly an invention of Proust's, or whether his refined and tortuous dithyrambs on the subject were inspired by an actual Sonata which the dullest may purchase at a Paris shop.

Well, the answer to this hypothetical question, like all real answers to all genuine questions, is "Yes" and "No." For the Ayes there is the statement by Proust in a letter to a friend printed in the memorial number of the *Nouvelle Revue Française:* "The little phrase of that Sonata . . . . is . . . . the charming but on the whole mediocre passage of a sonata for piano and violin by Saint-Saëns."[1]

Explosion! Thus are our idols shattered! Even Proust's deprecating "mais enfin médiocre" does not prepare for this shock the sturdy English connoisseur who likes only the best. Proust tells his friend that he can point out the precise passage, which is several times repeated; and adds—cunningly—that its execution was a triumph for Jacques Thibaud.

He continues that, during the same evening, when the piano and violin are described as murmuring like two birds in a dialogue, he was thinking of a sonata by Franck (especially as

* From *Marcel Proust—An English Tribute.*

[1] "La petite phrase de cette Sonate ... est ... la phrase charmante mais enfin médiocre d'une sonate pour piano et violon de Saint-Saëns. ..." *Nouvelle Revue Française,* No. 112 (n.s.), January 1923, pp. 201–2.

The friend is M. Jacques de Lacretelle. [—C. K. S.-M.]

played by Enesco). The tremolos over the little Saint-Saëns phrase when played at the Verdurins' were, he says, suggested by the Prelude to *Lohengrin*—he does not tell us, this time, in whose rendering, but that actually they were recalled that evening by a trifle from Schubert. The same evening, he tells us, as a final scrap of information, there was played "un ravissant morceau" for the piano by Fauré.

What are we to make of all this? Well, I am struck by the composite character of Proust's material. It shows that his art consists in his power of making an exquisite synthesis of his sensibility by reprecipitating his sensations in a more generalised, more abstract form than that in which they came to him.

17. *Proust as Creator**

JOSEPH CONRAD

.... WHEREAS before we had analysis allied to creative art, great in poetic conception, in observation, or in style, [Proust's] is a creative art absolutely based on analysis. It is really more than that. He is a writer who has pushed analysis to the point when it becomes creative. All that crowd of personages in their infinite variety through all the gradations of the social scale are rendered visible to us by the force of analysis alone. I don't say Proust has no gift of description or characterisation; but, to take an example from each end of the scale: Françoise, the devoted servant, and the Baron de Charlus, a consummate portrait—how many descriptive lines have they got to themselves in the whole body of that

* From *Marcel Proust—An English Tribute.*

immense work? Perhaps, counting the lines, half a page each. And yet no intelligent person can doubt for a moment their plastic and coloured existence. One would think that this method (and Proust has no other, because his method is the expression of his temperament) may be carried too far, but as a matter of fact it is never wearisome. There may be here and there amongst those thousands of pages a paragraph that one might think over-subtle, a bit of analysis pushed so far as to vanish into nothingness. But those are very few, and all minor instances. The intellectual pleasure never flags, because one has the feeling that the last word is being said upon a subject much studied, much written about, and of human interest—the last word of its time. Those that have found beauty in Proust's work are perfectly right. It is there. What amazes one is its inexplicable character. In that prose so full of life there is no reverie, no emotion, no marked irony, no warmth of conviction, not even a marked rhythm to charm our ear. It appeals to our sense of wonder and gains our homage by its veiled greatness. I don't think there ever has been in the whole of literature such an example of the power of analysis, and I feel pretty safe in saying that there will never be another.

*18. A Moment to Spare**

George Saintsbury

I have at last found time, or rather, for it expresses our relations better, Time has been gracious enough at last to find *me*—in regard to *Swann*. It was a

* From *Marcel Proust—An English Tribute.*

As to this article, Mr. Scott-Moncrieff wrote: ". . . . It is only fair, to both critic and reader, to explain that Mr. Saintsbury had read nothing of Proust save *Swann,* new and satisfactory experience. His reality is extraordinary—at least in the main part of the book . . . .

Has anybody said that he partakes *both* of De Quincey and of Stendhal? He does to me, and I'm shot if I ever expected to see such a blend! You see, there is in him on the one hand a double measure of the analytical and introspective power that Beyle's admirers make so much of; with what they also admire, a total absence of prettification for prettification's sake. Yet he can be pretty in the very best sense, while Beyle never can, in the best or any other. Then, too, I at least find in him much less of the type-character which, though certainly relieved by individuality in the *Chartreuse de Parme* and other books (especially *Lamiel*), is still always more or less there. But the oddest and to me the most attractive thing is the way in which he entirely relieves the sense of aridity—of museum-preparations—which I find in Stendhal. And here it is that the De Quincey suggestion comes so unexpectedly in. For Proust effects this miracle by a constant relapse upon—and sometimes a long self-restriction to—a sort of dream element. It is not, of course, the vaguer and more mystical kind that one finds in De Quincey, not that of *Our Ladies of Sorrow* or *Savannah-la-Mar,* but that of the best parts of *The English Mail Coach.* In fact, it is sometimes Landorian rather than De Quinceyish in its dreaminess. But, however this may be, the dream quality is there, to me, as it is in few other Frenchmen—themselves almost always poets. Now, the worst of the usual realist is that, being blinder than any other heathen in his blindness, he tries to exorcise dream, though sometimes not nightmare, from life. Such a mixture as Proust's I remember nowhere else.

and that only in an inadequate translation. On the other hand, it was as impossible for the editor to contemplate a book of this sort without a promise of collaboration from his old friend and master as it was, at the moment, for the doyen of English (if not of European, which is to say the world's) critics to qualify himself for saying more than is printed on this leaf."

*19. A Real World in Fiction**

G. S. Street

My presence among those who are offering a tribute to Marcel Proust would be an impertinence if the request for it had not been continued after I had confessed the poverty of my knowledge. . . . . I have to read a good deal for my bread, and the reading I can do for pleasure is limited by debility of eyesight; M. Proust's books are long and in a language I read less easily than my own. . . . . My slight study has produced opinions which, I am convinced, further study will only confirm, and it is a pleasure to record them. . . . .

We all have our views as to what, for us, distinguishes great fiction from that which is less than great. Mine has always been that it causes me to live in a real world of visible, audible, and intelligible people—a world in which, however novel it may be to start with, I am at home and able, with sureness, to exercise my powers of understanding to the full; this last point matters, for of course the superficial may be superficially alive. . . . . Well, M. Proust has done this most considerable service for me, in those two volumes I have read in translation. . . . . That is the first thing for which I am grateful. The second is the sheer intellectual joy with which, time and again, I came upon an achievement of divination in the subtleties of human emotion which caught one's breath by its compelling truth. Jealousy of a man for a woman may have been more grandly expressed, but have all the subtleties of its tortuous and agonising course ever been so completely exposed as in the case of M. Swann? Or the feelings of a sensitive and imaginative boy

* From *Marcel Proust—An English Tribute.*

in his first affections? . . . . For these two things I have a sincere gratitude which I propose to increase. But the wretchedness of my present qualifications must terminate my expression of it now.

20. *The Birth of a Classic**

EDGELL RICKWORD

. . . . WITH A certain resemblance to the achievement of the Impressionists who revealed the fabric of a world worked-over with conceptual images, Proust breaks up the moulds into which our feelings are generally poured. He is curious to note the sensual deceits which agitate the mind no less profoundly than the reality would have done, and to separate the social stratagem . . . . from the intention of which it was the paraphrase. He is dissociative only to that extent—a necessary one, since dissimulation is the mind's first nature. But he is not at all destructive; for an action never really is a separate entity, cut off by crystalline walls from the mother-liquor of our lives. In the style which he created that glittering illusion is re-dissolved into the saturated mental life of which it is an inextricable component.

. . . . Wishing to convey the shifting aspect of things, or perhaps the composite pile of aspects which represents, at any moment, our realisation of a thing—and as objective description reintroduces the pictorial *cliché* so far avoided,—he utilises the vast fabric of memory, shot, like iridescent silk, with many indefinable moods. To specify his method more exactly would not at present be easy, nor is there any enjoyment equal to the

* From *Marcel Proust—An English Tribute.*

mere following of this marvellous web into the still obscure future, where half is, to our chagrin partly and to our delight, yet hidden. . . . . There is a delicious state . . . . in which a book, having shaken off the first fever of novelty, is in a condition to be most artfully savoured, and at length. The classic features will never be dearer to us than while they are still flushed with contemporaneity. The classics are at least readable in so far as they are modern, but the modern, once firmly on his pedestal, is not all approachable. So it is a great and marvellous privilege to be awake to this exquisite dawn, at the moment this many-leaved bloom is suspended in all its freshness which tomorrow—

> To-morrow will find fallen or not at all:

fallen, if the worst comes to the worst, ... to a greatness in its decay and neglect more moving than the spick-and-span of a smart little subaltern of immortality. It is impossible to imagine how this titanic fragment can be trundled from age to age; nor is the future likely to have much time to spare from the production of domestic utensils which are so badly made that they must be continually replaced. *Remembrance of Things Past* is not one of those things which are replaced, like the novel of the moment, but exactly what part of it is most likely to be saved the present cannot decide. There will always be some to follow the whole sweep of the Master's gesture, which evokes the hours of adolescence flowering in the shade of girlhood and rebuilds the tormented cities of the plain; now stooping to dissect a snob or soaring to stroke a horizon, but never theatrical and never grandiose. Perhaps in the ray of this most intimate limelight we draw the greater part of our pleasure from the recognition of our own movements; the heirs of our sensibility will find there the original of many impulses which they accept as part of human nature.

21. *A Casuist in Souls**

Arthur Symons

Pater, who desired to find everywhere forces producing pleasurable sensations, "each of a more or less peculiar and unique kind," says: "Few artists, not Goethe nor Byron even, work quite clearly, casting off all *débris,* and leaving us only what the heat of their imagination has wholly fused and transformed." Has the heat of Proust's imagination fused and transformed his material as Balzac and Rodin transformed and fused theirs? Are his characters creations? Has he the strange magical sense of that life in natural things, which is incommunicable? I think not; there is too much *débris* in his prose which he has not cast off.

. . . . Proust, with his adoration of beauty, gives one an equal sense of the beauty of exterior things and of physical beauty; with infinite carefulness, with infinite precautions, he gives one glimpses of occult secrets unknown to us, of our inevitable instincts, and, at times, of those icy ecstasies which Laforgue reveals in *Moralités légendaires.* . . . .

In his feverish attempt to explain himself to himself, his imaginary hero reminds me of Rousseau, ... who, being avid of misunderstandings, was forced by the rankling thorns of his jealousy to write his *Confessions,* in which he unburdens himself of the exasperation of all those eyes fixed upon him, driven, in spite of himself, to set about explaining himself to other people—a coward before his own conscience. There is no cowardice in the conscience of Proust's hero; his utter shameless sincerity to the naked truth of things allows him "avec une liberté d'esprit" to compete, near the end of the last volume, in

* From *Marcel Proust—An English Tribute.*

his unveiling of M. de Charlus, with the outspokenness of Restif de la Bretonne in *Monsieur Nicolas*. . . . .

Proust has some of the corrupt mysticism of Huysmans, but not so perilous as his; nor has he that psychology which can be carried so far into the soul's darkness that the flaming walls of the world themselves fade to a glimmer; he does not chronicle the adventures of this world's Vanity Fair: he is concerned with the revelation of the subconscious self; his hero's confessions are not the exaltation of the soul. He is concerned, not so much with adventures as with an almost cloistral subtlety in regard to the obscure passions which work themselves out, never with any actual logic. With all his curiosity, this curiosity never drives him in the direction of the soul's apprehension of spiritual things. He does, at times, like Mallarmé, deform ingeniously the language he writes in; and, as in most of these modern decadents, perversity of form and perversity of manner bewilder us in his most bewildering pages.

I find to my surprise that a French critic, Carcassonne, compares Proust with Balzac. As an observer of society, yes; as a creator, no. "Never," he writes, "since Stendhal and Balzac has any novelist put so much reality into a novel. Stendhal, Balzac: I write those great names without hesitation beside that of Marcel Proust. It is the finest homage I can render to the power and originality of his talent." . . . . I should place Proust with those rare spirits whose *métier* is the analysis of difficult souls. Browning wrote in regard to his *Sordello:* "My stress lay on the incidents in the development of a soul: little else is worth study; I, at least, always thought so." This certainly applies to Proust; and, as he seems to me to derive some of his talent from Stendhal and from no other novelist, I can imagine his casuistical and cruel creation of the obscure soul of M. de Charlus in much the same fashion as Stendhal's when he undresses Julien Sorel's soul with a deliberate and fascinating effrontery.

. . . . A novelist with style will not look at life with an entirely naked vision. There is no naked vision in Proust; his vision is like a clouded mirror, in whose depths strange shapes flash and vanish . . . . in Proust's style there is something paradoxical, singular, caustic; it is coloured and perfumed and exotic, a style in which sensation becomes complex, cultivated, the flower of an elaborate life; it can become deadly, as passion becomes poisonous. "The world of the novelist," I have written, "what we call the real world, is a solid theft out of space; colour and music may float into it and wander through it, but it has not been made with colour and music, and it is not a part of the consciousness of its inhabitants." This world was never lived in by d'Annunzio; this world was never entered by Proust. All the same, there is in him something cruel, something abnormal, something subtle. He is a creator of gorgeous fabrics, Babylons, Sodoms. Only, he never startles you, as Balzac startles you.

22. *The Last Word**

ARNOLD BENNETT

Two OF THE contributors to the stout Proust memorial number of *La Nouvelle Revue Française* remind me that I met Marcel Proust many years ago at a Christmas Eve party given by Madame Edwards (now Madame José Sert) in her remarkable flat on the Quai Voltaire, Paris. (Not that I needed reminding.) With some eagerness I turned up the year, 1910, in my journal. What I read there was this: "Doran came on Sunday night for dinner. We went on to

* From *Marcel Proust—An English Tribute.*

Misia Edwards' 'Réveillon,' and got home at 4 A.M." Not a word more! And I cannot now remember a single thing that Proust said.

I have, however, a fairly clear recollection of his appearance and style: . . . . I would not describe him as self-conscious; I would say rather that he was well aware of himself. . . . . He sat at the hostess's own table and dominated it, and everybody at the party showed interest in him. . . . .

A few weeks before his death, while searching for something else in an overcrowded bookcase, I came across my first edition of *Swann's Way,* and decided to read the book again. . . . . The *longueurs* of it seemed to me to be insupportable, the clumsy centipedalian crawling of the interminable sentences inexcusable; the lack of form or construction may disclose artlessness, but it signifies effrontery too. Why should not Proust have given himself the trouble of learning to "write" in the large sense? Further, the monotony of subject and treatment becomes wearisome. . . . . On the other hand, at the second reading I was absolutely enchanted by some of the detail.

About two-thirds of Proust's work must be devoted to the minutiae of social manners, the rendering ridiculous of a million varieties of snob. At this game Proust is a master. . . . . His interest in human nature, if intense and clairvoyant, is exceedingly limited. Foreign critics generally agree that the English novelist has an advantage over the French in that he walks all around his characters and displays them to you from every side. I have heard this over and over again in conversation in Paris, and I think it is fairly true, though certainly Balzac was the greatest exponent of complete display. Proust never "presents" a character; he never presents a situation: he fastens on one or two aspects of a character or a situation, and strictly ignores all the others. And he is scarcely ever heroical, as Balzac was always; he rarely exalts, and he nearly always depreciates—in a tolerant way.

Again, he cannot control his movements: he sees a winding path off the main avenue, and scampers away further and further and still further, merely because at the moment it amuses him to do so. You ask yourself: He is lost—will he ever come back? The answer is that often he never comes back, and when he does come back he employs a magic but illicit carpet, to the outrage of principles of composition which cannot be outraged in a work of the first order. This animadversion applies not only to any particular work, but to his work as a whole. The later books are orgies of self-indulgence; the work has ruined the *moral* of the author: phenomenon common enough.

Two achievements in Proust's output I should rank as great. The first is the section of *Swann* entitled *Swann in Love*. He had a large theme here—love and jealousy. The love is physical and the object of it contemptible; the jealousy is fantastic. But the affair is handled with tremendous, grave, bitter, impressive power. . . . .

The second achievement, at the opening of *Sodom and Gomorrah* is the psychological picture of the type-pederast. An unpromising subject, according to British notions! Proust evolves from it beauty, and a heartrending pathos. Nobody with any perception of tragedy can read these wonderful pages and afterwards regard the pervert as he had regarded the pervert before reading them. I reckon them as the high-water of Proust.

Speaking generally, Proust's work declined steadily from *Swann*. . . . . That Proust was a genius is not to be doubted; and I agree that he made some original discoveries in the byways of psychological fiction. But that he was a supreme genius, as many critics both French and English would have us believe, I cannot admit.

23. *The Text of Marcel Proust**

EDWARD MARSH

SIR,—May I make a respectful appeal through you to the Editors of the *Nouvelle Revue Française* to take a nail out of the coffin of the Entente by presenting English readers (if they will not do it for their own countrymen) with a tolerable text of the masterpieces which the death of this enchanting writer has left to their mercies? They have made an entire issue of their magazine into a monument to Marcel Proust in which almost every contemporary of mark has placed a stone of praise and devotion; but they continue to print his books in a form which the most corrupt authors of antiquity need hardly envy.

To take a small point first, I could easily fill a column with maimed or distorted words which though not perplexing are provoking: *gourvernés, curioristé, présurseur, insouscieuse, adémicien, atrice, trite:* let these suffice. It is worse when the intruding word is a real one, *décrivant* for *décriant, forme* for *femme, défend les portes* for *devant les portes.* Punctuation is a still more important matter. The fascinating Saint-Simonian syntax of Proust's more elaborate passages makes the same kind of demand on an English reader's attention as that of the speeches in Thucydides or the later autobiographical writings of Henry James; and the strain is wantonly increased when the comma, which can be such a useful little creature under control, is allowed to gambol among the long paragraphs like an ignis fatuus. Proust himself seems to have taken but little interest in his commas, even when they were "inverted"; but this

* From "Correspondence," *The London Mercury,* May 1923.

makes it all the more incumbent on his Editors to keep them in their places.

The most serious complaint is to come. No one who has seen a proof of Proust's in facsimile will blame the compositors for losing their way; but surely there should be someone over them who can distinguish a style from a pepperpot, and perceive, for instance, that "on peut appartenir à une famille princière, et à une famille par le sang, par l'esprit fort populaire" (*C. de G.,* II, 176) is a jigsaw which should be arranged as "on peut appartenir à une famille princière par le sang, et a une famille fort populaire par l'esprit": that in "le navire ..., ainsi que dans une toile apparaissait impressionniste, ... comme si on n'eut fait que découper son avant" (*J. F.,* II, 97) the word "apparaissait" has jumped from its place before "comme": that the paragraph "Bloch s'était montré enchanté ... à l'ambassadeur" on p. 196 of *C. de G.,* I, belongs after "C'est justement ce qui vous enrhume" on the opposite page: and that Proust cannot have meant the sentence at the top of *S. et G.,* II, ii, 122, to survive, after he had rewritten it in the far more polished and pointed form in which it appears at the bottom of p. 121. I could multiply such awful examples. Upon my word, we ought to be thankful that the actual titles of the books have been kept from coalescing, and that there is no volume labelled *A la Recherche des Jeunes Filles Perdues.*

Proust himself (small blame to him, considering the scale of his work, and the conditions in which he did it) committed many inconsistencies and oversights. His great ladies hop from perch to perch in the peerage, and one can never be sure, when next one meets with Mme. d'Arpajon, Mme. de Marsantes, or Mme. de Surgis-le-Duc, whether she will be vicomtesse, comtesse, marquise or duchesse. I defy the most earnest student to give a connected account of the movements of Bloch and M. de Norpois at Mme. de Villeparisis' tea-party; or to reconcile the two versions of that lady's marriage; or the first two appearances of Mme. de Souvré. If Proust had remembered that he had made a joke of Mme. de Montpeyroux being nicknamed "Petite" because she was enormous, he would hardly have repeated it about Mme. d'Hunolstein. It is demonstrable that at the Princesse de Guermantes' reception the entrances of the two undesirable Embassy staffs are really alternative drafts (as it were, an Elohistic and a Jahvistic) of the same incident, only one of which should have been printed. But these accidents, and others like them, are now, alas! irremediable. All the more reason why the publishers should do what is still possible to produce the books in a worthy form.

Mr. Arnold Bennett, who has laid it down that nobody can read Proust except Mr. Walkley, will think this letter a sad waste of space. I hope, sir, that in spite of this Bull you may think it of interest that there should be discussion of even these comparatively noteless blots on a remembered name.—Yours, etc.

E. MARSH

5 RAYMOND BUILDINGS, GRAY'S INN, March 26th, 1923.

24. *The Café Royal**

ARTHUR SYMONS

. . . . TO TELL the same story, without mere repetition, no less than ten times over, to make each telling at once the same and new, a record of the same facts but of independent impressions, to convey by means of each monologue a sense of the speaker not less vivid and life-like than by the ordinary dramatic method, with a yet more

* From *The Café Royal and Other Essays,* privately printed by Beaumont Press, 1923.

profound measure of analytic and psychological truth, and finally group all these figures with unerring effect of prominence and subordination, to fuse and mould all these parts into one living whole: to achieve all this is surely one of the most extraordinary feats of which we have any record in literature. As a mere *tour de force* it is unique.

Proust's method is as difficult and as intricate as Browning's. Certain critics have compared him with Meredith. . . . . Proust's characters are less vivid than Meredith's, and yet they fascinate us. Both face the same problems of race and culture; both are equally impartial in their judgment. Proust glides over scabrous situations like a "smooth-lipped serpent, surely high inspired," as Heine did. . . . .

Proust's conception of the novel is certainly not that of the Goncourts; and yet in certain ways he resembles them; for there is in his work a morbid sensibility, and with this something almost incalculable which seems to come from diseased nerves, which sharpens the acuteness of every sensation to an almost vanishing point in space and which causes him to see life chiefly through this medium. . . . .

The novel as Balzac conceived it . . . . has created the modern novel, but no modern novelist has followed, for none has been able to follow, Balzac on his own lines. Those who have tried to follow him most closely have, sooner or later, branched off in one direction or another, most in the direction indicated by Stendhal. . . . . He discovered for himself and for others after him, a method of unemotional, minute, slightly ironical analysis, which has fascinated modern minds, partly because it has seemed to dispense with those difficulties of creation, of creation in the block, which the triumphs of Balzac have only accentuated. We know something of Julien Sorel's soul; . . . . has the hero of Proust's novels, who is certainly the writer himself, ever given us the vision of his soul? Has he given that peculiar knowledge which the anatomist alone possesses, of the dead body he has dissected? I should be the last to say that he is not a creation; but neither he nor M. de Charlus are creations after the order of Balzac or of Stendhal or of Laclos. . . . . Modernity—art always has its modernity—is as essentially revealed in Wagner as in Manet, Degas, Whistler, Baudelaire and Verlaine. When he lived, the Greeks imagined and rightly that Aristophanes was modern. So, as modernity had a fashion of shaking off the disgust it was at times deluged with, which might lead to the perilous half-way house of a corrupt mysticism, one finds Proust somewhere between these two theories, which are mutually antagonistic. Huysmans said, "That is what impressed me, particularly at that time, to suppress the traditional intrigue, possibly even passion, the woman, to concentrate one's brush on a single character, to create, at any cost, something new."[1] Proust neither suppressed passion nor the woman; only, unlike Balzac, to him women and passion are cruelly contrived in order to play into one another's hands—as when one dices—who play, one imagines, an endless game. Proust, who creates in M. de Charlus an amazing Sadist, never ventured to diagnose, as Huysmans did, a case of sadism in a woman, Madame Chanteleuve of "Là-Bas"; yet he concerns himself with many troubling problems, as he studies hysteria which can at times merge into a mystical corruption. He is wonderful in his intricate analysis of a series of states of nerves, sharpened by tragic ennui, deepened by pathological excesses; he reveals the excesses and the nerves of those who move in an atmosphere of his creation, who endure hallucinations, who are morbid and beautiful and odious; none of whom are quite normal; . . . .

It seems that the modern spirit of analysis and of disillusion, which sheds some of its morbid reflections on the surface of the

[1] "Moi, c'était cela qui me frappait, surtout à cette époque, supprimer l'intrigue traditionnelle, voire même la passion, la femme, concentrer le pinceau sur un seul personnage, faire à tout prix du neuf."

mirror in which Proust sees the images of his creations appear and vanish, wafted thither by blasts from hell or from heaven, has come to admire "L'Education Sentimentale" more than that unsurpassable, perfect and flawless masterpiece "Madame Bovary." . . . .

Only, when Proust casts from one of his magical mirrors a sinister light on some of his evil characters, his irony reminds me of Racine's; Phèdre's incestuous passion becomes insane and abnormal (abnormal in a different sense from M. de Charlus) and yet, strangely enough, logical: that logic which is part of the French temperament. . . . . Now comes Pater's almost cynical comment on certain of Flaubert's confessions: that his almost endless hesitation had much to do with diseased nerves. "Endless hesitations!" Surely, without endless hesitations, no man of genius can create. Rodin would go on working merely because the model was there, and, after two hours' work, discover suddenly the beauty of this living thing which was turning into a new kind of life under his fingers. . . . . Merely to have turned over, as I have, Proust's revised proofs, where hardly an inch of the printed text remains, so intricate are those revisions, so like cobwebs, is to realise what is meant by the phrase "endless hesitations." . . . .

Baudelaire, whose instinct was infallible, said of Balzac: "From the highest of the aristocracy to the lowest of the mob, all the actors in the 'Human Comedy' are keener after living, more alive and cunning in their struggles, more staunch in endurance of misfortune, more ravenous in enjoyment, more angelic in devotion, than the comedy of the real world shows them to us. In a word everyone in Balzac, down to the very scullions, has genius." No one could say this of Proust's characters. They seem always to be on the verge of doing or saying something wonderful: they never do or say anything wonderful. None of these people are tragic: none of these women, such as the wonderful women of Villiers, have in them the immortal weariness of beauty, who do good and evil with the lifting of an eyelid. And yet it is part of his curiosity in souls—as in the equally sinister curiosity of Baudelaire—to prefer the complex to the simple, the perverse to the straightforward, the ambiguous to either. Baudelaire in the preface to *Les Martyrs Ridicules* (1862) of Léon Cladel, points out the fantastic fashion with which he handles sin with the intense curiosity of a Casuist, analysing evil and its inevitable consequences. In the same sense all Hawthorne's work is one form or another of "handling sin": he had the Puritan instinct in his blood, and the power to use it artistically in the brain. Baudelaire notes in Cladel as I note in Proust, "Power with a sinister gift for caricature."[1] But it is in two sentences that he sums up supremely, the beginning and the end of realistic and imaginative art. *"The Poet can still be seen, beneath his mask. The supreme artistic achievement would have been to remain cold and impenetrable, and to leave to the reader the full merit of indignation."*[2]

25. *The Doctor Looks at Literature**

JOSEPH COLLINS

FORCE OR ENERGY in a new form has come into fictional literature within the past decade, and I propose to consider it as it is displayed in the writings of those who are mostly responsible for it: James Joyce, Dorothy

[1] "La Puissance sinistrement caricaturale."

[2] "Le Poète, sous son masque, se laisse encore voir. Le suprême de l'art eût consisté à rester glacial et fermé, et à laisser au lecteur tout le mérite de l'indignation."

* George H. Doran Co., New York, 1923.

Richardson, Marcel Proust, and to consider some of the younger English novelists from the point of view of psychology. . . . . —INTRODUCTION

MARCEL PROUST: MASTER PSYCHOLOGIST AND PILOT OF THE "VRAIE VIE"

Marcel Proust may justly be hailed as the greatest psychological novelist of his time. He was to normal psychology what Dostoievsky was to abnormal psychology: an unsurpassed observer, interpreter, and recorder of men's thoughts and conduct.

It would be hazardous to attempt to estimate the place he will eventually have in literature. . . . . But the volumes . . . . that have appeared . . . . justify the statement that with the death of their author . . . . France lost a writer whose fame will rank with that of Balzac. It is not likely that he will ever have a popularity comparable to Balzac or even Bourget, Barbusse, or several other contemporaries, for M. Proust is an author for writers. He will never be read by the large class of novel readers who create the market demand for novels of action and plot; nor will he appeal to that hardly less numerous class—chiefly women—who find the emotional novel palatable food. However, those who, like the writer, cannot punish themselves by struggling through a detective story and by whom the most skillfully contrived plot can be endured only if the harassment which it causes is counterbalanced by the charm of its literary style or its interpretation of the personality of the author reacting to conditions more or less common to all mankind, may find in M. Proust a novelist whom they can ill afford to ignore. And no writer of fact or fiction today would be just to himself were he to proceed with his art without making the acquaintance of this master artificer and psychologist. Proust will be remembered as a pioneer who explored the jungle of the unconscious memory, and a marvellous interpreter of the laws governing associated memories. I doubt not his name will be as inseparably connected with the novel of the future as that of de Maupassant or Poe has been with the short story of the last few decades, even while his wares will still find scant sale, save to writers, dillettantes, professional students of letters, of form, and of psychology.

. . . . In *Sodom and Gomorrah* he did the impossible. He talked with frankness and with a tone of authority of an enigmatic, inexplicable aberration of nature, inversion of the genesic instinct. . . . . He divested it of pruriency; he rescued it from pornography; he delivered it from pathology; and at the same time he made the penologist pause and "normal" man thoughtful.

. . . . It will mark an epoch in modern civilization when this strange variation from the normal shall be subject to study by such investigators as Mendel, de Vries, Tschermak, and the host of biologists who are slowly solving the mysteries of heredity. Meanwhile the preparation for such work is the formation of public opinion, and probably there is no better way to accomplish it than that adopted by M. Proust. . . . .

The power not only of reproducing scenes and events, but also of revivifying states of consciousness long past through invoking associated memories, is utilised with an effect rarely parallelled in literature. . . . .

Associative memory depends upon the fact that though the grouping of the stimuli is novel, the elementary components are individually similar to previous stimuli, and Proust avails himself of this established fact. These elementary stimuli leave retention traces in the central nervous system. When the same stimuli recur in a new grouping the pathways and centres that bear such traces are brought into connection and are combined in new ways. This modifies the form of the response. As the separate retention traces were due to conditions resembling the present, the new response will tend to be adaptive. This associative memory is known in psychology as mnemonic combination. . . . .

Without doubt M. Proust had a definite idea in mind, a determination to make a contribution: to prove that the dominant force in mental life is association, the chief resource of mentality reminiscence. Thus the primitive instincts of mankind and their efforts to obtain convention's approbation furnish the material with which he has built. It is extraordinary how large association bulks: individuals remind him of famous paintings, not merely the general characters of the people whom he encounters in his daily life, but rather what seem least susceptible of generalization, the individual features of men and women whom he knows. For instance, a bust of the Doge Loredan by Antonio Rizzo, is suggested by the prominent cheekbones, the slanting eyebrows, in short a speaking likeness to his own coachman Rami; the colouring of a Ghirlandajo, by the nose of M. de Palancy; a portrait by Tintoretto, by the invasion of the plumpness of the cheek by an outcrop of whisker, the broken nose, the penetrating stare, the swollen eyelids of Dr. Bolbon.

. . . . Like the monk who seeks God in solitude, like Nietzsche who sought Him in reason, M. Proust has sought to reveal his soul, his personality, the sum total of all his various forms of consciousness by getting memory to disgorge her contents, the key to the chamber being association. . . . .

It may be beside the question to inquire the intention of the author in painting his picture of high society and then dwelling on aspects of it that can only cause disgust. His words at times seem to reveal a sarcastic intention. His descriptions are so full of minute details and so rich in incidents of extreme naturalness that it is impossible to believe that even a lively imagination could fabricate them. One easily sees that they are fragments of real life. This keeps the interest alive, despite the involved style. His periods are so twisted and turgid with associated thoughts, so bristling with parenthetical clauses that often profound effort is required to interpret them. There is none of the plain, clear, sane, sunny style of Daudet, or of Paul Bourget. This causes a sensation of discomfort at times, especially when the author indulges in introspection that reveals a morbid imagination and pathological sensitiveness; as, for instance, in the distinction between abiding sorrows and fugitive sorrows; on how our beloved departed ones live in us, act on us, transform us even more than the living ones; and how those who are dead grow to be more real to us who love them than when they were alive.

We feel an unhealthiness under it all. We have to stop and analyse, to unravel the main idea from the tangled skein in which it is hidden. But it is a work that brings its own reward. It brings real jewels of *"finesse de pensée et d'observation."* . . . .

But to discover such treasures one has often to wade through a series of long and indigestible sentences of thirty or forty lines.

I recall reading in an English magazine, a number of years ago, an article entitled "A Law in Literary Expression." Stated in its plainest terms, the law is this: that the length of the phrase—not the sentence, but its shortest fraction, the phrase—must be measured by the breath pause. M. Proust breaks this law oftener than any citizen of this country breaks the prohibition law, no matter how imperious may be his thirst. . . . .

M. Proust's work is the first definite reply in the affirmative to the question whether fiction can subsist without the seductive power due to a certain illusory essence of thought. Whether in this respect he will have many, if any, successful followers is to be seen. But his own volumes stand as an astonishing example of an organic and living fiction obtained solely by the effort to portray truth.

Because of the unique qualities of his novels and the fact that they are developed on a definite psychological plan, more than the usual interest in a favorite writer is attached to the personality of M. Proust. During his lifetime inaccessible both because of aristocratic taste and of partial invalidism, his figure is likely to become more familiar to the reading world—even to those who never read his books—than the figures of great authors who walked with the crowd and kept the common touch.

Neither Proust the man nor Proust the author can be considered apart from his invalidism. It shows all through his writings, although what the malady was which rendered him, if not a de facto invalid, certainly a potential invalid, is not known. Some of his friends accused asthma, others a disease of the heart, while still others attributed it to "nerves." In reality his conduct and his writings were consistent with neuropathy and his heredity. And if the hero of *Remembrance of Things Past* is to be identified with himself, as is popularly supposed, he was from early childhood delicate, sensitive, precocious, and asthmatic, that is profoundly neuropathic. . . . .

His social activity may have been deliberate preparation for his work, as his fifteen-year apprenticeship to Ruskin was preparation. Or it may have been a pose, much the same as his mannerisms, habits, customs, and possibly some features of his invalidism were a pose. Surely he enjoyed the reputation of being "different."

He ruminated on Rousseau and studied Saint-Simon. When he arrived at the stage where he could scoff at one and spurn the other, he learned Henry James by heart. Then he wrote; he had prepared himself. The deficit which art and endeavor failed to wipe out was compensated by his maternal inheritance.

One may infer whither he is going by reading Proust once, but to accompany him he must be read a second time. Those who would get instruction and enlightenment must read him as Ruskin, his master, said all worthwhile books must be read: "You must get into the habit of looking intensely at words and assuring yourself of their meaning, syllable by syllable."

The discerning reader must look intensely at M. Proust's words. If he looks long enough they seem to take on the appearance of *Mene, Tekel, Phares.*

26. *The Ego and the Universe**

RENÉ LALOU

SINCE THE *Jean-Christophe* series, no one had undertaken to construct a monument comparable in its proportions to *Remembrance of Things Past;* but, while Jean-Christophe's life was told in the third person, the narrative here is entirely subjective, mingling autobiography and the memories of an observer without however there being any question of an automatic development. Proust, indeed, attempted the resurrection of a life by means of memory . . . . "the spaces of my memory became covered little by little with names which, by arranging themselves, by composing themselves with regard to each other, by forming more and more numerous relations among themselves, imitated those finished works of art in which there is not a single isolated touch, in which each part in its turn receives from the others its *raison d'être* as it imposes its own upon them." This sentence from *The Guermantes Way* defines his method. Hence the importance he attaches to Names, the syllables of Balbec or Guermantes absorbing for him the place or the woman they designate, the real

* From *Contemporary French Literature,* by René Lalou, translated from the French by William Aspenwall Bradley, Knopf, 1924.

individuals having but a secondary importance for him who pursues "an aesthetic pleasure," not "an historical curiosity," in a quest where everything relates "to the narrator who says I and who is not always I," if the author is to be believed. . . . . The Past, that is his domain, the present in his narrative being merely an instant of the past upon which he focuses the light of other moments of a past more or less distant. To appreciate his extraordinary skill, one must read the comparison between the two performances of La Berma, or this passage: "Before going to sleep, I thought so long I could not that, even when asleep, I had a little thought left. It was a mere gleam in the almost obscurity, but it sufficed to reflect in my sleep, first the idea that I could not sleep, then, reflection of this reflection, the idea that it was in sleeping I had had the idea I was not asleep, then, by a new refraction, my awakening . . . . to a new nap in which I wanted to tell some friends who had entered my room, that just now, while sleeping, I had thought I was not sleeping. These shadows were scarcely distinct. It would have required a great and very vain delicacy of perception to seize them. Thus later, at Venice, long after sunset, when it seemed to be quite dark, I saw, thanks to the echo, invisible however, of a last note of light indefinitely held on the canals as if by the effect of some optic pedal, the reflections of the palaces unfurled as if forevermore in blacker velvet on the twilight grey of the waters."

Such an example shows the difficulty of speaking precisely of this art without basing each observation upon multiple quotations. At least it permits us also to see by what successive gradations Proust depicts his object, how he corrects the harshness of the words by mobilizing about the affirmation pictorial and melodious combinations which take away its dryness. "I think," he wrote (apropos of Flaubert in whom he admired "the eternal imperfect"), "that the metaphor alone can give a sort of eternity to style." He seeks incessantly the image, nourishing with it his most difficult scenes such as the meeting of Charlus and Jupien in *Sodom and Gomorrah.* He owes it his happiest successes, whether he makes us feel "Rachel balanced by two infinities" or "that privilege of being abruptly present at our own absence" or the pianist "who is only a window looking out on a masterpiece" or this definition in *Within a Budding Grove:* "Beauty is a series of hypotheses narrowed by ugliness which bars the road we saw already opening on the unknown."

There has been much discussion concerning the composition of these thousands of pages. Proust defined it as "rigorous though veiled" and denied obeying "the fortuitous laws of the association of ideas." . . . . His order is sometimes purely verbal and does not seem to him so evident that he can dispense with reminders and warnings. For he is by turns verbose in a parenthesis and concise in a long sentence where several different ideas rise one above the other, mutually enlightened. . . . .

On this immense tapestry certain perfect bits stand forth. A volume of essays will certainly be extracted from *Remembrance of Things Past:* names, images, sickness, death, sleep, music, and snobbishness, sexual inversion (for Proust here had the courage to face a success easy to foresee and, in treating his subject, to disappoint comic hopes). The fact that chapters entitled *Les Progrès irréguliers de l'oubli* (Grief and Oblivion) or *Les Intermittences du cœur* (The Heart's Intermissions) may be isolated from his narrative exactly indicates the strength and the weakness of a work which André Gide has compared to Montaigne's *Essais*—adding however a surprising eulogy: "What I most admire is, I think, his gratuitousness. I know no work more useless or one which seeks to prove less." To which we would willingly reply that *Les Caves du Vatican* is not more partial than this *Remembrance of Things Past,* an apology—against creative imagination—of the passing memory.

It is true Proust has mentioned "that detached, smiling, almost sympathetic benevolence by which we reward the object of our disinterested observation for the pleasure it procures us"; but he has warned us equally that he "places in the last volume his whole theory of art concerning unconscious recollections" which are for him realities after the fashion of Vinteuil's little saying that the musician has not invented but simply liberated. Now does this not come back again to the dangerous generalization of *Les Plaisirs et les Jours:* "Later I was often ill, and for long days I too had to remain in the Ark. I then understood that never had Noah seen the world so well as from the Ark, in spite of its being closed and of its being dark on earth"?—a sentence which explains that curious comment on the sonata in the *Budding Grove,* where Proust denies intelligence, individual or collective, the power to grasp immediately a new beauty. So that, of this art entirely based upon the slow absorption by the ego of the elements time has deposed in it—of this art which leaves the various parts of *Remembrance of Things Past* the aspect of vast mines unequally developed—the last work is perhaps less the love of analysis than the hatred of synthesis.

27. *The Critic's Armoury**

CYRIL FALLS

THERE ARE WRITERS who make their own way to their readers through that jungle which is modern literature, and others who have it hewn for them by the critics. The late Marcel Proust had a good deal of assistance

* Published by Richard Cobden-Sanderson, London, 1924.

from these woodmen in his own country; but in England he had a great deal more. . . . . Most of the English critics of note have set themselves with enthusiasm to the task, and have, in the space of about five years, secured for him an extraordinary notoriety. . . . . As a result, this Frenchman is today as widely discussed as any of our home-bred novelists. . . . .

That Proust is a considerable writer is obvious to all who have given him intelligent study, even if short. But is he really all that he has been claimed to be? Is he, for example, our modern—and not decadent—Balzac? I am not prepared to answer No; yet were there put a stake upon my answer, I should say No rather than Yes. In truth I marvel at the temerity of my fellow-critics. They seem to have no doubts, whilst I find myself full of doubt. Proust appears to me to be very difficult to criticize justly. It is a notable young vintage, doubtless, that suits the present taste; though, even while I say so much, I fancy I detect, like Sancho Panza's kinsmen, some foreign matter in it. That question, however, is not the most urgent. The real difficulty lies in this: how will it "lay down"? And so, in this short study, I shall attempt to make no definite judgment, because I have reached none. Short of that, the personal impressions of each one of us who has been interested by a writer so extraordinary may have their value in helping to unravel the problem of his position.

Consider first the man's manner of writing, since that is so far away from the common that it is what inevitably first strikes one on picking up any of his books. The critics have exhausted their adjectives in striving to describe its subtlety. Subtlety it has, to be sure, but that is, alas! by no means its sole prominent characteristic. The prose of Marcel Proust is finely expressive, but not in the finest fashion. He does not achieve his object by the happy choice of a word which we feel to be inevitable once we have read it, as is so often the case with M. Anatole France; but rather by the use of many words, by a sustained effort, very conscious and very apparent. It is only rarely that he makes his point at once; more often he approaches it like a hunter stalking game. In his inconsequence, his "asides," he sometimes reminds us of Sterne, save that with Proust there is never any jerkiness, but a solid and sustained flow of even language, however much caprice there may be in the thoughts to which he is giving expression. That effect of solidity comes in part from the merely mechanical tricks of his style: no chapters or few, long paragraphs, the absence of commas where we should normally expect them. I have found that I experience pleasure at first in reading a passage, renewed each time that I pick up one of his books; but that after an hour or less there comes weariness and an inclination to turn over two pages at a time. Too often he pursues an idea, a joke, a phrase, to the death. . . . . He is forever explaining, and explaining too much.

And yet, the effect of all these deviations and moralizings and descriptions is in its fashion as remarkable as anything in modern literature. The pictures of men and women, the analysis of their emotions, which they achieve, are bewildering in their perfection and comprehension. It were unjust to compare him in this to a Dutch painter, for the detail of that school is lifeless by comparison with the vitality of Proust's portraiture. Harking back to Balzac, it is at least possible to assert that there has been, since his, no such collection of types in French literature. The analysis of their thoughts goes further than the description of their persons. It is not merely personal but universal; so that at his best he seems to give us the analysis of the secret thoughts of all mankind in microcosm.

Proust is also a wit of a high order. Yet here again we often find lacking that exquisite sharpness and clarity of outline which marks the finest Gallic wit. With his *mots* the edges are generally blurred, though they may be delightful none the less. . . . .

The matter of Proust springs from his style more directly even than is the case with most great novelists. This is because his descriptions of personages and of *mœurs*—that admirable word which covers both our "manners" and "morals"—are what really matter. Of action throughout his series of books there is little. He is never so happy nor so interesting as when he has gathered a party of choice spirits into a room and set them to listen to music and to talk. On such occasions he does continue to keep his reader's full attention for a length of time so great that few authors would dare to attempt the feat. . . . . we have here the world of the modern French salon depicted. . . . .

The aristocratic *salon* is, indeed, his own world. He resembles Balzac in this respect at least, one rare among writers of the past democratic hundred years, that he is an aristocrat in spirit and sympathy. But he had this advantage over the elder: Balzac, despite his particle of nobility, was a plebeian. Poor, rough in manners, a recluse and a slave to his work, he had to depend for his pictures of the great world mainly upon his magnificent imagination; and sometimes even that failed him. Proust, on the other hand, lacking the particle, went about in Parisian society and saw its life from the inside. He may laugh at the Faubourg Saint-Germain, but it is quite apparent that it is to him the most interesting thing in this world. . . . .

This passion appears to have disturbed some of our critics, amid all their enthusiasm. Yet there is little doubt that it is his study of the French aristocracy which is the most notable contribution of Proust to literature. The charm of that world, which so greatly appealed to him, is very real.

. . . . snobbery and injustice counted against him, it is in the picture of the aristocratic life of France and in the realization of its significance that lies the triumph of Marcel Proust. It is because, though he became an ironist instead of a worshipper . . . . because he never lost altogether that sense of what this world had meant in old times, that his heaviness has its moments of inspiration. It is by reason of this, if at all, that he can be ranked among the great novelists. . . . .

There is another side of his work which cannot be neglected, since it fills so large a space in his version of the *Comédie Humaine* . . . . That is his preoccupation with sexual perversion. It is exemplified especially by M. de Charlus and the girl Albertine. Now M. de Charlus is one of the greatest figures among all the *dramatis personae* of Proust. . . . . While he holds the stage there may be intervals of heaviness, but they are continually dissipated by bright flashes. Yet it is M. de Charlus and not his theme that holds us. . . . . I confess that I have never read completely through the first volume of *The Captive.* It appears to be not only gloomy but aimlessly so. Analysis of the tortures of jealousy and dissection of women's methods of lying may be admirably done, but do we want to revolve about them for ever and ever? The only remedy for my feelings that I could discover was to skip ten pages when the strain became too great.

. . . . From *Swann's Way* and *Within a Budding Grove* to *The Captive* the descent is dismal. The last few volumes will probably have to hang precariously to the reputation of the first half dozen. What is to be the final fate of these?

It seems to me not impossible that they may recede considerably into the shade as time goes on. In many respects they are too up-to-date. That may help to account for their present success, but what is topical to one generation is stale to the next, and sets the third a-yawning. That interminable analysis, carried so far that it often seems pointless, is likely to decline rather than grow in favor as its setting changes and grows dim in the memory. I do not know, nor, having from the first striven to describe merely the writer's effect upon my own mind, will I attempt a comprehensive prophecy. To be quite definite in one's verdict is to be very sure of oneself, or very careless of the weight of one's words, or a *poseur.* I know I am not the first, and I trust I am not the second or third. Yet I cannot think that the charm with which Proust endows the life of the "Faubourg" will ever wholly disappear. It at least should assure him a certain position, if not, as his devotees claim now, one among the highest. The earliest of his books appeared but a few years ago, and he died the other day, yet those pictures seem to take on already the air of an "old master"; at risk of damnable iteration I add once more, possibly a minor "old master" only.

28. *A Gallery**

PHILIP GUEDALLA

THE VOGUE has risen into a cult; and the cult, embracing the cultured masses, has deepened into a wave; until the whole of our literary taste is threatened by the towering line of this tidal, this positively Marcel, wave.

. . . . Believed at first by large numbers of people to be a misprint for M. Marcel Prevost, he approached the critical consciousness of these islands with certain radical advantages. He had a singularly attractive personal mythology; and for the English, who have always preferred their geniuses dead, it counted for something that he was dying. His works, when they reached England, were almost posthumous; and their reception was pitched in a becoming tone of slightly lugubrious appreciation. The sick room was felt to be no place for criticism; and M. Proust's earlier readers tip-toed in and out with the proud air of privileged callers. That was, perhaps, permis-

* G. P. Putnam's Sons, New York, 1924.

sible. But since his death, whilst the volume of his published work continues to grow at a rate that most of us find formidable even on a falling exchange, the demeanour of his official admirers begins to do him a singular disservice. Their solemn airs, their hieratic manner, their almost ritual handling of these pleasing works of fiction conspire to render him nearly unreadable. A grave company was recently assembled by an energetic editor, to whom his English readers owe so much. The intention was to lay a wreath of English prose on his grave. But one feels that the gesture was somehow lacking in spontaneity; and it is almost distressing to observe how many of the more distinguished contributors came to bury Caesar, not to praise him. The hysterical commendation of the young (and Mr. Walkley is eternally young) is apt to be outweighed by the frank bewilderment of Mr. Saintsbury, the desperate endeavour of Mr. Conrad to say something polite, and the candid yawns of Mr. Arnold Bennett. On the whole there is not much to be said in favour of these organised *feux de joie* over literary reputations. But how maliciously M. Proust would have described an evening party of his devotees—unless, indeed, he could not face the lamentable shortage of Duchesses. And so few of them could keep an eye-glass in for half a paragraph.

But how far all these solemn gentlemen are from that charming, interminable inventory of a young man's sensations, which was the work of M. Proust, "essayant de me souvenir, sentant au fond de moi des terres reconquises sur l'oubli qui s'assèchent et se rebâtissent."[1] That was the Grail of the whole *Remembrance of Things Past.* It is idle to object that the quest was not worth making, that the contents of a man's spiritual trouser-pockets are hardly the most appetising material for the exercise of art. That, in the dear jargon of the Nineties, is a

[1] "trying to remember, sensing deep inside of me territories won back from oblivion, drying out and building up once more."

question for the artist. The reader is at liberty to close the book whenever he wants to. But when he does, he will have a haunting memory of long days in French provincial gardens; of shadowy aunts; of church towers and the finer shades of snobbery; of vulgar little ladies and of Duchesses, how vulgar their proud creator never knew; of sunshine, and sickbeds, and concerts, and days in the country, and all the little pieces which fit together into life. He will remember *Swann;* and in that memory he may forget the heavenly host of his admirers.

1925

29. *The Writing of Fiction**

EDITH WHARTON

. . . . THE MORE ONE READS of Proust the more one sees that his strength is the strength of tradition. All his newest and most arresting effects have been arrived at through the old way of selection and design. In the construction of these vast, leisurely, and purposeful compositions nothing is really wasted, or brought in at random. If at first Proust seemed so revolutionary it was partly because of his desultory manner and parenthetical syntax, and chiefly because of the shifting of emphasis resulting from his extremely personal sense of values. The points on which Proust lays the greatest stress are often those inmost tremors, waverings, and contradictions which the conventions of fiction have hitherto subordinated to more generalized truths and more rapid effects. Proust bends over them with unwearied attention. No one else has carried as far the analysis of half-conscious states of mind, obscure associations of thought and gelatinous fluctuations of mood; but long and closely as he dwells on them he never loses himself in the submarine jungle in which his lan-

* Charles Scribner's Sons, New York, 1925.

tern gropes. Though he arrives at his object in so roundabout a way, that object is always to report the conscious, purposive conduct of his characters. In this respect he is distinctly to be classed among those whom the jargon of recent philosophy has labelled "behaviourists" because they believe that the proper study of mankind is man's conscious and purposive behaviour rather than its dim unfathomable sources. Proust is in truth the aware and eager inheritor of two great formulas: that of Racine in his psychology, that of Saint-Simon in its anecdotic and discursive illustration. In both respects he is deliberately traditional.

Out of all the flux of judgments and theories which have darkened counsel in respect of novel-writing, one stable fact seems always to emerge; the quality the greatest novelists have always had in common is that of making their people live. . . . .

M. Jusserand, in his *Literary History of the English People,* says of Shakespeare that he was *un grand distributeur de vie,* a great life-giver; it is the very epithet one needs for Proust. His gallery of living figures is immense, almost past reckoning; so far, in that ever-growing throng, it is only the failures that one can count. And Proust's power of evocation extends from the background and middle distance (where some mysterious law of optics seems to make it relatively easy for the novelist to animate his puppets) to that searching "centre front" where his principal characters, so scrutinized, explained, re-explained, pulled about, taken apart and put together again, resist in their tough vitality his perpetual nervous manipulation, and keep carelessly on their predestined way. . . . . Ah, how they all live, and abound each in his or her own sense—and how, each time they reappear (sometimes after disconcertingly long eclipses), they take up their individual rhythm as unerringly as the performers in some great orchestra!

The sense that, through all his desultoriness, Proust always knows whither his people are tending, and which of their words, gestures and thoughts are worth recording; his ease in threading his way through their crowded ranks, fills the reader, ... with the feeling of security which only the great artists inspire. Certain novels, beginning very quietly—carelessly, almost—yet convey on the opening page the same feeling of impending fatality as the first bars of the Fifth Symphony. Destiny is knocking at the gate. The next knock may not come for a long time; but the reader knows that it *will* come, as surely as Tolstoy's Ivan Ilyitch knew that the mysterious little intermittent pain which used to disappear for days would come back oftener and more insistently till it destroyed him.

There are many ways of conveying this sense of the footfall of Destiny; and nothing shows the quality of the novelist's imagination more clearly than the incidents he singles out to illuminate the course of events and the inner workings of his people's souls. . . . .

Proust's pages abound in . . . . anticipatory flashes, each one of which would make the fortune of a lesser novelist. A peculiar duality of vision enabled him to lose himself in each episode as it unrolled itself before him . . . . and all the while to keep his hand on the main threads of the design, so that no slightest incident contributing to that design ever escapes him. This degree of saturation in one's subject can be achieved only through something like the slow ripening processes of nature. Tyndall said of the great speculative minds: "There is in the human intellect a power of expansion—I might almost call it a power of creation—which is brought into play by the simple brooding upon facts," and he might have added that this brooding is one of the most distinctive attributes of genius, is perhaps as near an approach as can be made to the definition of genius.

Nothing can be farther from the mechanical ingenuities of "plot"-weaving than this faculty of penetrating into a chosen subject and bringing to light its inherent properties. Neither haste to have done, nor fear lest the reader shall miss his emphasis, ever affects the leisurely movement of Proust's narrative, or causes him to give unnatural relief to the passages intended to serve as signposts. . . . .

It was one of the distinctive characters of Proust's genius that he combined with his great sweep of vision an exquisite delicacy of touch, a solicitous passion for detail. Many of his pages recall those mediaeval manuscripts where the roving fancy of the scribe has framed some solemn gospel or epistle in episodes drawn from the life of towns and fields, or the pagan extravagances of the Bestiary. Jane Austen never surpassed in conciseness of irony some of the conversations between Marcel's maiden aunts, or the description of Madame de Cambremer and Madame de Franquetot listening to music; and one must turn to "Cranford" for such microscopic studies of provincial life as that of the bed-ridden aunt, Madame Octave . . . .

. . . . just as the reader is sinking delectably into the feather-bed of the small town, Proust snatches him up in eagle's talons and swings him over the darkest abysses of passion and intrigue. . . . .

Every reader enamoured of the art must brood in amazement over the way in which Proust maintains the balance between these two manners—the broad and the minute. His endowment as a novelist—his range of presentation combined with mastery of his instruments—has probably never been surpassed.

Fascinating as it is to the professional to dwell on this amazing virtuosity, yet the lover of Proust soon comes to feel that his rarest quality lies beyond and above it—lies in the power to reveal, by a single allusion, a word, an image, those depths of soul beyond the soul's own guessing. The man who could write of the death of Marcel's grandmother . . . . —the man who could touch with so sure and compassionate a hand on the central mysteries of love and death, deserves at such moments to be ranked with Tolstoy when he describes the death of Prince Andrew, with Shakespeare when he makes Lear say: "Pray you, undo this button. . . . ."

In writing of a great creative artist, and especially of one whose work is over, it is always better worth while to dwell on the beauties than to hunt down the blemishes. Where the qualities outweigh the defects the latter lose much of their importance, even when, as sometimes in Proust's case, they are defects in the moral sensibility, that tuning-fork of the novelist's art.

It is vain to deny, or to try to explain away, this particular blemish—deficiency, it should be rather called—in Proust's work. Undoubtedly there are blind spots in his books, as there are in Balzac's, in Stendhal's, in Flaubert's; but Proust's blind spots are peculiarly disconcerting because they are intermittent. One cannot dismiss the matter by saying that a whole category of human emotions is invisible to him, since at certain times his vision is acutest at the precise angle where the blindness had previously occurred.

A well-known English critic, confusing the scenes in which Proust's moral sense has failed him with those (far more numerous) in which he deliberately portrays the viler aspects of the human medley, suggests that timorous readers might find unmingled enjoyment in the perusal of *Remembrance of Things Past* by the simple expedient of "thinking away" M. de Charlus—as who should propose "thinking away" Falstaff from the plays in which he figures! It would, in fact, be almost as difficult to dismiss M. de Charlus with an "I know thee not, old man," as Falstaff; and quite as unnecessary. It is not by daring to do "in the round" a mean or corrupt character—an Iago, a Lord Steyne, a Philippe Bridau, or a Valérie Marneffe—that a novelist diminishes the value of his work. On the contrary, he increases it. Only when the vileness and the cruelty escape him, when he fails to see the blackness of the shadow they project, and thus unconsciously flattens his modelling, does he correspondingly empoverish the picture; and this Proust too often did—but never in drawing M. de Charlus, whose ignominy was always as vividly present to him as Iago's or Goneril's to their creator.

There is one deplorable page where the hero and narrator, with whose hypersensitiveness a hundred copious and exquisite passages have acquainted us, describes with complacency how he has deliberately hidden himself to spy on an unedifying scene. This episode—and several others marked by the same abrupt lapse of sensibility—might be "thought away" with all the less detriment that, at such moments, Proust's characters invariably lose their *probableness* and begin to stumble through their parts like good actors vainly trying to galvanize a poor play. All through his work there are pages literally trembling with emotion; but wherever the moral sensibility fails, the tremor, the vibration, ceases. When he is unaware of the meanness of an act committed by one of his characters, that character loses by so much of its life-likeness, and, reversing Pygmalion's gesture, the author turns living beings back to stone.

But what are these lapses in a book where countless pages throb with passionate pity and look at one with human eyes? The same man who thus offends at one moment, at the next has one by the heartstrings . . . . And it is almost always at the very moment when the reader thinks: "Oh, if only he doesn't fail me *now!*" that he floods his squalid scene with the magic of an inexhaustible poetry, so that one could cry out, like Sigmund when the gale blows open the door of the hut: "No one went—someone came! *It is the spring.*"

M. Benjamin Crémieux, whose article on Proust is the most thoughtful study of his work yet published, has come upon the obstacle of Proust's lapses of sensibility, and tried, not very successfully, to turn it. According to this critic, Proust's satire is never "based on a moral ideal," but is always merely "complementary to his psychological analysis. The only occasion" (M. Crémieux continues) "where Proust incidentally speaks of a moral ideal is in the description of the death of Bergotte." He then cites the beautiful passage in question: "Everything happens in our lives as though we had entered upon them with a burden of obligations contracted in an anterior existence; there is nothing in our earthly condition to make us feel that we are under an obligation to be good, to be morally sensitive (*être délicats*), even to be polite; nor, to the artist, to begin over again twenty times a passage which will probably be admired only when his body has been devoured by worms. . . . . All these obligations, which have no sanction in our present life, seem to belong to a different world, a world founded on goodness, on moral scruple, on sacrifice, a world entirely different from this one, a world whence we come when we are born on earth, perhaps to return there and live once more under the rule of the unknown laws which we have obeyed here because we carried their principles within ourselves, without knowing who decreed that they should be; those laws to which every deep intellectual labour draws us nearer, and which are invisible only—and not always!—to fools."

It is difficult to see how so deliberate a profession of faith in a moral ideal can be brushed aside as "incidental." The passage quoted would rather seem to be the key to Proust's whole attitude: to its weakness as well as to its strength. For it will be noticed that, among the mysterious "obligations" brought with us from that other "entirely different" world, he omits one; the old stoical quality of courage. That quality, moral or physical, seems never to have been recognized by him as one of the mainsprings of human action. He could conceive of human beings as good, as pitiful, as self-sacrificing, as guided by the most delicate moral scruples; but never, apparently, as brave, either by instinct or through conscious effort.

Fear ruled his moral world; fear of death, fear of love, fear of responsibility, fear of sickness, fear of draughts, fear of fear. It formed the inexorable horizon of his universe and the hard delimitation of his artist's temperament.

In saying so one touches on the narrow margin between the man's genius and his physical disabilities, and at this point criticism must draw back, or linger only in reverent admiration of the great work achieved, the vast register covered, in spite of that limitation, in conflict with those disabilities.

Nietzsche's great saying, "Everything worth while is accomplished notwithstanding (*trotzdem*)," might serve as the epitaph of Proust.

30. *Men Seen**

PAUL ROSENFELD

[IN *Remembrance of Things Past*] . . . . Proust has treated himself as the stuff of fiction; detached himself and seen himself in three-dimensional perspective. . . . . It is well nigh the history of a libido, which is set before us. What Henry James sought all his days to do, to approfundize his own sensations, to explain why a certain place, a certain person, a certain name, stirred him as it did; and what James for some timorousness was never quite able to do, that this nervous Parisian laboriously achieved. . . . .

. . . . in the process of finding the past, Proust was making his roundabout run for liberty. The search for time that was passed was with him, indeed, a rigorous appreciation of the past, a judgment of the value of the past, and consequently, a stripping off of it of the purely irrational glamour with which

* The Dial Press, 1925.

the yearnful, nostalgic unconscious has invested it. . . . . The *Remembrance of Things Past* seems therefore to have been an attempt to give the present and the future the fair chance which the backward-flowing libido would deny to it.

The dense prose mass which has been set forth in the course of this process is a deep stilly moving tide. The nearly *maladif* refinement of his sensibilities, the depth of his psychological insight, has drawn forth from the granary of Proust's mind a stream of the most delicate and subtle detail, and this thick body of material moves in slow, noiseless, deep progression. . . . . Something of the dreaminess and vagueness of the writing of George Moore is in this style, too, although Proust wrote at once more journalistically and carelessly, and more finely and nervously than his Irish brother. The sentences growing out of Proust's orchid-like malady are almost singular in the museum of French literature for their many branchedness, their capricious turns and drops and excursions. . . . . Proust drew his analogies and similes, which arose in him with astonishing spontaneity, from many regions of human exploration. He seems to have learned from history and from botany, and from art, as well as from human intercourse. But his prose is for the greater part quite anti-lyrical . . . . Proust is one of the great psychological instructors; it has been said that one could gather a new LaRochefoucauld from this novel. . . . .

With Proust, the novel of analysis, after almost a century of quiescence, returns to the center of the literary stage. The brothers De Goncourt, Renan, perhaps even Ruskin, helped make possible the subtle effects of this prose; but the work of Proust itself touches hands with the French novel which antedated Balzac and the realistic orientation. . . . . Balzac and Flaubert knew with the greatest exactitude what people did, what they said, how they appeared. But it was rarely that they concerned themselves with the manner of sensation of their characters . . . . The Russians, Dostoievsky in particular, may have situated the actions of their novels largely in the minds of their characters and shown us the subjective world. The French remained without; or, if they wished, as did Flaubert in *La Tentation de Saint Antoine,* to represent the tragedy of thought, they pictured the mind, characteristically enough, in the form of hallucinatory vision. But with Proust there begins again the chain of those novelists whose interest is the complexity of the human heart. . . . . But the fine French critics of the hour, M. Jacques Rivière, for instance, are able to perceive underneath the epidermic differences the blood-relationship, and will tell you no classic novelist has more fully obeyed the classic precept that the novel be "a discourse on the passions," than has this latter-day Parisian. . . . .

Of the qualities which charm in the novel of Marcel Proust, this light, telling painting of a singular and moribund little world will doubtless remain the most durable . . . . There are certain books to which men go for a special sort of evocation. Saint-Simon's memoirs are one of these. The memoirs of Casanova, of a very different flavor, form another; for no one quite knows the sporty life of the eighteenth century who has not wandered about in them. And will not *Remembrance of Things Past* eventually form another of this special series of books which deform a reality and create in its place a superior one? . . . . Proust has not the grand freshness and nobility of manner that was Saint-Simon's; nor the gorgeous sanguineness of the self-styled Chevalier de Seingalt; he remains always the neurasthenic. . . . . He has to show a gallery of portraits of masters and lacqueys, swells and cocottes, of all sorts of people who figured in society in the nineties, which stands almost Balzacian in its largeness of conception and brilliance of detail. And while there are born men of the world and students of human nature and people curious of aristocratic groups with traditions and names and singular manners, he will remain the hierophant of charming mysteries.

1926

31. *Memoirs of Léon Daudet**

. . . . ABOUT HALF-PAST SEVEN, a young man used to drop in to the Café Weber in the Rue Royale. He was pale, with eyes like a deer, always nibbling or pulling one end of his drooping brown mustache, and wrapped up in woolens like a Chinese idol. He would ask for a bunch of grapes and a glass of water, declaring that he had just got out of bed, he had the grippe, he was going home, and the light hurt his eyes. He would look about, anxiously at first, then mockingly; finally he ended by breaking out in a delighted laugh, and not leaving after all. Soon he began to talk and from his lips there flowed, in hesitating, hurried tones, extraordinarily original remarks, and diabolically clever comments. His surprising figures played about in the upper regions like a kind of celestial music, such as one might have heard floating above the Globe Tavern, among the companions of the divine Shakespeare. This young man had something of Puck, something of Mercutio, about him, and pursued several trains of thought simultaneously. He was clever in finding excuses for his good nature, but was devoured by ironic scruples, was naturally complicated, quiveringly sensitive, strangely silky. He was the author of an original, rather mad, book, full of promise, called *Swann's Way*. His name was Marcel Proust.

* Constable & Co., Ltd., London, 1926.

"I beg your pardon, sir, don't you think that . . . ." thus the insidious fellow would begin a conversation, and his unsuspecting prey would fall a victim to his powers of analysis, working somewhat in the manner of a thousand laborious ants. For while Proust, with part of his brain, admires and enjoys the sight of something, he criticises it with another part, and with a third stands off watching indifferently what the other two are doing. I am not surprised that Proust is always tired. I never knew anyone so perpetually haunted by the psychology and physiology of his contemporaries and their forbears, nor anyone who can so completely take their point of view. He is a master of metempsychosis, a phenomenon of auto-creative imagination. On the other hand, he can act for himself and prove his will power when he needs to.

For instance, one evening as he entered the restaurant, Marcel thought he heard an elderly and elegant diplomat named Monsieur de Lagrenée, saying something disagreeable about him. He came over to me. "Monsieur, I cannot bear a thing of this kind. I dislike to make a fuss; nevertheless I shall be greatly obliged to you if you will ask Monsieur de Lagrenée whether he intended to insult me, and if he did not, ask him to present his apologies."

Robert de Flers, the playwright, the most tactful of men, was asked to co-operate with me. We were much worried, for the offender, at least the man we took to be the offender, although no longer young, was a crack shot and expert swordsman, while Marcel was nothing of a warrior. But everything passed off smoothly. Monsieur de Lagrenée said to us: "Gentlemen, I declare on my honor that I never had the slightest intention of insulting Monsieur Proust, whom, as a matter of fact, I have never met. I will add that I do not in the least object to having a young man so touchy. In fact his sensitiveness makes me like him." Then he turned to me: "Your grandmother, Monsieur Daudet, was a friend of my dear sister, a fact which does not help me seem any younger. It was necessary that Monsieur Proust should take offence at a remark not intended for him, in order that you and I should meet. How interesting life is!" This is an instance of the magical atmosphere floating about Marcel and anything one happens to undertake for him.

Marcel Proust hates the country. It upsets his carefully arranged sedentary life, the voluntary confinement in which he reads, dreams, and thinks, and which releases him from the obligations into which his excessive kindness and friendliness would lead him. We once met, some twenty years ago, at the Hôtel de France et d'Angleterre, in Fontainebleau, where we spent a week. During the day Proust kept to his room but in the evening he allowed himself to be persuaded to take a drive through the forest under the stars. He proved the most fanciful, the most whimsical, the most delightful of companions. It was as though a will-of-the-wisp had lit on the cushions of the victoria. Since Marcel does not see what others see, he does see what they do not. It is as if he slipped behind a tapestry and studied its pattern, all the details of its fabric, even at the risk of being taken for a rat by Hamlet. Proust has made a mosaic composed of his observation of actual things, a sort of abstract world in which he dwells quite happily, separated from everything and everybody by a sort of transparent screen.

On another occasion, my brother Lucien managed to persuade him to pay us a visit in Touraine. He came down on the evening train, spent the night in a cloud of Espic cigarette smoke, which he uses for his asthma, and left the next morning declaring that the tranquil magnificence of the Loire is unequalled. This sick meteor, however, left a trail of light in its wake, and I quite believe that our friend Proust has become phosphorescent through excess of intellectual brilliancy.

At the very height of the political conflict in 1901, in other words in the midst of the Dreyfus Case, Proust conceived the idea of giving a dinner party with sixty guests of various shades of opinion. Every piece of china was liable to be smashed. I sat next to a charming young person, looking like a portrait of Nattier or Largillière, who, I afterwards learned, was the daughter of a prominent Jewish banker. Anatole France presided at the next table. The bitterest of enemies ate their *chaud-froid* within two yards of each other, for the currents of understanding and benevolence which originated in Marcel flowed about the guests and enveloped them in coils. For the space of two hours the greatest imaginable good-will reigned among the warriors. I doubt if anyone except Proust could have accomplished that feat. As I was complimenting the host on his achievement he replied modestly: "But, monsieur, really it all depends on the first reaction to each other of the different characters." I gathered that he realized the danger of his experiment and was pleased to see it succeed.

Proust has an ultra-refined taste in literature. He has explored the authors of the seventeenth, eighteenth, and nineteenth centuries down to their very foundations. He can write Michelet that is better than Michelet and turn out Bossuet by the yard. At the same time he can listen with the expression of an attentive school boy to two fools quarreling over the respective merits of Bossuet and Michelet. In fact, he enjoys the depths of their absurdity. He has a sense of caricature, and appreciates how a human being is twisted by his habits, his mannerisms and surroundings. In Proust is the acute vision of La Bruyère and of Meredith, obscured by a mist of childishness rising from his reminiscences of his own childhood, which are unbelievably vivid. I feel Proust is haunted by memories of himself, that he hears constantly the sound of a thousand tiny streams flowing through his veins which have their sources in the hearts of his ancestors and his own youth. If he can manage to guide his steps, to control himself, to establish firmly his literary point of view, he will one of these days write on the margin of life itself something quite extraordinary. All the material is within his reach. . . .

32. *From Pascal to Proust**

G. TURQUET-MILNES

WE HAVE HAD French writers who were sick men before Proust, and the epithet of madmen has not been sparingly applied to them by the healthy, but these thinkers, like great Pascal or subtle Maine de Biran, following the classic French tradition, sought to turn their sickness to good use, neglecting their self, or at least studying it only in so far as such study should be beneficial to humanity. When suffering threw them upon their own resources, their mind being thus forced to produce from its own meditation or memories, some rule of life, gained in depth, and thus acquired psychological knowledge that no outside teaching could reveal. In a measure this is true also of Proust; he could not escape that law which forces every thinking being to concentrate and reflect upon the problem of its destiny, and it is as well to admit at once that he owes it to his unhealthy—deliberately unhealthy—sensitiveness, that he studied himself, watched himself living with so infinitely careful an attention that he surpasses the great self-analysts, Benjamin Constant or Amiel or Meredith. He uses his malady as a microscope which shows him on an enormously enlarged scale all the molecules which swarm and seethe in his heart. That is how he came to give us a new perception of Duration which makes it fitting to set his name beside that of Bergson.

* Boni & Liveright, New York (Butler & Tanner, Ltd., Frome and London), 1926.

There is then in Proust an unhealthy attraction about illness for illness's sake, just as in his work there is a morbid attraction about vice for vice's sake, a liking for what is base or vile just for the pleasure of forcing us to admit that there are base or vile elements in human nature. . . . . Marcel Proust in love is very like Marcel Proust in sickness. Both seek deliberately the art of self-torture; the one after shutting himself up in a close room, wrapped in innumerable shawls, suddenly runs out to what seems to him to be the pleasures of his worldly *clique:* the other, when he loves, uses all his ingenuity for seeing only the ugly cruel side of his idol. He reminds us of the negroes in Central Africa who can worship only a horrible divinity with grinding teeth.

Whilst then the sick men of genius—a Pascal or a Maine de Biran—being chiefly preoccupied with their soul's salvation or the functions of their brain, seek to drive out of their minds all that is false or merely artificial, and above all "all lusts of the flesh or of the eyes, all pride of life," the better to be penetrated by eternal truths, Marcel Proust, enslaved by his education and his instincts, remains always imprisoned in the dominion of the senses. He has neither ability nor desire to escape from his painful love: "Love is time and space made sensible to the heart." . . . . Far too from any religious feeling. Proust never enters that realm which for want of a better word we call "Grace" and with which were well acquainted men so different as Pascal, Blake, or Dostoievsky, and which Epictetus approached. "Difficulty, abnegation, martyrdom, death, are the allurements that act on the heart of man," wrote Carlyle. Quite different are the feelings that act upon the heart of Marcel Proust. He makes no spiritual ascent: he climbs to the top of his artistic cathedral guided by Ruskin, the better to embrace his own age. But he is no nearer to God for that. . . . .

Somewhere in his *The Captive* Proust evokes the presence of Dostoievsky, he writes very acutely about him, and he is very careful to note the original trait in the Russian which makes him see that "love and bitter hatred, kindness and treachery, timidity and insolence, are but degrees in one and the same nature." There is something of that in Proust. . . . .

The vision of immortal sin would seem to exhilarate Proust like some horrible concierge primed with low gossip. We should tremble for him were it not that an art about which he has written wonderful passages comes to save him from himself, the art of music. Clearly Proust is of Stendhal's opinion that we enjoy music only in the dreams it brings us. . . . .

Proust offers us an original, but not a new answer to the question asked by countless ages: What is the purpose of music? The answer is more or less of a commentary on the famous myth of the music of the spheres. Music, according to Sir Thomas Browne, is "a shadowed lesson of the whole world," but the lesson must be read with Plato's remark that music is character in the soul of the composer and in the soul of the listener. Leibnitz added that music was *arithmetica nescientis se numerare animi*—the arithmetic of our soul not knowing that it is counting, which is putting epigrammatically the effect of music so idealised that it is no longer space but time. Proust, by very reason of his being steeped in Bergsonian philosophy, comes very near this conception. For without wishing to depreciate Proust's undeniable talents, it is perhaps not pedantic to point out here that in a sense he is following exactly the same path as Bergson in his effort to understand the audible and inaudible harmony of the world. . . . .

For the moment one thing matters: music is the work of our self which changes so completely that what we thought even today no longer belongs to us. Just as human personality is divided into countless numbers of beings ceaselessly in pursuit of one another, so music with its fluidity, its harmonies, its discords and its syncopations, is composed of a ceaselessly changing becoming.

That is why Bergson and Proust attach so great importance to memory, the unconscious and dreams. According to Bergson memory is something other than a function of the brain, and there is not a difference of degree, but of kind, between perception and recollection. We have on this point the exceedingly profound pages of *Matter and Memory*. . . .

In his first book, and later in his others,[1] Proust from time to time comes back to this "terrible recreative power of memory." He is emphatic that it is involuntary, and on this point is in close agreement with Bergson, who declares in every way that our past is automatically preserved within us. Proust must have read Bergson very carefully. Of all novelists he is certainly the one who by slightly modifying the philosopher's system, adapting it for the cultivated reader, adorning it with all the seduction of his own style, has striven hardest to prove to us that memory by purifying reality allows us to grasp reality and essentials. "The flowers you show me today do not seem to be real flowers . . . . reality is formed only in the memory."[2] Robert de Montesquiou has been here, but the main responsibility is Bergson's. . . . .

M. Crémieux's study of Proust is a very penetrating one, but it has a grave fault of omission—we miss the Bergsonian statue on the threshold of this Proustian edifice. The novelist loses none of his originality—on the contrary—for plunging his root into the rich soil of a philosophic system whose greatness is undeniable: far from becoming a destroyer—as has been so often said—Proust becomes a true constructor. This philosophy enables him to revolutionise the novelist's art: since he may devote many pages to a happening which could have lasted only a few instants, while, like the astronomer, he may condense mathematical time into a few lines, one might almost say a few figures.

It may be well to point out that Proust is in this point less

[1] *Swann's Way,* I, 45; *Within a Budding Grove,* I, 196. [2] *Swann's Way,* I, 170.

of an innovator than may at first appear. Long before Proust, Marivaux and his disciple Sterne had written novels like the cinema moving at infinitely diminished speed. Proust's enemies should study his illustrious predecessors . . . . Read Sterne again after reading Proust, and you cannot fail to be struck by the resemblance between a certain aspect of their brains; both have a comic gift, the salt of mockery, mimicry which will ever keep their work fresh.

. . . . No writer has analysed as he has the world of sleep: his pages on "that inner Lethe with sextuple folds" are a most brilliant commentary on Bergson's study of dreams. The two . . . . complete each other in the happiest fashion. Bergson is colder, calmer, more scientific, Proust is livelier, more thrilling. He puts aside his terrestrial covering just as we, entering those vague dream-states, put aside everyday reality to penetrate into another truer, deeper reality in which we may be visited by our dead coming to prove the truth of Auguste Comte's dictum that it is they who guide the course of the living.

Herein Proust rose above his time—far above all that overflow of Asiatic art composed of all too frequently gross sensations, vulgar sadness, sickly religiosity, which abounds in French prose from 1890–1914.

. . . . In his best mood, above all when writing on music, Proust has written pages which would be the pride of any writer, nor should the critic be in a hurry to declare that behind so many new and striking beauties lurks a pharmaceutical or physiological mystery, a physical anomaly—a drug's action.

. . . . Side by side with his indifference to morality (which is not the same thing as immorality) there is in Proust an almost Puritanical strain, a hardness with much more energy than at first appears, and which cannot be understood unless we remember that on his father's side Proust belongs to that old French bourgeoisie whose solid virtues are based upon a high conception of duty. Proust belonged, or wished to belong, to that Parisian world for whom everything appertaining to etcher's-needle or mahl-stick, pen or palette is sacred, but only those things, a world which denies the existence of sin and which counts it as an honour to number among its members lettered monsters or dilettanti bandits. The memory of our own time will furnish curious reading to our grandchildren, who will see that pre-war Paris—or a part of it—was a veritable pandemonium, ennobled by art.

. . . . M. Crémieux declares that Proust rejects from his work everything which is moral action and practical reason: I think he is mistaken. In Proust's soul is waged a mortal combat, in which he goes under. That is the tragedy of Proust's life.

His conception of the universe—which he owes partly, we must remember, to Spinoza and to Bergson, is that of a philosopher for whom current ideas of morality are meaningless. The conscience animating the universe is an endless vital impetus guided by nothing. It is a prodigious invention of marvellous, curious and new works of which nothing gives us warning, and which no one can foresee. . . . .

In Proust, then, though he hides it as best he can in order to appear more modern, more Parisian, war is declared between the aesthete who wishes to "live his life his own way," and who consequently denies the existence of morality, and the moralist whose desire is to be good, virtuous, altruistic, wise according to the ancients' formula: between the artist who desires to follow his instincts, and the philosopher who, perceiving that society is but dupery, desires only to be, and frequently succeeds in being, a pamphleteer. There is in Proust a craving to be revenged upon life which eludes him—for he knows he has received his death sentence—and at the same time a morbid hunger for its enjoyment at any cost: complex feelings which explain the fascination certain of his pages exercise upon the psychologian.

Like Don Juan, Proust wants to enlarge his personality by new conquests, but he does not succeed in escaping from what his friends would call sheep-morality. There are in life primordial feelings from which no man can escape—among others that most primitive and most painful of feelings—jealousy. Never has novelist analysed this feeling so acutely as Proust. He pursues it to its most secret hiding places, and in many pages the portrait he draws of himself in this torment is that of an *écorché*—a man stripped of his skin and every quivering nerve laid bare. . . . .

It is surprising that the French critics have not seen how deeply Proust was obsessed by the idea of God, though he only speaks of Him once and then only indirectly. No, virtue is no meaningless word for him.

. . . . Many reasons may be proposed to explain his real thirst for justice, chief of them is probably the naturally good foundation of his nature. This happy honest character in Proust explains not only the evangelical indulgence with which he looks on some of the ways in which our feelings lead us astray, but also that imperious need of sincerity which rules him and makes him rebel against all hypocrisy. . . . .

Proust is above all sincere; he is perhaps the only novelist who is not afraid to contradict himself. If there be a theory he holds dear it is assuredly that of the multiplicity of our self. Yet he also notes that "Swann was no longer capable of renewing his way of loving, the way he had used for Odette still served him for another." This is in direct contradiction with that other thought so dear to him—and true, too—that one person can have a thousand ways of loving, it merely depends upon one of his avatars.

If posterity reads Proust it will be for his symbolic rather than for his literary value. . . . .

The critic who is interested in the "natural history of minds" cannot but be astonished as he reads his Proust after reading his Pater at the very striking resemblances between the two. . . . . Proust is really a second Marius the Epicurean who lives in the real and the concrete, and, to use Pater's phrase, "by system in reminiscence." Proust's intellectual activity has never been so well summed up as by Pater some thirty years before his time: "a strange trick memory sometimes played him; for, with no natural gradation, what was of last month or of yesterday, of today even, would seem as far off, as entirely detached from him, as things of ten years ago."

Proust is a hedonist to whom the grace of God . . . . or Plato was mainly lacking, because he never *really* loved nature. Pater has an illuminating little sentence which tells us a very great deal about Marius and explains his spiritual end: "In those grand hot summers he would have imprisoned the very perfume of the flowers." Not so Proust, he was never more than the toy of the tropical garden in which he shut himself. The hothouse wherein he breathed the heavy perfumes of most deadly flowers was that little select world in Paris which has no place for a really religious man. In all Pater's work we see the ghost of Pascal overshadowing him, and in the end Pater died, pen in hand, trying to understand the author of the *Pensées*.

But Proust in his eternal pursuit of singular sensations understood that he would never be so completely himself as when relating his own past. Thenceforward humanity is resolved into juvenility. He is always the *"Child in the House."* Universal man in his work becomes nothing more than a grown-up child. Sensitiveness becomes the source of all knowledge. Proust's real field is the pursuit of the obscure forces of the human being, the impressionism of the infinitesimal. Whatever may be the final judgment passed on his work we should be grateful to him for taking us behind the scenes of the unconscious and for having reclaimed a little ground from the seas of mystery encircling us.

1927

33. *Aspects of the Novel**

E. M. Forster

. . . . Rhythm in the easy sense is illustrated by the work of Marcel Proust.

Proust's conclusion has not been published yet, and his admirers say that when it comes everything will fall into its place, times past will be recaptured and fixed, we shall have a perfect whole. I do not believe this. . . . . The book is chaotic, ill constructed, it has and will have no external shape; and yet it hangs together because it is stitched internally, because it contains rhythms.

There are several examples (the photographing of the grandmother is one of them), but the most important, from the binding point of view, is the "little phrase" in the music of Vinteuil. The little phrase does more than anything else . . . . to make us feel that we are in a homogeneous world. We first hear Vinteuil's name in hideous circumstances. The musician is dead—an obscure little country organist, unknown to fame—and his daughter is defiling his memory. The horrible scene is to radiate in several directions, but it passes.

Then we are at a Paris salon. A violin sonata is performed and a little phrase from its andante catches the ear of Swann and steals into his life. It is always a living being, but takes various forms. . . . .

That seems all. The little phrase crosses the book again and again, but as an echo, a memory; we like to encounter it, but it has no binding power. Then, hundreds and hundreds of pages on, when Vinteuil has become a national possession, and there is talk of raising a statue to him in the town where he has been so wretched and so obscure, another work of his is performed—a posthumous sextet. The hero listens—he is in an unknown rather terrible universe while a sinister dawn reddens the sea. Suddenly for him and for the reader too, the little phrase of the sonata recurs—half heard, changed, but giving complete orientation, so that he is back in the country of his childhood with the knowledge that it belongs to the unknown.

We are not obliged to agree with Proust's actual musical descriptions (they are too pictorial for my own taste), but what we must admire is his use of rhythm in literature, and his use of something which is akin by nature to the effect it has to produce—namely a musical phrase. Heard by various people—first by Swann, then by the hero—the phrase of Vinteuil is not tethered; it is not a banner such as we find George Meredith using—double-blossomed cherry tree to accompany Clara Middleton, a yacht in smooth waters for Cecilia Halkett. A banner can only reappear, rhythm can develop, and the little phrase has a life of its own, unconnected with the lives of its auditors, as with the life of the man who composed it. It is almost an actor, but not quite, and that "not quite" means that its power has gone towards stitching Proust's book together from the inside, and towards the establishment of beauty and the ravishing of the reader's memory. There are times when the little phrase—from its gloomy inception, through the sonata, into the sextet—means everything to the reader. There are times when it means nothing and is forgotten, and this seems to me the function of rhythm in fiction; not to be there all the time like a pattern, but by its lovely waxing and waning to fill us with surprise and freshness and hope.

34. *Marcel Proust—His Life and Work**

LEON PIERRE-QUINT

WHEN *Swann's Way* first appeared, the work was held to be confused, full of digressions, over-luxuriant, burdened with too great detail. Its true significance was not apparent. Proust had set himself an immense task of the fathoming of depths. What was to him an exploration in the interior of beings and things seemed to others to be no more than minute descriptions. And some time was necessary before the sense of his method could be appreciated.

This method is first and foremost a painful, almost agonized effort to penetrate to the very bottom of nature and of men. It is directed to the prizing open of secrets, and it lays bare unsuspected treasures. And in this way it comes in the end to certain great laws: a law of movement, a law of evolution, a law of the unconscious. . . . .

The psychology of Marcel Proust is something that surpasses the quality of mere observation. The analysis is based upon the personal impressions of the writer. His novel, as he himself said, is real, because nothing is more real than the contents of one's ego. . . . .

. . . . The style of Proust reveals his extraordinary undertaking: to reach by intuition and to express by intelligence the most fleeting sensations of the inner life. . . . .

* From *André Gide, His Life and Work,* Alfred A. Knopf, New York, 1927.

The undertaking of Marcel Proust calls for a new style. The language is so original that it is necessary to learn it, as if it were a kind of foreign tongue, all the words of which would be already known to us. The reason is at first rebuffed by the lengthy and entangling sentences, as a pupil is by exercises in diction or solfeggio, but then he grows accustomed to the difficulties and is astonished to find that his reading has become easy. . . . .

Proust . . . . is attempting to enclose within one single period, not only a moment of the life of our consciousness, but further to enclose within it the *milieu* or the landscape, the characters near us, our occupation in that moment, our ego seen from within and from without at one and the same time. . . . .

Writing to Louis de Robert, Marcel Proust said: "My concern is only in that which seems to me to unfold (in a sense analogous to that of the carrier-pigeon) some general laws." And so this distracted quest after the most fleeting sentiments of our consciousness leads the writer to the discovery of certain great ideas. An artist first and foremost, he has not sought to develop them. No work is less of a thesis than his. A certain world has imposed itself upon him. He knows that by courageously penetrating it to a sufficient depth a spontaneous philosophy will be set free. "Every great artist," he wrote, "who voluntarily leaves reality to expand in his books forgoes the appearance in these of an intelligence, a critical judgment which he holds inferior to his genius."

But to the attentive reader there emerges first and foremost this great idea, that our inward life is not intelligible. If Proust dissects and reconstructs states of consciousness by means of the logical processes of language, it is only to tell us that logic does not apply thereto. The passages which, from a literary point of view, are the most remarkable of the novel lead us to this conclusion: that the emotional life has its own particular laws differing altogether from those of the intelligence. There exists an association and a memory of sentiments, which are not the association and memory of ideas. Their obscure workings are hidden under the unconscious, which itself forms the most essential part of our ego.

Marcel Proust reaches the same ultimate conclusions as the modern philosophers. By these it is stated at the present day that the conscious is only one lighted point on the vast, dark expanses of the unconscious. Some, such as Freud, declare that the unconscious is so vast that its deepest parts remain always obscure, always suppressed, and are visited only occasionally by the troubled light of our dreams.

This is just what Proust realized. And this is why sleep, the great manifestation of the unconscious, interests him so much . . . . it is from out of this unconscious, as from a hiding place, that Proust draws forth the wonderful treasures which he proceeds to analyse in the light of intelligence. Dreaming and sleeping make up one of the great sources from which the novel gradually emerges.

One of these treasures is the emotional memory . . . .

Baudelaire was perhaps the first to demonstrate the poetic charm of odours and tastes. Proust explains the part which they play in the mechanism of the unconscious. The perceptions of each of his senses remain, for him, linked with emotional memories. . . . .

. . . . Marcel Proust always reaches the conclusion that the intelligence is incapable of recalling to us the reality of our joys and sorrows. And it is no less impotent to bring back to life our beloved dead. The love we bear them is hidden in the unconscious and the unconscious alone is capable of awakening them . . . .

. . . . In an unpublished letter Marcel Proust explained himself in this connexion: "It is a book," he wrote, "of the utmost reality, but *supported,* in a way, in order to imitate the involuntary working of the memory (which in my opinion, although Bergson does not make this distinction, is the only true one, the memory of the intelligence and of the eyes giving us back the past only in inaccurate facsimiles, which do not resemble it any more than the pictures of bad painters resemble the spring, etc. . . . .) by abrupt recollections. One part of the book is a part of my life which I had forgotten and suddenly find again in eating a piece of cake which I had dipped in a cup of tea . . . . Another part of the book springs up again from those moments of awakening, when one does not know where one is, and imagines one is in another country, and two years ago. But all that is the *scaffolding* of the book. And what it conveys is real, impassioned" . . . . from these various phenomena, there will emerge 'a whole theory of memory and knowledge' though not promulgated directly in logical terms. . . . .

"We bathe not twice in the same stream," wrote Heraclitus. The world of our sentiments is an uninterrupted flow—a continuous gushing, say the modern philosophers. It is to this thought that we are led by the psychology of Proust. Our ego is modified every moment. Every sensation, every sentiment, grows old by the very fact of its duration. And here lies the second great idea of Proust's: that our conscious and unconscious life is an unceasing process of evolution. . . . .

. . . . In spite of the criticisms of the ignorant or foolish, the work (Proust's novel) is so magnificently constructed that its conclusion is already enclosed within its starting point and is only one great expansion. In the two themes of the unconscious and of evolution it is present in its entirety. One proceeds from memory to art, the other from birth to death; the first is developed in our inner duration, the second in time itself. And Proust teaches us that all that exists in time is lost, that what is in our own duration is a treasure revealed.

In this way alternate these two leading motives, with the

aid of which the writer, in accordance with a superior order, expresses his creative genius. . . . .

Marcel Proust, it may be, passed a great part of his life in listening to the conversation of his friends, the people in a drawing-room, and in ceaselessly provoking answers to his questioning "But tell me, please . . . .?" But he had a reason: with him there was no better light into the hearts of men than their language. Guided by their own peculiar phraseologies, he descended into their consciousness, as a miner follows the veins of ore through the obscurity of the galleries. . . . . The Verdurins, the Guermantes—he plays them on the stage of his novel Unable to let himself be heard or seen by the reader, grimacing, waving his arms, changing his intonation, laughing, he makes them speak, in monologue or dialogue, and he makes his commentary, with the aid of parentheses—or incidents placed within dashes—their nervous tricks or their eccentricities.

It is of course, the most familiar, the most everyday, of their conversations that he reproduces. . . . .

How does the reader succeed in extracting his most secret states of consciousness from his most commonplace conversation? . . . . by the pathology of the language, interpreted in all its exactitude, that Proust reveals his characters to us. . . . .

. . . . What interests the writer is not what his characters are thinking of each other; it is the manner in which they express what they are thinking. Proust is too much of a Bergsonian not to be aware that words never correspond to the fineness of our sensibilities. Language was created by man when he was seeking his nourishment, when he struggled against the beasts of the wild, when he was contriving instruments of war, of iron, for utilitarian ends. So language is precise and supple when it is applied to the sciences, but vapid and clumsy when it is obliged to convey our states of consciousness. . . . .

When Freud declares that *lapsus linguae* are not simply

matters of distraction, but correspond with certain obscure feelings pushed back within us, is he not working on the same lines as Proust? . . . .

But Proust goes further. As in life itself, where the slightest thought of other people's could not pass unnoticed by this veritable wizard, so, attentive in listening to Albertine's conversation, he seized hold in this way of the tiniest movement of her mobile conscience. . . . .

No doubt the merit of a novel is not made by its philosophic ideas. But when a novel has the vastness of *Remembrance of Things Past,* it is they alone that allow us to penetrate it. They are the true keys to the work, those keys which the public has sought for every character among our contemporaries, and sought so vainly. It is true that to-day "Time Recaptured" is still unpublished, but I think that the detailed study of each aspect of the work, so far as it has already appeared, allows us to fill up this lacuna without difficulty. "Time Recaptured" will probably not be so much an intellectual surprise as a splendid artistic confirmation.

Human consciousness, to take the Bergsonian image no doubt dear to Proust, is covered with a thick crust into which our habits, the feelings customary to us, have solidified. It is there, in this outer covering of consciousness, that we find the machinery mounted, the ready-made sentiments, requisite for our everyday work and conversations. But beneath this superficial layer there lies in us the richer part, the essential part of our self, which scarcely ever intervenes in our daily activities. For the truth is that we are perpetually playing one single part, like those actors or actresses who are La Dame aux Camélias, or L'Aiglon, to their dying day. We cry out, we laugh, we even shed real tears, but all without our deeper personality's having to come upon the stage. Our reflexes, our memory-habit, make us perform the necessary gestures and utter mechanically the necessary words. . . . .

The artist, on the other hand, is free. It is from the heart of his individual consciousness that he draws the sources of his art. "Vinteuil . . . . with all the strength of his creative effort, attained his own essence at those depths where, whatever the question that faced him, it was with the same accent, his own particular accent, that his essence responded." And Bergson writes: "Between nature and ourselves, or rather between us and our own consciousness, a veil is interposed, a veil that is opaque for the generality of men, but thin, almost transparent, for the artist and the poet." And he adds, giving a definition of art which is almost that of Proust: "Art has no other object than to set aside the symbols of practical utility, the generalities that are conventionally and socially accepted, everything in fact which masks reality from us, in order to set us face to face with reality itself." Thus, according to the writer, the reality of the external world lies in the inner life of things and of ourselves, and this reality, if art did not give it expression, would remain forever unknown to us. It is upon art that the Proustian universe is founded. . . . .

A legend takes shape with rapidity: Marcel Proust—novelist of memory and of the life of fashion. Nevertheless, it is forgotten that he is first and foremost an artist, that no one loved art, the supreme goal of life, more passionately and more disinterestedly than this so-called "snob."

His articles on Baudelaire and Flaubert, his prefaces to the translations of Ruskin, bear witness, as does the whole of his existence, to his passion for the labour which is the artist's lot. The works created by the artist, Proust brings back to life in his own books; and the astonishing intensity with which he has done this has not perhaps been adequately noticed. Most novelists when they have to speak of some work of art in their books, will cite some definite historic masterpiece—the Sistine Chapel, or the Cathedral of Rouen. But such works are not given a name in Marcel Proust's pages. Following his usual procedure, he borrows from Debussy, from Wagner, from Saint-Saëns, different phrases of their music, and makes a literary re-composition of the sonata and the Vinteuil quartet, a sonata and a quartet which emanate entirely from his own imagination—and a sonata greater perhaps than any real sonata, for it allows the reader to enshrine within it the corpus of his own most cherished musical memories. He is not here performing the functions of an art critic. He does not expound the beauties of the Wagnerian *Nibelungen* cycle, or the charm of a painting by Vermeer. He does not talk like most professional critics of the *colour* of this music, or of the *singing* tone of that colour, resting content with these transpositions of the values of an art from one direction to another. In his pages he re-creates a work, the sonata, the quartet, the church at Balbec, and, investing it with an abstract and general character, he penetrates it and sinks into it so deeply that it becomes animate and enduring, making us dream of the morality and philosophy which, by virtue of art, lies there within it. . . . .

We are brought finally to the conclusion that from Proust's books there emerges the same lesson as from his life. This writer, whom love and pleasures played false, who might easily seem to be a man given over to despair, suddenly recovers his strength as admirer and idealist. This man who gave up so many of his years to the life of fashion, is in reality nothing less than the type of the pure artist.

Proust, while turning back to the classics, loved to discover new forms of art. He was too strongly imbued with the spirit of evolution and of life for his taste to remain fixed, or for it not to seek out the art that creates itself, that is born, that comes, the art like his own. . . . . among a few pure artists Marcel Proust is the most astonishing: it was after he had made study of men, of duels, of love, of the vices, that he withdrew like a monk into his chamber, and began his adoration of art as of his God. . . . .

35. *Time and Western Man**

Wyndham Lewis

In his *Time and Western Man,* which Wyndham Lewis offers as a "comprehensive study of the 'time' notions which have now, in one form or another, gained an undisputed ascendancy in the intellectual world" he says: "How the 'timelessness' of Einsteinian physics, and the time-obsessed flux of Bergson, merge in each other; and how they have conspired to produce, upon the innocent plane of popularization, a sort of mystical time-cult is shown. . . . . With this end in view I have chosen to open the discussion among books such as those of Proust or Joyce, which have been widely read, and which are popularly accessible, and in which I consider that, with a very little attention, the *time-cult* can be observed in full operation. . . . .

"That Joyce and Proust are both dedicated to Time is generally appreciated, of course; Joyce is often compared to Proust on that score. Both Proust and Joyce exhibit, it is said, the exasperated time-sense of the contemporary man of the industrial age; which is undeniable, if the outward form of their respective work is alone considered . . . . Bergson and his time philosophy exactly corresponds to Proust, the abstract for the other's concrete . . . ."

But, to Lewis, Proust differs from Joyce, in that Joyce "collected like a cistern in his youth the last stagnant pumpings of Victorian Anglo-Irish life. This he held steadfastly intact for fifteen years or more—then when he was ripe, as it were, he discharged it, in a dense mass, to his eternal glory. That was *Ulysses.* Had the twenty-year-old Joyce of the *Dubliners* not

* Harcourt, Brace and Company, Ltd., New York, 1927.

remained almost miraculously intact, we should never have witnessed this peculiar spectacle."

"That is, I believe, the true account of how this creative event occurred with Joyce; and, if that is so, it will be evident that we are in the presence of a very different phenomenon from Proust. Proust *returned* to the *temps perdu.* Joyce never left. them. He discharged it as freshly as though the time he wrote about were still present, because it was *his* present. It rolled out with all the aplomb and vivacity of a contemporary experience, assisted in its slick discharge by the latest technical devices.

"So though Joyce has written a time-book, he has done it, I believe, to some extent, by accident. Proust on the contrary, was stimulated to all his efforts precisely by the thought of compassing a specifically time-creation—the *Remembrance of Things Past.* The unconscious artist has, in this case, the best of it, to my mind. Proust, on the other hand, romanticizes his Past, where Joyce (whose Present it is) does not."

In another passage Lewis places Proust amid what he calls "the child-cult." This cult, he holds, "is connected with the cult of the *primitive* and *savage,"* is the "same impulse that takes the romantic painter Gauguin to the South Sea paradise, takes a similarly romantic person of today to the Utopia of childhood"—and concludes that this "was really Proust's Utopia, too. And the great appeal of that author is partly because he shows a method for capturing and retaining that spirit—*Remembrance of Things Past*—and partly because he so feverishly expresses the will to that particular dream. As we read him, the 'I' of his books is that small, naif, Charlie-Chaplin-like, luxuriously-indulged, sharp-witted, passionately snobbish, figure, a model for many variations bred thickly everywhere."

Finally: "In Proust . . . . one of the ideal examples of a projection on the grand scale, in narrative form, of the philosophy of 'time'—we have in a sense a new type of historical practitioner. Proust embalmed himself alive. He died as a sensational creature in order that he should live as an historian of his dead sensational self, which expired about the time that lyrical poets are supposed to snuff out. Or rather he did in a sense really die; when those complicated and peculiar meeds of admiration exacted by his slight, ailing, feminine body, with deep expansions of bottomless vanity, were in the nature of things no longer forthcoming, and life's (for him) paradoxical receptive trance was terminated, he bleakly awoke; in his wakeful industrious nights he began stealthily revisiting the glimpses of the sun of the past time-scene. That was his way of making himself into an historical personage, by embalming himself in a mechanical medium of 'time'."

1928

36. *Hogarth Essays**

E. M. Forster

And Proust—how amazingly does Proust describe not only French society, not only the working of his characters, but the personal equipment of the reader, so that one keeps stopping with a gasp to say "Oh! how did he find that out about me? I didn't even know it myself until he informed me, but it is so!"

37. *Pleasures and Days*†

Anatole France

Why did he ask me to stand sponsor to his book, and why did I promise to undertake that very pleasant but quite superfluous task? His book is like a

* New York, 1928. Reprinted by permission of Doubleday, Doran & Co., Inc.

† From *Prefaces, Introductions, and Other Uncollected Papers,* translations, notes and foreword by James Lewis May, Dodd, Mead and Company, New York, 1928.

young poet, full of rare and delicate charm. It bears with it its own commendation; it pleads its own cause and offers itself in its own despite.

Of course it is young. It is young with the author's own youthfulness. But it is old too, as old as the world. It is the leafage of springtime on the ancient branches of the age-old forest; yet it might be said that the fresh shoots sadden over the immemorial past of the woods and robe themselves in sorrow for so many dead springs.

To the goatherds of Helicon, the grave Hesiod sang the *Works and Days*. It would be a sadder task to sing *The Pleasures and Days* to the fashionable men and women of our times, if there be any truth in the saying of that English statesman who averred that "life would be tolerable were it not for its pleasures." And so our young friend's book shows smiles tinged with languor, attitudes of fatigue which are not devoid of beauty or nobility.

In its sadness it will touch many soft and divers chords, sustained as it is by a marvellous spirit of observation, by a penetrating and truly subtle intelligence. This calendar of the *Pleasures and Days* portrays alike the moods of nature by harmonious pictures of sky and sea and forest, and depicts the moods of man by faithful portraits and by *genre* paintings of wonderful minuteness.

Marcel Proust takes equal pleasure in describing the lonely splendours of the setting sun and the restless vanities of a worldly heart. He excels in the telling of exquisite sorrows, of artificial sufferings, which are at least as cruel as those which Nature lavishes upon us with maternal generosity. I confess that these farsought sufferings, these sorrows discovered by human ingenuity, these factitious griefs, strike me as wonderfully interesting and valuable, and I am grateful to Marcel Proust for having studied them and furnished a few choice examples.

He attracts us and holds us in an exotic atmosphere amid cultivated orchids whose strange and morbid beauty is nourished on no earthly soil. Suddenly through the heavy-scented air, there strikes a shaft of light, a flash which, like the ray of the German scientist, traverses the body. In an instant, with a single stroke, the poet has probed the hidden thought, the longing unavowed.

Such is his manner, his art. He displays in it a sureness of aim surprising in so young an archer. He is not in the least innocent. But so sincere is he, and so true, that he takes on a character of naïveté, and that in itself conveys a charm. In him there is something of a depraved Bernardin de Saint-Pierre and an ingenuous Petronius.

Fortune has smiled on this book of his. It will fare on its way through the town adorned and perfumed with the flowers which Madeleine Lemaire has showered upon it with that divine hand which scatters both roses and the roses' dew.

*38. Introduction to "Swann's Way"**

LEWIS GALANTIÈRE

AS THIS IS NOT a critique, but an introduction, I shall not discuss Proust's . . . . method except to warn against the assumption that he may have anything in common with other contemporary writers. Careless critics have coupled his name with that of an equally great artist, James Joyce. Two artists could not be more unlike. Proust is "introspective" only in so far as he descends for his materials within himself; once he has found his materials he deals with them

* Modern Library, New York, 1928.

objectively (and not, as Joyce does in his later work, subjectively). He is in the major line of French novelists and moralists . . . . in that he reflects continuously, analyses ceaselessly, portrays through dissociation of motives. In him the "creative imagination" seems to me to be replaced by sensibility, by an unmatched curiosity and a vibrant neural apprehension of human joys and anguish, combined with a power of intellectualising his intuitions which is as great as that of any properly "realistic" writer. He had certain obsessional preoccupations which I think a little absurdly melodramatic. I should not be astonished to learn that here and there he has paid off a personal score. (How any attentive reader can see snobbishness in what is frequently the most tranquilly cruel portrayal of *le beau monde* is something I have often asked myself). And he is not "universal" as Balzac was, or Shakespeare; there are passions upon which he does not touch; he was limited essentially in his interest to the movements inspired in man by considerations of love and the vanities of the world of fashion; but here, in this field itself immense and fertile as is no other, he stands higher than any novelist I have ever read. Nor should I omit to add that no man, unless it be Havelock Ellis, has been more profoundly tender and tolerant of human frailties, and more especially of those aberrations looked upon generally as monstrosities, than Marcel Proust. Even when he is cruel, his is the cruelty of truth, of life; and he compensates his characters for this by a plenitude of affectionate recognition of their qualities that is deeply moving. Finally, he lived disinterestedly for the art he practiced. I do not of course mean merely that theses will be written upon his language, his impeccable ear (his French, by the way, is the most various to be found in any writer of France), his sense of beauty, the immense scale and originality of his form. I mean that this weakling, reared like Homer's Dolon among women, moved by a passion for his art, had the organising genius of a

Napoleon and that unshakable will without which the consummation of vast creative projects is impossible. He was a neurotic and an invalid, but he possessed a serenity of soul which raised him far above himself and the raw materials of his labour and permitted him, lying in a cloud of fumigation, on his back, to give the last thirteen years of his life to the most exhausting travail imaginable. Even for us who are Americans he was a great man, since he loved his work and died—in the common phrase—"in the harness."

39. *Morbidity, Perversity, Snobbery**

SISLEY HUDDLESTON

. . . . IT IS, in my opinion, unfortunate that a writer of the class of Marcel Proust—substantial, "innombrable," as the French say, extraordinary for his power of psychological observation, should figure in the category of authors who brave the ultimate conventions. There is so much in him that it is a pity to narrow him down to the nauseous Baron de Charlus. Nevertheless, whatever be our view of Proust, we are bound to note that he appears to some of his compatriots as significant chiefly from the point of view of the "noncomformist."

François Porché, poet and dramatist, and, shall we add, the husband of the great actress Madame Simone, in his book *"L'Amour qui n'ose pas dire son nom,"* begins by announcing the appearance in French literature, just before the war, of Charlus. It was on the eve of mobilisation that a fragment of Proust's work, published in the *Nouvelle Revue Française,*

* From *Paris Salons, Cafes, Studios,* J. B. Lippincott Co., Philadelphia and London, 1928.

solemnly introduced Charlus into the world of letters. He entered elegantly but severely dressed, now distracted and haughty, now scrutinising hidden things with a piercing glance, surveying adolescents of the lowest type. In 1919 Marcel Proust obtained the Prix Goncourt and became illustrious. So did Charlus. Translations of *Within a Budding Grove* and *Swann's Way* appeared in England and America. Admirable translations they were, made by C. K. Scott-Moncrieff, a young man whom I had met in the office of the *Times* in London, and who was designated to join me in Paris in 1922. English and American writers were loud in their praises. I am not sure that they were quite prepared for what was coming in *Sodom and Gomorrah.* Until that volume the Baron was relatively discreet. That is to say, his morals had only been suggested in his manners. In 1921 he abandoned all precautions and unmasked himself.

Let me quote a passage from François Porché. "That constituted a new fact. In a prosopopoeia now celebrated and indeed magnificent, Proust evoked an immense sect with its ceremonial, its emblems, its secret language, its physical stigmata and its moral blemishes, its notes of infamy and its marks of honour, its eternal inquietude, its boundless pride, its incurable bitterness. Charlus was no longer alone—an entire species, to which he belonged, surrounded him: it comprised several races, numerous classes, a multitude of varieties. The deviation of instinct from that time did not appear as exceptional, as singular, as the fantasy of a degenerate aristocrat. It became a sort of obedience to another law, a reformed religion. The new church united in its ranks kings and lackeys—many lackeys—dukes and cabmen, artists and butlers, lift-boys, the chestnut-seller of the corner, the concierge, the tailor, the policeman of the crossways, the fireman . . . . The street suddenly showed an unexpected side; and after the street, the city; and after the city, the globe."

. . . . A new frankness was discernible in the works of Rémy de Gourmont. Binet-Valmer was positively brutal. Francis Carco painted a curious milieu. In 1911 André Gide wrote "Corydon"—which he locked in his drawer. But Proust, as it were, opened that drawer. . . . .

Today, it is taken for granted, in various literary and artistic quarters which it has been my lot to frequent, that the third sex, as it is called, veritably exists. It does not seek to hide itself. The snippety periodicals are full of equivocal anecdotes. If you go to cabarets you will hear chansonniers making the most ribald jokes at the expense of persons who are well known—and those persons do not protest. Several popular books on the subject have made their appearance which do not represent the vice as unusual.

I have said that it is unfortunate that Marcel Proust should be associated especially with this aspect of his work. For Proust had great talent and if there is much that is unpleasant in his volumes there is much that is of deep interest. His style is heavy, but his personages live, and he had an almost unexampled faculty of painting them in their most intimate details . . . . "We are irremediably solitary," he said; and in his solitude, surrounded by the desert of the world, he watched the passage of time and saved from oblivion his sensitive impressions of other days. His imagination did not work in the present but in the past. In the realm of memory were the only realities, realities which had been rescued from the tyranny of time. In art he found his consolation. There alone was permanence, and line by line he constructed a permanent world. The insatiable curiosity of the intellect gathered up a mass of material, and, rearranging it, saved it from the havoc of the years. Whatever has disappeared from space is the substance of his books, and, with all its tedious passages, the gigantic work of Proust will live because of its occasional dramatic quality, its irony, its pity, its clearness of detail. His people live as perhaps they did not live in what we call real life. Therefore, nobody deprecates more than I do the unsavoury reputation that has been fastened, not without reason, on the central personage in the magnum opus which Proust patiently achieved in the solitude of the sick-room. . . . .

The cult of Proust is of course overdone. Paul Souday, the literary critic of the *Temps,* one of his admirers, made in a salon which I frequented an extremely sound remark: "Proust resembles in many ways the Goncourt Brothers as a writer, and will probably be found to occupy the same rank." . . . .

Robert Dreyfus is a man of letters who may be described as a seeker after curiosities. . . . . He has given us his souvenirs of Marcel Proust, not sparing Proust's defects, revealing his inquietude, his fatuity, his suffering, his labour, and finally representing Proust as almost heroic. "We doubted his power to construct a work. We would have sworn that the refinement of his sensibility would never have been perceptible to the public—that to understand Proust, to tolerate his bizarre manners, and to submit to his grace, it would always be necessary to have known him in person and sometimes to have smiled at his extravagances."

40. *Proust**

Clive Bell

. . . . Not . . . . till the spring of 1919 did I hold a copy of *Swann* in my hand; and then the introduction was contrived by a lady. She had fallen in love with the book and through the book with the author—as ladies will; and I, instead of feeling grateful for having been brought acquainted with a masterpiece, felt jealous—as will men. I began reading *Swann,* not in hope of a new experience, but with a view to picking holes in a rival. In so Proustian fashion does the adventure open.

I began reading in a hypercritical, not to say cantankerous, frame of mind; and, as things have turned out, that was no bad beginning. Soon enough I was seduced. . . . . By 1925 Proust meant for me what seventy-five years earlier I suppose Balzac must have meant for people of my sort. Here was a contemporary possessing imaginatively and giving form to the vague, half-conscious experience of two generations; here was a path cut into an unexplored shrubbery of that back-garden men call life; and here were the memoirs of my age. Also, it will be, I

*Hogarth Press, Letchworth, England. Harcourt Brace & Co., New York, 1929.

surmise, with Proust's contribution to experience as it has been with Balzac's: something will remain, something will be discarded, much will be lost. . . . . The most variegated periods tend, at a distance, to appear monochrome; wherefore one of Proust's most delicious gifts for us, his gift of rendering temporal colour, inevitably will cease to charm as the age of which he is the memorialist loses its bloom. Now because I began to read in a faultfinding spirit, because I have known what it is to feel definitely and ungenerously hostile, because there was a moment when I refused to surrender myself to the slightly vicious pleasures of actuality, I believe, or like to think, that I have had a glimpse of this early twentieth-century masterpiece through the eyes of 1950. . . . .

After my conversion the adventure became more Proustian than ever. It was a *ménage à trois*. . . . . The book with its moods lived on through ours—gay, agitated, intense, cynical; not only did everything about it become of consequence, everything about the author became interesting. God forgive me, I tried to look at the drawings of Mlle Lemaire: I re-read a few pages of Ruskin. And at last, drawing level with my accomplice, I met the master. It was at a supper-party after a first night of the ballet; and at half-past two in the morning up popped Proust, white gloves and all, for all the world as though he had seen a light in a friend's window and had just come up on the chance of finding him awake. Physically he did not please me, being altogether too sleek and dank and plastered: his eyes were glorious however. Though he was infinitely gracious, the call was not a success. In paying Stravinsky a compliment he paid Beethoven a better: Ansermet failed to keep the peace: *ça finissait mal.* Still, I had seen Proust; there was fresh food for enthusiasm, something new to write home about, more to discuss.

How I have talked! Have I friend or acquaintance whom I have not implicated in long and presumably tedious conversations about Proust and his ways? To boot I have read most of what has been written on the subject. Wherefore I warn those who do me the honour of reading this essay that sooner or later they are sure to hear some echo of their own voices, to come across some reminiscence of what they have read elsewhere. Does it matter? . . . .

Two thousand five hundred years of philosophy notwithstanding, truth is rarely absolute; that is why Proust's sentences are interminable. They are a string of qualifications. For him short sentences would have been mere literature—words corresponding with no reality. His object was to tell the truth about life as he saw it; wherefore he intended originally to write a book without a single paragraph or chapter, so unlifelike—so unreal—did these arbitrary and convenient divisions appear. For the same reason he may have had a horror of full stops. He was to render his sense of life—of something which has relations in space, and is also, as he saw it, a mode of time. But time, he may have argued, is what the hymn says it is—an ever-flowing stream, not a ball of string cut into neat lengths. Time overflows punctuation. Also, how is a style to be anything but complicated and prolix when an artist is trying to say four things at once—to give a bird's-eye view and "a close up" at once in time and space?

. . . . Dichotomy for Proust is begging the question. It is a complete experience he pretends to give—his whole experience, as a whole, not in detail: that sort of thing cannot be done in the style of Voltaire. Wherefore, when we complain that Proust's sentences are unarchitectural, illogical and endless, let us add that not otherwise could he have said what he had to say, and that what he had to say had never been said before. . . . . If Proust was not a stylist after the manner of Flaubert, or of Gautier even, Proust had his reasons. And, in fact, he cared so much for the sound of his sentences that he would not use a foreign word or phrase—so at least one of his friends affirms—till he had made sure of the correct pronunciation. For if the rhythm depended on a mispronunciation, manifestly to an educated ear the sentence would be unrhythmical. It is characteristic of the artist, I think, that he should have written for the one just ear rather than for the nine hundred and ninety-nine.

. . . . Proust is comparable with the seventeenth-century writers in that his style may be considered periodic; and this is worth noting because it may help us to understand the workings of Proust's mind when he sat down to express the truth that was in him. The period was invented by Thucydides and perfected by Demosthenes as a means of giving cohesion to the disjointed statements that tumble from the mouth of an unpractised narrator. . . . . You may, if you please, compare a periodic writer with a musician who as long as he decently can keeps back the resolution of his harmonies. Proust, like the seventeenth-century masters, is periodic: only, whereas the great prose writers of that age deal generally in general ideas, Proust is plaiting very particular strands of emotion and sensation experienced by a very definite individual, and experienced simultaneously. That is why the interminable dependent clauses, instead of following one another duckwise, go side by side, like horses driven abreast, and sometimes higgledy-piggledy like a flock of feeding starlings. . . . . Proust composed in the periodic manner in that his meaning is often not revealed till the close, or near the close, of the sentence. Often a careless or sleepy reader will find himself at the end of the sentence with a principal verb on his hands which he hardly knows what to do with. This shows that the period has been well sustained and that the periodic structure has served its purpose. He who would understand Proust must attend to every word he utters. This means stiff reading. Hence fatigue: hence, also, the revelation. I see no reason for supposing that Proust acquired his style by the study or imitation of other writers. Like all styles worthy the name it was an instrument developed gradually to serve the single purpose of self-expression; it is the nearest Proust can get in words to an equivalent for what Proust felt and thought and Proust's way of thinking and feeling. We laugh when it is suggested by a lady—by a duchess to be sure—that the literary style of Marcel Proust is a transcription of M. de Montesquieu's conversation. The style of Proust was the mind of Proust, which was sensibly different from that of M. le Comte. But is it much less fanciful to suppose that Henry James was an influence? Proust hardly knew English. From his heroic effort to translate Ruskin he may have picked up something. But what is there common to Ruskin's verbiage and Proust's press of words —each corresponding to some twist or start of the mind? Rather the style of *Remembrance* seems to me a quite natural development—but what a development!—from the style of *Les plaisirs et les jours:* at its best it is the precise equivalent of the recaptured and detached experience of the author at his best. How simple art is!

In my jealous irritation I complained that Proust was not only tedious but clumsy. He is clumsy; again I was right, and again wrong in not seeing that as a rule he is clumsy in order to be something else. Proust's passion was for truth, the whole truth, the truth about oneself, the untold truth. "Beauty is Truth, Truth Beauty," was his aesthetic creed; it usually is the creed of those who care more for truth than for beauty—albeit the coiner of the aphorism was of the other sort. . . . . He [Proust] knew that to tamper with words is to tamper with sense; that to change the shape and sound of a sentence is to change its meaning: and it was to the exact expression of his hideously complicated meaning—the expression of that and not a scruple more or less—that he devoted his uncompromising genius. . . . . Proust wanted to speak his mind and his was a mind not easily spoken.

Proust wanted to tell the truth as he knew it. He has a passion for the fact. And this pursuit of truth, of reality I had rather say, is the only begetter and conditioner of his style. It was the contemplation, the realisation, of facts which provoked the poet that was in him. He kept his eye on the object much as the great impressionists had done, he observed, he analysed, he rendered; but what he saw was not what the writers of his generation saw, but the object, the fact, in its emotional significance. And, like the impressionists, he has taught the more sensitive of a new generation to see with him. . . . . Because Proust was an observer who analysed his experience his mind was full of abstractions; because he was a poet these abstractions were seeking ever to give themselves concrete forms. He burst into images, in other words he wrote poetry.

. . . . Proust [and] . . . . Flaubert . . . . had things in common: for instance, a passion for verifying references (the passion for truth) and a habit of not always getting them right. Flaubert travelled to where Carthage was before writing *Salammbô,* and Proust, fearful of having misused a technical term in describing a fourteenth-century ornament, pestered Billy with interrogatory letters. But for the Flaubert-Maupassant doctrine—the doctrine that the artist should stand outside the work, observe and record—Proust had no use at all. Facts, yes: he adored facts, but he would not leave them alone. Proust, the master commentator, the born showman, had no notion of standing aside. On the contrary, he rarely states a fact without commenting and criticising and reminiscing at enormous length, reminding one in this of another seventeenth-century master, of Bayle of the *Dictionnaire historique,* with his two lines of text to two pages of notes: also, in both cases, the notes are the better part. Proust's comment, *qua* comment, never jars: it displeases, when it does displease, because it is silly not because it is misplaced. No mere observer and recorder of facts, no Goncourt, but a psychologist writing out of himself, digging deeper, ever deeper, lowering his bucket to the very bottom of his own subconsciousness, Proust brings nothing to the surface which is irrelevant to his subject. How should he, seeing that the subject of Proust's book is Proust?

Nevertheless, to return to my grumbling, Proust was clumsy. He can be grossly and, what is worse, unwittingly so. He could not leave out. Insignificant facts, platitudinous reflections, the obvious, the well-worn, the thrice-told, all, all are set down beside what is stranger, subtler and truer than anything that has been set down in imaginative literature since Stendhal at any rate. Because he will not eliminate he is indiscriminate. He will treat facts as though he were a man of science rather than an artist. Indeed, in his way of piling instance on instance he reminds me sometimes of Darwin; also for piling thus high he has the man of science's excuse—he accumulates that truth may prevail. Proust was too profoundly in earnest not to be repetitious sometimes. Subtlest of analysts, subtlest of observers, he is not a subtle expositor. Far too much of what he says is redundant. Really he seems not to know which of his ideas and observations are surprising and which are trite. Occasionally his lack of finesse makes one positively uncomfortable, and his humour becomes so elephantine sometimes that one hardly knows which way to look. . . . .

Proust had a sense of humour; but in his writings he was rarely witty, except of course in his parodies. In life he seems to have been delicious often. . . . .

Whatever we may think of Proust's aesthetic we cannot deny that he was the perfect aesthete in that for him art came first. Art and thought he set above all things: his detestation of Philistinism was, I suppose, what made him enthusiastic about Ruskin. Only he protests too much. We begin to feel uncomfortable when for the tenth time we have been given to understand that a minor poet is immeasurably superior to a marquis. We cannot help suspecting that he is beating down an innate propensity with an acquired. But when he insists on the duty of sacrificing life to art he is impressive because he is sincere. . . . .

Proust was a snob. And what does it matter? He was an artist of genius who has revealed an age to itself and has created something which possibly for a thousand years will have some value for people who think and feel. . . . .

To catch truth, truth as a whole, which is something different from the whole truth, to take the deep-sea monster alive, not to dissect the corpse, that was Proust's intention. . . . .

Proust deals with time as modern painters deal with space. The painter will not allow scientifically ascertained spatial relations and laws of perspective to restrict his imagination. . . . .

Remembrance of Things Past is a shape in time; it is not an arabesque on time. It is constructed in three dimensions, and may be described as architectural if we bear in mind that the blocks of which it is built are time-blocks. They are arranged in an order, conceived and determined by the architect with a view to expressing truth, which is not necessarily chronological order. . . . . Better to think of the book as a picture—an oil-painting not a fresco—in time. Because one time mass stands before another in the composition it does not follow that it precedes it in history; for, like the modern painter dealing with space-masses, Proust moves his hither and thither regardless of their chronological relations.

. . . . A sense of the lapse of time and of time's ineluctable triumph was ever present to the author of *Remembrance of Things Past,* at once agitating and consoling, and moving him so profoundly that on occasions it could make him dramatic. An author who deals in states, not actions, will not be that often or for nothing; but Proust is dramatic, subtly and unostentatiously, when he allows us suddenly to become aware that the new Princesse de Guermantes is the old Madame Verdurin; . . . .

Of course Proust was an artist; only he was not the greatest kind of artist. He gives us little or nothing that life would not give if only we could press life hard enough. If you care for paradoxes you may say that Proust was a story-teller, a poet story-teller, a Chaucer, an Ariosto, a Crabbe; only his stories are about things which no one ever told stories about before. Primarily he is an observer and a psychologist. Now a psychological artist (I am not going to pay Behaviourism the compliment of taking it seriously) must depend on his own experience: none but himself can he know well enough for his purpose. He must write out of himself. The profound and complicated spiritual states analysed and described in *Remembrance* are the author's own; only the secondary characters are constructed from external observation. . . . . The unconvincingness of Albertine, ... may be due rather to the fact that Proust seems never to have known quite whether the character was a girl or a boy. . . . .

An opinion is held—why, unless it has something to do with the title of the book, I cannot tell—that Proust was interested only in the past . . . . Proust wanted to know what was going on. He wanted to know what the young were writing and painting, he tried to understand the most abstruse thought of his age. Not only was he the first to read the last Cocteau and Giraudoux, he struggled with Einstein and Freud. To the end of his days he was in the movement. As we may infer from the preface he wrote for *Propos de peintre* and from the correspondence arising out of that preface, M. Jacques-Emile Blanche became for him a thing of the past about the time that Mr. Aldous Huxley, whom in *Remembrance* he names and nicely distinguishes from his even more illustrious grandfather, became an actuality. . . . . He observed banalities after the manner of his beloved Impressionists, staring at familiar objects till they gave up their secrets, till he had penetrated the dust and dirt of familiarity and discovered underneath that thrilling reality which is the thing itself. And it was this fixed stare, concentrated on people and things, which revealed to him, as it had revealed to them, the poetry of the world in which he lived. . . . .

Need I add that these sixteen volumes, in so far as they are memoirs, are memoirs of a world of the artist's imagination, that *Remembrance of Things Past* is not a *roman à clef?* I suppose so since there are still people to assert the contrary. . . . .

And is there a moral? To be sure there is; a philosophy of life at all events. It is not very new, but it is true enough. Proust has explored depths hitherto unplumbed, he has stripped the dirt and varnish from reality till his fingers ache and our eyes, he has seen life from a new angle and described what he saw with a frankness and precision unmatched in prose; and the conclusion to which he has come is the conclusion to which came the Preacher—and Shakespeare:

> All is vanity . . . .
> . . . . it is a tale
> Told by an idiot, full of sound and fury,
> Signifying nothing.

Not quite nothing: Proust had his illusions. He believed that art and thought did signify something. Shakespeare knew better.

What Proust knew . . . . about the nature of the universe is unimportant; it is what he knew and still more what he could tell about that microcosm which is man, which is the marvel of our age. From the unsurveyed mines of subconscious memory he dragged up experience vital yet stingless and made the past live sterilised in the present. Then, on a pin's point, he held his living captive till he had described it, and describing created a world. . . . . From exaggeration he was not saved; but he is never vulgar, never sentimental. . . . . he avoided those messy pits into which most modern creators . . . . have fallen.

*41. The Impuritans**

HARVEY WICKHAM

UPON THE FACE of things, no man would seem to have been less influenced by Puritanism—and hence by any degradation of Puritanism—than was Marcel Proust. . . . .

His early associations were picturesquely Romish; but his youthful mind was innocent either of Moses or St. Peter. So Bergson became his mentor, Anatole France his admirer, and Léon Daudet his friend.

These men are certainly Impuritans, though they belong to that Protestant revolt which still goes on but no longer calls itself Protestantism, and is Puritan in nothing save its dislike of the Vatican and its exaltation of individual judgment, good or bad. . . . .

Anatole France professed not to understand him, saying that one can comprehend one's own generation and the generation immediately following but not one's intellectual grandchildren. Doubtless this was intended as flattery. Unquestionably it is nonsense. Proust is by no means as futuristic as all that. There is a certain cleanliness about the very latest in philosophy—a spirituality at last decently dead and awaiting resurrection. . . . . But Proust is an old heart flowering in its second childhood, an old brain ravaged by cancer—both marvellously articulate.

. . . . He never invented in the sense of trying to make things up out of whole cloth. Barring certain philosophies, which he lamentably took from books instead of from observation or experience, he wrote of what he knew, had seen and felt.

* Dial Press, New York, 1929.

And he saw everything which came before his eyes—with a detail approaching the miraculous. . . . . With Proust, language forbore its tyranny of conventionalized figures, and permitted a thought to be expressed as in that instant when it is born, when it is as yet unmixed with hearsay, and lies naked in all its integral uniqueness—a ripe thought withal, re-created by maturity, a child seen and understood by its father. Reborn experience, in short, with quick emotions slowly and painstakingly recorded. For once realism and romanticism met in just proportions. For once facts were made to give up their spirit without giving up the ghost, made to reveal those ideal connexions which reduce life and nature to that lesser but more vivid and humanly comprehensible thing which calls itself a work of art. . . . .

It is as a philosopher that Proust exposes his Achilles' heel to the critic. Sex he treated in a falsely romantic fashion. Unquestionably the greatest novelist of his generation, he here fell into propaganda and permitted himself to suppose what he did not know. And it is to the mistakes he made in supposing, that he owes that vast notoriety which has obscured his proper fame.

. . . . Proust began filling those twenty enormous notebooks which posterity, if still under the impression that genius achieves its effects without effort, may well regard with profit. They record the most minute observations ever made of the secular manners and motives of humankind. Were Behaviourism the study of behaviour as it ought to be, the novel which, when the author was well within the shadow of forty, began at last to take shape from these notes . . . . would certainly be its bible.

. . . . Proust alone saw snobbery to the bottom and laid bare its very heart. . . . . At the same time, it must be admitted that we have lost something with all our gain. In an age where everyone is as good as the next and even better, few men seem really to believe in their own superiority to the extent of feeling that sense of obligation which once went with it. So doth equality breed a new arrogance, even less lovely than the old. . . . .

He laboured in agony to find the "authentic impression" which was his very own—the little gift to himself of that God whom he denied. He knew by instinct that mere memory would accomplish nothing, that dead details raked together make but a pile of rubbish. So he waited always for flashes of another sort of memory, the sort which re-creates the past—what we ordinarily call inspiration, which has the marvellous power of taking incidents and seeing them unite in a new and vital order. . . . .

The evil that men do lives after them. Proust's evil consists chiefly in his theoretical idea of love, ...

Almost all his characters, male or female, are homo-erotic. He paints a world whose rain of fire and brimstone is long overdue. . . . .

No man can be expected to re-create the world altogether in his own interior image. He must play the historian, and piece it out with fragments from other images. But Proust lacked the critical faculty which would have enabled him to distinguish between true and false inferences in matters beyond his personal habit, even if they came under his eye. And when it came to passing judgment upon the alleged facts which he found in print, he was hopeless. Nine people out of ten know him as the pretended Pepys of the next-door neighbors of Lot—which is the same as saying that nine-tenths of his present reputation is shoddy and destined not to wear.

That time will take the remaining tenth and gnaw upon it in vain, I have not the slightest doubt; for this tenth is no garment of rags, but a living body, which can but grow. To put it in other words, he is an oak which attained to stupendous and lovely proportions in spite of all attempts of mistletoe to strangle it. Some day the world will see the tree. Just at present it is the foreign parasite which most attracts attention.

The root of this parasite sprang, as might have been expected, from a flaw in the native wood. Proust was a solitary. His probable habits one does not like to think of. Yet auto-eroticism has only this in common with homo-eroticism: it viciously avoids nature's saving differentiation. His love for his mother was so intense that it prevented him from looking upon other women in a normal fashion. But here was no life with wings sufficient to keep it *always* above the flesh. Therefore he failed to associate the fleshly excitation with gonochorism at all. And not wishing to fill his fictional world with men altogether like himself, he chose to fill it with Charli, perverts of a drastic and dramatic order. He was enough like them to make the attempt half a success; enough unlike them to make it, unsupported as it was by either science or sound philosophy, half a failure.

He treats inversion everywhere as if the taint were a compulsory, hereditary force. The Guermantes are what they are because of one, Gilbert, their ancient *mauvais sire.* He even attempts to idealize this peculiarity, calling it "a vice which Nature herself has planted in the soul of a child, perhaps by no more than blending the virtues of its father and mother as she might blend the colours of their eyes." This is pure moonshine, and founded upon no well-established truth of human experience. Proust acquired the notion from undigested reading-matter.

. . . . System is the one thing which Proust cannot let alone. He must always have his "law." Thus, the hero in *The Past Recaptured,* speaking of his observations upon human character, enquires: "Was it not worth more than these gestures that they made, these words which they spoke, their lives, their nature, that I should attempt to describe the curve of it, and from this to disengage its law?"

The answer must be an emphatic *no,* though generalizing is a well-known stratagem of the fiction-writer, a technical trick intended to lend a spurious air of importance to his goods —a showman's ballyhoo, in short. But Proust, super-showman that he is, makes us run the risk of taking it seriously.

There is his precious "general law" that inverts make their wives happy—happier, I gather, than the wives of normal men. . . . .

Proust's genius was intellectual. His best work is wisely malicious—for without malice, that is, without a vision of the unloveliness of natural man—literary immortality is impossible. But when Proust tries to make *bestémmia e il turpiloquio* into something charming and sublime, his rational power leaves him. He becomes ridiculous and sentimental—the inevitable penalty for giving honor where no honor is due.

Sometimes his humour saves him, however, even from his philosophy. . . . .

His snob-philosophy at least hangs together, and he follows it wherever it leads—like a printer following copy out of a window. It is inversion which is too much for him, since he is determined to make it noble, romantic, and artistic, and at the same time congenitally pathologic, scientific, and contemptible. . . . .

Proust's unnamed hero, drawn so unmistakably from himself, stands almost unique among his other characters in being a lover only of the opposite sex. The theory that inversion arises when a man has the soul of a woman is here abandoned, for this hero is effeminate and yet no monster. The heroines whom he loves, the delicate petals of *Within a Budding Grove,* are more feminine still. What makes the abnormality is the fact that they are Lesbians. He can hardly imagine himself as loving anything but a woman. So the rivals he fears are not men but women. How is one to account for this strange state of things?

The explanation, I think, lies in that unhealthy gynaecian bringing-up to which the male body of Proust was subjected by the domestic situation surrounding his boyhood. His was the intermediate sex, evolved in the only way it is ever evolved, by a pernicious education. He was not so much his mother's lover as her shadow. She had wrapped his heart in a petticoat. Women are jealous of women, not of men—that he could understand. . . . .

And yet another element enters into the situation here. He was a lover of self. Being, crudely speaking, a man, he lived too closely to this man—the only one he deeply knew. So he could, though with some difficulty, think of himself as Charlus. But he could not actually have followed in the steps of the Baron; for it is one thing to dream, and quite another to put a nightmare into practice. Reality has sharp edges. Reverie softens them as a mist softens a rugged mountain.

The general result of all this was that Proust considered himself free to wander at large in the region of forbidden things. His body was contradicted not by plasms but by mental wont. He could discover unheard-of abominations in a garden of innocent flowers, and innocent flower-like passions in Sodom and Gomorrah. Most often we wonder that we are not more offended. The secret lies in this chameleon heart, infecting us and changing the superficial garments of our gender at its will.

42. *Five Masters**

J. W. Krutch

Proust himself, it will be remembered, spoke of the various *themes* whose full significance would not be clear until, in the later volumes, they had begun to combine; and this remark of his gives the key to his method . . . . of an elaborate musical composition. One may, if one likes, study it first in some small unit like the first volume—much as one might begin to study the structure of a symphony by considering the first movement alone. Thus in the first part of that first volume one might note how the incident of his mother's failure to kiss him good night is first referred to on page thirteen, is dropped like a musical phrase, reappears successively on pages twenty-six, twenty-eight, thirty-two, and forty-four, but does not receive its full development until just fifteen volumes later when the narrator is standing in the anteroom of the Guermantes residence. Moreover this method is the one consistently followed throughout the book in which the themes play about one another like the themes of a fugue. Each separate scene is related to others by the fact that some general emotion, or thought, or observation recurs in each. . . . .

The motifs appear one by one. It would be possible to go through the work and to note, as one would note in a sym-

* From *Five Masters: A Study in the Mutations of the Novel,* Jonathan Cape & Harrison Smith, New York, 1930.

phony, that at this point or that each one of the themes—love, taste, manners, etc.—is introduced for the first time merely in passing before it is returned to again and again for more and more complete development. . . . . And one result of this arrangement is to make the novel in another respect like a piece of music, for of it may be said, more truly even than of most great novels, that the second reading is more rewarding than the first. To know what is coming does not detract from the pleasure—is indeed necessary to the full enjoyment of it—since each incident is, like a musical theme, only enriched by a knowledge of the variations to follow.

This original and perfected form has its own self-justifying beauties, but to consider the intention which determined its choice is to be led back again to that obsession with Time whose influence is discoverable in every detail of Proust's work and which gives it its unity. Thanks to the method which disregards chronology he was able to bring together, for purposes of contrast or comparison, widely separated periods. . . . . Moreover it was necessary for his puropse to do just this because the full horror of Time had to be revealed in order that the miraculous joy which comes through the escape from it might be properly appreciated. . . . .

Very diverse opinions have been expressed concerning the rank which ought to be accorded to Proust as a novelist, and when such matters are discussed it is as well not to enter into dispute. But perhaps it is . . . . worth while remarking that at least he very perfectly realized the conception of the artist which was formulated by his philosophical master, Bergson.

The latter, it will be remembered, held that artistic vision is distinguished from ordinary vision by the fact that it manages to escape from the effects of habit and to see a thing itself rather than the conventionalization of it with which we happen to be most familiar. . . . . The artist, combining sensations afresh with the aid of nothing except his own intelligence, is enabled to conceive of them as forming patterns hitherto unrecognized and to make others see them under forms totally new.

And whatever other qualities Proust may or may not have, one can hardly deny him his freshness of vision which makes his novel very unlike any other. . . . . We enter the pages of *Remembrance of Things Past* as we might enter a realm totally unfamiliar, and before we are aware of the fact we have closed a door behind us, forgetting the standards and the conventions of familiar life as completely as we forget its personages. For the world which the novel reveals is more than merely strange; it is also so consistent, so self-sustaining, and so logically complete that we are never by any reference led back to the other world of our ordinary concerns. . . .

Moreover, it must be admitted that . . . . the spiritual world of Proust has elements of charm lacking in most contemporary novels because of the fact that the sensibility everywhere exhibited is of an extraordinary sort . . . . he managed somehow to recapture the feeling of romantic love without introducing any of those illusions which the modern finds it all but impossible to enjoy. And perhaps this love of his, this emotion which is so obviously neither the sacrament of the conventional romanticists nor the devaluated amusement of the cynic, might be made the type of his sensibility, for in many other respects also he manages to attain an attitude poised somewhere between the extremes which have so often seemed inevitable alternatives. He was disillusioned enough with many things—with morals for example—and he had neither any code nor any standards beside those which his taste supplied. Yet in the midst of what might seem to be anarchy there were still capacities and faiths which he retained. He still believed, for example, in the sufficiency of the senses—at least as furnishers of the material which contemplation might transform. But, on the other hand, he never, like so many moderns, found himself in a universe limited and debased by the impossibility of escape from psychology, anthropology, and Freudianism. The world was still absorbingly, still amazingly, interesting. Women—most women—were to him magical and mysterious. Conversations were witty, artists incalculably great. In a word, he respected his desires, his tastes, and his amusements and hence, though experience might be predominately painful, it was neither meaningless nor mean. And that perhaps is the secret of the individual charm of his world. It is one viewed with the critical freedom of modern thought and one in which scepticism rules. Yet it is somehow glamorous as well. Nor is it, perhaps, impertinent to remark that in this respect (though assuredly in this only) Proust was like Boccaccio, since both were faced with the task of creating a world out of the ruin into which an accustomed world had been thrown by the decay of the principles upon which it had rested. Boccaccio had had to do without the aid of the theology which had given shape and meaning to the universe of the Middle Ages; Proust had to do without most of the dogmas which had got themselves established since the Renaissance.

Some have not failed to reproach him with a lack of reticence, of decency even, and they have pointed to certain scenes, like that in which the narrator is represented as eavesdropping upon Jupien the tailor and the perverted de Charlus, as evidence of the fact that he lacked, as well, even the most elementary instinct of a gentleman. But to raise such objections is to forget that Proust, having retired out of active life as completely as though he had been dead, was no longer "playing the game" and accordingly had no concern with the rules. With nothing to gain and nothing to lose, he no longer cared even for the opinion which others might form of him, and he was accordingly as little concerned with the moral judgments which might be passed upon him as with those which might be passed upon his characters.

To make the most exquisitely minute discriminations always, but to judge between the things discriminated never—that is the essence of his method. . . . . No man was ever more completely than Proust a slave to sensations; no man ever lived more entirely by and for the nerves; but by shutting himself off from all but the memory of these sensations he not only recovered them with unexampled fullness but recovered them in a state more nearly pure than would have been possible for anyone who had a living future which could occupy him with plans and desires—recovered them, that is to say, unmixed either with his own personal concerns or with those moral fervours and antipathies which, for such at least as he, are in fact no part of a personal concern.

But the reasons which lead certain critics to hesitate to grant Proust the supreme place among novelists of the twentieth century are more often of a sort somewhat subtler than these just referred to and seem to find their roots in a feeling that, however excellent his work may be in its kind, the kind is, nevertheless, not the one demanded of the Great Novelist whose coming they have been so long awaiting.

Nor can it be denied that Proust's work fails to afford that "synthesis of modern life" which has been the subject of so much discussion or that, indeed, it fails even to treat the themes which the age seems to impose. Thus—to consider the most obvious aspect of the fact—his work is wholly without what some would describe as social consciousness, and from it alone one would never guess that, for at least seventy-five years, nearly every novelist of first rank has expounded—explicitly or implicitly—some attitude towards the problems raised by our universal concern with social justice. Most of the novelists of the nineteenth and twentieth centuries felt constrained to take life seriously in a sense that Proust does not, since, and with a clear conscience, he permits himself to live the charmed life of a dilettante, not troubling himself much about the fate of civilization, acting as though there were nothing more important than the careful discrimination between shades of feeling, and devoting himself with the selfishness of the contemplative saint to the achievement of his own private salvation. He surrenders the effort so characteristic of our fiction to be in some sense dynamic, to master the life it treats. He does not hope to dominate or even to influence the civilization of which he is part but instead—and again like the most other-worldly of monks—only to find some way of accepting the evil inevitably woven into the fabric of any life which takes place in time.

Moreover, even among those who are content that the novel should detach itself from sociological concerns, there are some who are chilled by the subtler aspects of Proust's detachment from the problems which seem the problems of contemporary existence. *Remembrance of Things Past* is, they would insist, simply not concerned with the things which the modern novel has the duty of concerning itself with, simply shirks that obligation which other contemporary novelists . . . . have at least accepted. No one who had been told in 1913 that a very great work of fiction was about to appear could have imagined that it would be anything like what this one turns out to be; no one could have dreamed that a novel which was to be proposed as the most distinguished of our generation could possibly be, not only aloof, but essentially mystical as well.

But on the other hand, is it not true that these critics themselves have been demanding "form," that they have grown weary of mere document and discussion, and that here in Proust's novel they are presented with one of the most beautiful, one of the most accomplished, and one of the most perfect formal designs ever achieved by a writer of prose fiction? And is it not true, also, that, whereas they have longed for someone who should find a way of achieving order and peace for himself and his readers without removing them from modern life, Proust does just that? . . . .

43. *Axel's Castle**

EDMUND WILSON

MARCEL PROUST is the first important novelist to apply the principles of Symbolism in fiction. Proust had assimilated a great variety of writers from Ruskin to Dostoevsky, and he had acquired a remarkable technical virtuosity; but, born in 1871, he had been young in the eighties and nineties, when Symbolism was in the air, and the peculiar methods and form of his great novel certainly owed much to Symbolist theory. I have said that the influence on the Symbolists of Wagner was as considerable as that of any writer of books, and it is significant of Proust's conception of his art that he should have been in the habit of speaking of his "themes." His enormous novel, *Remembrance of Things Past,* is, in fact, a symphonic structure rather than a narrative in the ordinary sense. The shifting images of the Symbolist poet, with their "multiplied associations," are here characters, situations, places, vivid moments, obsessive emotions, recurrent patterns of behavior. . . . .

Proust had at one time had the idea of dividing his novel

* Charles Scribner's Sons, New York, 1931.

into three parts and calling them respectively: "The Age of Names," "The Age of Words," and "The Age of Things."

. . . . People who have stuck in the *Within a Budding Grove* and thus know only the subjective Proust must acquire a false idea of what his genius is like. We are now to be violently thrown forward into the life of the world outside. The contrast between, on the one hand, the dreams, the broodings and the repinings of the neurasthenic hero, as we get them for such long stretches, and, on the other, the rich and lively social scenes, dramatized by so powerful an imagination, is one of the most curious features of the book. These latter scenes, indeed, contain so much broad humor and so much extravagant satire that, appearing in a modern French novel, they amaze us. Proust, however, was much addicted to English literature: "it is strange," he writes in a letter, "that in the most widely different departments, from George Eliot to Hardy, from Stevenson to Emerson, there should be no other literature which exercises over me so powerful an influence as English and American." In the descriptive parts of the early volumes, we have recognized the rhythms of Ruskin; and in the social scenes which now engage us, though Proust has been compared to Henry James, who was deficient in precisely those gifts of vividness and humor which Proust, to such an astonishing degree, possessed, we shall look in vain for anything like them outside the novels of Dickens. We have already been struck, in *Swann's Way,* with the singular relief into which the characters were thrown as soon as they began to speak or act. And it seems plain that Proust must have read Dickens and that this sometimes grotesque heightening of character had been partly learned from him. Proust, like Dickens, was a remarkable mimic: as Dickens enchanted his audiences by dramatic readings from his novels, so, we are told, Proust was celebrated for impersonations of his friends; and both, in their books, carried the practice of caricaturing habits of speech and of inventing things for their personages to say which are outrageous without ever ceasing to be lifelike to a point where it becomes impossible to compare them to anybody but each other. As, furthermore, it has been said of Dickens that his villains are so amusing—in their fashion, so enthusiastically alive—that we are reluctant to see the last of them, so we acquire a curious affection for even the most objectionable characters in Proust: . . . .

It seems strange that so many critics should have found Proust's novel "unmoral"; the truth is that he was preoccupied with morality to the extent of tending to deal in melodrama. Proust was himself (on his mother's side) half-Jewish; and for all his Parisian sophistication, there remains in him much of the capacity for apocalyptic moral indignation of the classical Jewish prophet. That tone of lamentation and complaint which resounds through his whole book, which, indeed, he scarcely ever drops save for the animated humor of the social scenes, themselves in their implications so bitter, is really very un-French and rather akin to Jewish literature. The French novelist of the line of Stendhal and Flaubert and Anatole France, with whom otherwise Proust has so much in common, differs fundamentally from Proust in this: the sad or cynical view of mankind with which these former begin, which is implicit in their first page, has been arrived at by Proust only at the cost of much pain and protest, and this ordeal is one of the subjects of his book: Proust has never, like these others, been reconciled to disillusionment. This fact is clearly one of the causes of that method which we find so novel and so fascinating of making his characters undergo a succession of transformations: humanity is only gradually revealed to us in its selfishness, its weakness and its inconsistency. . . . .

Proust has created . . . . a sort of equivalent in fiction for the metaphysics which certain philosophers have based on the new physical theory. Proust had been deeply influenced by

Bergson, one of the forerunners of the modern anti-mechanists, and this had helped him to develop and apply on an unprecedented scale the metaphysics implicit in Symbolism. . . . . For modern physics, all our observations of what goes on in the universe are relative: they depend upon where we are standing when we make them, how fast and in which direction we are moving—and for the Symbolist, all that is perceived in any moment of human experience is relative to the person who perceives it, and to the surroundings, the moment, the mood. The world becomes thus for both fourth dimensional—with Time as the fourth dimension. The relativist, in locating a point, not only finds its co-ordinates in space, but also takes the time; and the ultimate units of his reality are "events," each of which is unique and can never occur again—in the flux of the universe, they can only form similar patterns. And in Proust's world, just as the alleys of the Bois de Boulogne which the hero had seen in his youth under the influence of the beauty of Odette have now changed into something quite different and are as irrecoverable as the moments of time in which they had had their only existence—just as his people, in spite of the logic of the processes by which they change, are always changing and will finally fade away, disintegrated by illness or old age; so love, of which we hope so much, changes and fails us, and so society, which at first seems so stable, in a few years has recombined its groups and merged and transformed its classes. And, ... the "events," which may be taken arbitrarily as infinitely small or infinitely comprehensive make up an organic structure, in which all are interdependent, each involving every other and the whole; so Proust's book is a gigantic dense mesh of complicated relations: cross-references between different groups of characters and a multiplication of metaphors and similes connecting the phenomena of infinitely varied fields—biological, zoölogical, physical, aesthetic, social, political and financial. (These similes seemed far-fetched and silly to the first readers of Proust's novel—but Proust insisted that one of his principal concerns was to discover the real resemblances between things which superficially appeared different. . . . .)

Proust, though all his observations seem relative, does, like Einstein, build an absolute structure for his world of appearances. His characters may change from bad to good, from beautiful to ugly, as Einstein's measuring-rods shrink and elongate, his clocks become accelerated or retarded; yet as Einstein's mathematical apparatus enables us to establish certain relations between the different parts of the universe, in spite of the fact that we do not know how the heavenly bodies are moving in respect to one another and no matter from what point of view our measurements have been made—so Proust constructs a moral scheme out of phenomena whose moral values are always shifting. (Perhaps the narrator's grandmother may be taken as playing for Proust the same role that the speed of light does for Einstein: the single constant value which makes the rest of the system possible!)

. . . . And in the long last sentence of the book the word "Time" begins to sound, and it closes the symphony as it began it.

The fascination of Proust's novel is so great that, while we are reading it, we tend to accept it *in toto*. In convincing us of the reality of his creations, Proust infects us with his point of view, even where this point of view has falsified his picture of life. It is only in the latter part of his narrative that we begin seriously to question what he is telling us. Is it really true, we begin to ask ourselves, that one's relations with other people can never provide a lasting satisfaction? Is it true that literature and art are the only forms of creative activity which can enable us to meet and master reality? Would not such an able doctor as Proust represents his Cottard as being enjoy, in supervising his cases, the satisfaction of knowing that he has imposed a little of his own private reality upon the world outside? Would not a diplomat like M. de Norpois in arranging his alliances?—or a hostess like Mme. de Guermantes in creating her social circle? Might not a more sympathetic and attentive lover than Proust's hero have even succeeded in recreating Albertine at least partly in his own image? We begin to be willing to agree with Ortega y Gasset that Proust is guilty of the mediaeval sin of *accidia,* that combination of slothfulness and gloom which Dante represented as an eternal submergence in mud.

For *Remembrance of Things Past,* in spite of all its humor and beauty, is one of the gloomiest books ever written. Proust tells us that the idea of death has "kept him company as incessantly as the idea of his own identity"; and even the water-lilies of the little river at Combray, continually straining to follow the current and continually jerked back by their stems, are likened to the futile attempts of the neurasthenic to break the habits which are eating his life. . . . .

I have said that Proust's novel was a symphony, and I have indicated its relation to Symbolism—and I have explained Proust's special idea of the kind of symbols which were valid for literature, the kind of symbols of which his own novel was to be made. Like all the graduates of the Symbolist school, Proust was a determined opponent of Naturalism: in the last part of *Remembrance of Things Past,* when he explains the plan of his novel, he expresses himself emphatically and at great length on the futility of trying to represent reality by collecting and organizing the data of the external world, and he handles with what is evidently deliberate carelessness all those facts which a Naturalistic novelist would have been scrupulous to have consistent and precise. What is more, there is no explicit logical connection between the different elements of *Remembrance of Things Past.* . . . .

That he could doubt what seem to be the book's basic assumptions is indicated by one of his letters in which he confesses to having cut out a long passage of *Remembrance of*

Things Past, in which he had asserted that reciprocal love was not merely difficult and rare, but universally impossible—leaving only an expression of skepticism as to whether anyone was any better off than he. And I believe that those aspects of his novel which seem ambiguous or distorted are due to Proust's own uncertainty as to whether he is exemplifying universal principles of human conduct or projecting by images sometimes monstrous the elements of a personality which he knew to be morbid and special. . . . .

In spite of all the less reassuring or less agreeable aspects of Proust which appear more plainly in his letters and the memoirs of him than in *Remembrance of Things Past*—his self-coddling, his chronic complaining, his perversity, his over-cultivated sensibility—we get the impression from them, as we do in his novel, of an intellect and imagination vigorous, comprehensive and deep. One of the things which strikes us most is his capacity for keeping in intimate touch with various circles of friends, as with various fields of activity, sympathizing with the emotions, understanding the interests, and following the affairs of each, though of the several groups already represented by the memoirs which have so far been published, all seem pretty well independent of each other and some scarcely at any point to overlap. And in spite of all his parade of weakness, in spite of all his masks and indirections, we remember him as a personality of singular magnanimity, integrity and strength. . . . .

We must recognize in Proust, it seems to me, one of the great minds and imaginations of our day, absolutely comparable in our own time, by reason both of his powers and of his influence, to the Nietzsches, the Tolstois, the Wagners and the Ibsens of a previous generation. He has recreated the world of the novel from the point of view of relativity: he has supplied for the first time in literature an equivalent on the full scale for the new theory of modern physics.

Imaginatively and intellectually, Proust is prodigiously strong; and if we feel an element of decadence in his work, it may be primarily due to the decay of the society in which he lived and with which his novel exclusively deals—the society of the dispossessed nobility and the fashionable and cultivated bourgeoisie, with their physicians and their artists, their servants and their parasites. We are always feeling with Proust as if we were reading about the end of something—this seems, in fact, to be what he means us to feel: witness the implications of the bombardment of Paris during the War when Charlus is in the last stages of his disintegration. Not only do his hero and most of his other characters pass into mortal declines, but their world itself seems to be coming to an end. And it may be that Proust's strange poetry and brilliance are the last fires of a setting sun—the last flare of the aesthetic idealism of the educated classes of the nineteenth century. If Proust is more dramatic, more complete and more intense than Thackeray or Chekov or Edith Wharton or Anatole France, it may be because he comes at the close of an era and sums up the whole situation. Surely the lament over the impossibility of ideal romantic love which Proust is always chanting on a note which wavers between the tragic and the maudlin announces by its very falling into absurdity the break-up of a whole emotional idealism and its ultimate analysis and readjustment along lines which Proust's own researches, running curiously close to Freud, have been among the first to suggest. *Remembrance of Things Past* subsumes, in this respect, *The Great Gatsby, The Sun Also Rises, The Bridge of San Luis Rey,* the sketches of Dorothy Parker, and how many contemporary European novels! Proust is perhaps the last great historian of the loves, the society, the intelligence, the diplomacy, the literature and the art of the Heartbreak House of capitalist culture; and the little man with the sad appealing voice, the metaphysician's mind, the Saracen's beak, the ill-fitting dress-shirt and the great eyes that seem to see all about him like the many-faceted eyes of a fly, dominates the scene and plays host in the mansion where he is not long to be master.

44. *French Novelists from the Revolution to Proust**

FREDERICK C. GREEN

.... TO MARCEL PROUST the subconscious is our true self, our authentic ego. It is the hidden treasure house of our real and vital impressions, more real and more vital than those that can so easily and so mechanically be summoned up by the voluntary memory because they have sunk so deeply into the depths of our being. But it is not merely in sleep that these experiences succeed in detaching themselves from the underworld of the subconscious. Frequently a chance sensation, a perfume, a sound, a contact will evoke from what we loosely and wrongly call the Past one of those submerged fragments of brilliantly and intensely lived life. And it is such fragments dug out of the very depths of that rich inner lode—our true self—that constitute for Proust the only true realities of life.

So we must regard his long novel, *Remembrance of Things Past,* as the attempt of a great artist to evolve a new and more powerful instrument by which all of us may look at life in a new way, a magnifying glass thanks to which we may understand that what hitherto we took to be realities were not realities at all. And the literature, the art called "Realistic" is, says

* J. M. Dent & Sons, Ltd., London and Toronto, and D. Appleton-Century Company, 1931. Reprinted by permission of the American publishers.

Proust, entirely false because it confines itself to the notation of conscious impressions: . . . .

The vital realities lie hidden within us and are evoked by the most trivial things, so trivial in fact that our intelligence often ignores them. Yet we have all experienced, like Proust, the anxious insistence with which certain apparently unimportant things, a group of poplar trees, a chance phrase, the fleeting expression of a face, implore us not to forget them. But if we try to estimate their significance by the intelligence there is no reason why they should hold our attention for a moment . . . . It is because these material impressions are "fragments of existence abstracted from Time"; each one of them carries with it like an aura the self we were when it was first experienced by us . . . . This is the supreme achievement of Proustian art. It does not stop at the outward appearance of an impression, but dives deep into it as a bee into the calyx of a flower, sucking out its very essence: the outward impression, the glimpse of the name on a book, for example, or the aroma of coffee, is a mere symbol of a vaster reality.

For Proust the true reality of life is subjective and extratemporal. We must not think of the past as divorced from the present, since each one of us carries the past in his subconscious mind, from which it emerges to the surface of the conscious self, bringing with it, like a water-spider with its crystal bubble of air, a whole milieu rescued from Time and replete with life that was really lived because it was profoundly felt. The true artist, therefore, is he who will find a way of imitating this trick of Nature's and of expressing this rhythmic interweaving of "past" and "present." . . . . The genius of Proust, in order to express these realities, has created a style which, though at first it strike us as complicated, is actually the only skin that will fit the wrinkles of his thought.

Like Bergson, Proust jettisons the old mathematical conception of Time as something divided objectively into years, days, and hours, substituting for it what Bergson calls *durée mobile.* Mobile duration is Time measured from the subjective point of view of our individual consciousness, for which, as we all know, the term an "hour" may be hopelessly inadequate to indicate the duration of a state of soul which in reality may be much longer or much shorter. The whole of Proust's long novel, then, is an extraordinary *tour de force,* an unparalleled effort to see the world of men and things situated not in mathematical Time but in Bergsonian Time or Duration. Viewed thus, existence acquires a new aspect and becomes almost monstrously complex. . . . . Proust feels that to express the reality of his regret or of his jealousy he must resort to what he calls a "sort of psychology in space" different from the "plane psychology" of his predecessors. One must of course read his novel to understand how his psychology differs from that of novelists who see life in terms of conventional Time, and it is very difficult to express in a phrase what that difference implies. . . . .

Remembrance of Things Past is an experiment in a new psychology, and represents therefore an advance in the art of fiction. The novelist, for Proust, is primarily a translator, an interpreter whose function it is "to seek beneath matter, beneath experience, something different." And this is the key to Proust's method of notation, since it explains the fascination of his picture of aristocratic Parisian society from the eighties to the present day. His characters acquire a startling vividness, emerging, as it were, in volume. If we look at a photograph with the naked eye and then through a stereoscope we have a very feeble idea of the difference between a character presented by a novelist of the old school and as revealed by Proust. The complexity of the world appears in a new light, and where a Balzac showed the social interdependence of human beings Proust lays bare the myriad filaments, hitherto invisible, that link our souls. The great fallacy exposed by him is that we can observe life objectively or form an inkling of reality from appearances. Habit, passion, intelligence, amour-propre, erect a constant barrier between reality and our comprehension. . . . .

Obviously, in making Albertine an invert Proust has taken an extreme case the better to reveal the role played by jealousy in love, the better to demonstrate that we can never "possess the contact of the loved one's being with every point of Time and Space." For Proust love is entirely subjective and never reciprocal. The woman is the screen on which we project our *moi,* the *negative* of our sensibility. In herself she is of secondary importance, since she is merely the vase which contains the essence of our ideal and not the essence itself. Love is "a sort of creation—of a supplementary person distinct from the one who bears the same name in society and the majority of whose elements are drawn from ourselves." It is an effort to externalise our ego, to find in some other person the reflexion which our soul has projected in her. . . . .

No novelist, it is safe to say, has ever portrayed the passion of jealousy so luridly as has Proust. . . . . The author does not of course enter into the ethical aspect of his subject, nor does he, like M. Gide, solicit our sympathy for a Charlus or represent him as a Romantic *incompris.* He shows us a tragic figure, a great artist afflicted by an incurable malady. One wonders why Proust, whose sense of proportion is so very delicate, should not have confined himself more exclusively to the Charlus that interests us most, the Palamède of the *salons* where he terrorises all by his stupendous *morgue,* his daemonic consciousness of superiority. A somewhat similar objection can be raised in regard to Albertine. Proust would reply no doubt that the creation of these two characters was for him a necessity. His study of love, as he conceives this passion, would have been incomplete had it failed to take into account these two abnormal aspects of it. To an expert in the art of analysis, of course, the psychology of the invert must have presented itself as a difficult and therefore a fascinating exercise. But, granting the skill with which Proust isolates the terrible and tragic elements of his theme, it occupies far too large a place in the novel. . . . .

Proust is beyond doubt the greatest literary psychologist whom we have yet encountered in fiction, and though his field of observation is limited to the aristocracy and the higher bourgeoisie, his power of penetration is unsurpassed. . . . . It was Diderot, was it not? who said that the great literary types should be revised every fifty years. After Molière, after Balzac and Flaubert, Proust has something new to tell us, something which affords us new food for meditation on the queerness of the animal, man. The profound truth that emerges from his characterisation is that in every man there is an arrant fool. . . . . And, as Proust turned away from the spectacle of human vanity and selfishness, racked with spiritual and physical suffering, he made what for him was his supreme discovery. It is that happiness is to be found only in art, in the pursuit of that essential truth and beauty which all of us unconsciously extract from life and secrete in the cells within us. Most men, slaves of habit, seek the reality and the beauty of life in surface impressions, in the outward appearance of things. At times they are naively sad when these afford no lasting joy. The true philosopher, in Proust's eyes, is the artist who, like Elstir of the *Remembrance of Things Past,* looks for the roses in that *jardin intérieur* which is in all of us if, like him, we will only cultivate it.

The world unfolded by Proust staggers us by its complexity as it astounds us by its beauty. Is not that because, half emerged from the age of rationalism, we have grown accustomed to expect simple and material explanations of life's deepest problems and lost to some extent the sense of wonder? As a corrective to this attitude of mind, as a reminder of the profounder and more richly coloured spiritual existence which underlies our rational one, the work of Proust has an enduring value. In

Remembrance of Things Past the great forces of Idealism and Realism meet and coalesce in a blinding flash through which the dazzled eye of the reader seems to behold the image of a living reality. One thing, however, is certain. It is that Proust's work signalises the complete overthrow of an old dogma; for never again, surely, can novelists return to the nineteenth-century conception of a purely objective art, of a Realism which confines itself solely to the "scientific" notation of unidealised life.

1932

45. *Proust—The Invalid**

BURTON RASCOE

.... HE [PROUST] resolved to be [the] .... portrayer, historian, analyst, satirist and moralist .... [of] this society .... [which] was to be swept away, destroyed: the images of Pompeii, Sodom and Gomorrah, the first destroyed by the elements, the other two by the wrath of God, continually presented themselves to his mind, and he felt that a picture, a record of an analogous modern society was worth preserving. "The frivolous life of an epoch after ten centuries have passed over it is worthy of the most scholarly research," he once wrote. ....

In order to describe what one has known and seen and felt and loved, he said, it is necessary to withdraw from it, and then, having concentrated upon the plan of the work one has contemplated, to let memory, and the associations of memory, flow freely in an imaginary reconstruction. "I had already come to the conclusion," he said, "that we are not at all free in the presence of the work of art to be created, that we do not do it as we ourselves please, but that it existed prior to us and that

* From *Titans of Literature from Homer to the Present,* G. P. Putnam's Sons, New York, 1932.

we should seek to discover it as we would a natural law because it is both necessary and hidden." He did not manufacture, or follow a formula, least of all did he attempt to produce an intellectual work. He did not work from theory: "From this comes the vulgar temptation for the writer to produce intellectual works. A grave lack of feeling! A book in which there are theories is like an article from which the price mark has not been removed." He wrote from the depths of both his consciousness and subconsciousness, true to the record of his knowledge and experience.

To do this Proust had almost to invent a new language and a new syntax. Since the days of Voltaire and Racine the logic and form of the French language had become perfected and fixed. It had become a marvelous medium of clarity, simplicity, lucidity and urbanity; but it was made up almost entirely of clichés. Certain fixed rules had been established for saying certain things, to depart from which was not to write good French. From Montaigne through Renan, to Anatole France, the French language, in the great tradition, had reached its absolute limits in its purest expression of the characteristic of French thought, which is its logic. All that could be said had been said in that classic medium. But with the dawn of the twentieth century—and more apparently with the beginning of the World War—something new had come into the world, new ideas, new investigations, new interests, new regions of the mind and soul to be explored; and this called for a new syntax in Proust, for he had something unique to say.

He was not exercising a too conscious control over what came out of the reservoir of his feelings, judgments and impressions, a control always regarded by the French as necessary to preserve the classic purity of the language. He got away from the literary formula. He often said he would have preferred to write in German, as a language more resourceful than French, or failing German, to write in English, which he also considered more flexible, suggestive and capable of expressing shades of meaning impossible in French. He therefore wrote a French more like German in its syntax than like classical French, often placing the verb at the very end of an extremely long sentence, as being the logical place for it for the development and emphasis of what he was saying, and stringing out an idea to prodigious sentence lengths with subordinate clauses, parentheses, qualifying phrases and explanatory hesitancies (a practice frequently found in English literature but almost never in French literature). . . . .

I have, by the way, a suggestion for those who never have read Proust. In the first place, even if one reads French easily, it is best not to read him in the original, but in the superb transfusion into English made of the first six parts of *Remembrance of Things Past* by the late C. K. Scott-Moncrieff. In Scott-Moncrieff's translation Proust reads better than he does in French, as Proust himself realized. A bilingual French man of letters, familiar with English through studies at Oxford and Harvard, told me that it may be necessary to re-translate Proust from Scott-Moncrieff's English version back into French to secure for Proust the audience which the intrinsic *entertainment* value of his work possesses. After the death of Scott-Moncrieff, the final volume of the long work, entitled in English, *The Past Recaptured,* was attempted by Stephen Hudson, and that is the version published in England. It is extremely bad. The American publishers, however, intrusted the translation to Frederick Blossom with very happy results. It is more literal, closer to the text than is Scott-Moncrieff; Dr. Blossom even reproduces Proust's slips of grammar and occasional carelessness in leaving out words; and, while it is not a recreation of Proust into an English masterpiece like Scott-Moncrieff's, it is an excellent translation. My suggestion to the person who has never read Proust or who has tried to read him and found him difficult, is to begin with the last volume, the one translated by Blossom. There Proust tells entertainingly and at length just what he set out to do; he tells in straight narrative form about his early life, how he became interested in aristocratic society, how he got into it, how he met Charlus, how he felt there was a book in him that he must write, how he got the idea for his long novel, what problems he set for himself, how he analyzed the truth of other writers in relation to himself and resolved to improve upon the "reality" of these writers, how he withdrew from society on account of illness and how that illness enabled him to carry out his designs—how, indeed, toward the last he knew he was soon to die and how his only anxiety was that he should complete his work before he breathed his last.

1933

46. *The Years before the War**

COMPTON MACKENZIE

IT MAY HAVE BEEN the influence of the Russians, it may have been the reaction against the deliberately contrived tale, it may have been a sudden awareness that the development of external circumstances was forcing the novelist to extend his scope, or it may have been simply Plato's something in the air which produced almost simultaneously right across Europe a kind of novel which was beginning to be absolutely different from any kind of novel that had preceded it. Romain Rolland in France had just produced the eight or nine volumes of *Jean-Christophe,* and Marcel Proust in 1911 had just published the first volume of that huge work *Remembrance of Things Past.* I remember Edmund Gosse's telling me he had just read a French novel that seemed to him an example of the same kind of impulse which had led me into writing *Sinister Street,* and Charles Scott-Moncrieff told me later that while he was translating Proust's earlier volumes he always read *Sinister Street* to achieve an English rhythm with which he could break up Proust's sentences. What vandalism,

* From *Literature in My Time,* Rich & Cowan, London, 1933.

the Proustian *dévoté* will exclaim. Perhaps it was, but let him try to reproduce in English those exquisite involutions without altering the original architecture of the French. Some of those parentheses would have made even Henry James gasp.

47. *The Marquis de Chaumont**

HAROLD NICOLSON

. . . . THE PRIX GONCOURT was awarded to Proust for *Swann's Way*. Proust began to be lionised. He would lie in bed all day in his stuffy darkened room, and in the evening he would put on his elaborate evening clothes (those white kid gloves clasping an opera hat) and attend the receptions given to the members of the Peace Conference. He appeared there like Beethoven at the Congress of Vienna. He would flit about looking like a Goanese bridegroom. He would flit from Mr. Balfour to M. Venizelos, from Marshal Foch to M. Berthelot. He was very friendly, and ill, and amusing. He enjoyed hearing stories about the Conference. He seemed quite unaware of the early and enduring monument of his own impending fame. He drank a great deal of black coffee and he stayed up very late.

On one such occasion he said that he would like to introduce me to the Marquis de Chaumont. I said that this was unnecessary since I had known de Chaumont for many years. He begged me not to be so unintelligent and so gross. Surely I must realise the pleasure it gave him to take an Englishman by the arm, to propel him across the room, to say, "My dear

* In *Travelers Library*, compiled by W. Somerset Maugham, Doubleday, Doran & Co., Inc., 1933.

Jacques, allow me . . . ."[1] to hesitate and then to begin again, "Allow me, Sir, to present my dear friend, the Marquis de Chaumont."[2] For me it would be perfectly easy. I should only have to say, "Oh! but I know de Chaumont, we were at Oxford together." And then the three of us could sit on that sofa over there and talk about other people. "Don't you see," he said, "it's so simple. Let's go. Do not be unintelligent!"[3] I surrendered myself to this comedy. Proust purred like a small Siamese cat. De Chaumont, I am glad to say, was exquisitely polite. We sat on the sofa as arranged. As arranged, we talked about the other people. After a few minutes de Chaumont rose and left us. We then talked about de Chaumont. Proust was indignant with me for regretting that so bright a talent should have been ruined by an undue deference to foreground. He did not agree with me in the least. He said that there were a great many young men who could write much better than Jacques de Chaumont, and very few young men who could show so many quarterings. It was right and fitting that Jacques should concentrate on the qualities which he possessed in so highly specialised a manner. The world was becoming too diverse; it was necessary to specialise.

"He is merely cultivating his line! He is wise."[4]

"I shall now speak to you," he said, "on the subject of elegance."

. . . . We were interrupted by our hostess; Proust rose, and a few minutes later he drifted away. I leant against the window watching him. A little white face over there, those bruised eyes, that blue but shaven chin, those white gloves resting upon the opera hat. He was being universally affable. I never saw him again.

[1] "Mon cher Jacques, permettez ..."

[2] "Permettez, Monsieur, que je vous présente mon grand ami le Marquis de Chaumont."

[3] "Vous voyez bien c'est d'une simplicité. Allons-y! Ne soyez pas inintelligent!"

[4] "Il ne fait que cultiver sa spécialité! Il fait bien."

I walked away from that party with Jacques de Chaumont. I told him how excited I was by Proust, how Antoine Bibesco had promised on the following Sunday to take me to dinner with him in his bedroom. De Chaumont was not enthusiastic: "A remarkable man, assuredly, a remarkable man; but Jewish, Jewish."[5] And that dinner never materialised. I have recently seen the letter which Proust wrote on that occasion to Antoine Bibesco. It was a letter in which he begged the latter to come alone on Sunday and not to bring me with him. The letter was quite kindly worded.

A few weeks later we heard that Proust was again seriously ill. He had been working at *Pastiches et Mélanges* and the effort had exhausted him. De Chaumont came to see me in obvious tribulation, carrying a letter in his hand. I read the letter. It was from Proust, saying that he had written a short sketch in the manner of St. Simon and would Jacques mind if he figured in it by name? The latter was embarrassed how to answer. He did not wish to offend Proust, yet on the other hand, well, really . . . . I said that I, for my part, would have been in the seventh heaven had Proust showed any inclination to insert me in *Pastiches et Mélanges.* De Chaumont said, "it moight be jolly well all roight for a foreigner, but moy mother would not loike it." I told him that I had met his mother, and was convinced that she would not mind in the least. He was only slightly disconcerted. "Then there is moy aunt, de Maubize. She 'ates Jews." I began to get a little angry at this, and told him that I doubted whether Proust would live for long, that he was the greatest living writer, that Jacques was sacrificing a free gift of immortality, and that what on earth could it matter about his aunt? He sat there turning the letter over and over in his gloved hands. Suddenly he tore it up with a gesture of decision; he flung it into one of the large brass bowls that enlivened the foyer of the Majestic.

[5] "Un homme remarquable, évidemment, un homme remarquable: mais juif, juif."

"No, no indeed. It will make me lose the Jockey."[6]

The book appeared some months later and it contained no mention of Jacques de Chaumont. And the following year I met a member of the Jockey Club and asked him whether de Chaumont had been elected. He said that he had not been elected.

*48. Proust: The Two Ways**

PAUL ELMER MORE

THERE IS SOMETHING portentous in the life of Marcel Proust; something portentous in the vast work of fiction into which his life was poured; something equally portentous in the kind of homage given to that work by admirers, many of whom have read but a small portion of it. . . . .

. . . . the novel itself . . . . is portentous in its mere length and portentous in its power of combining unity of purpose with dispersion of method. The *Overture* to the first volume begins with a curious analysis of sleep and waking, and their merging together in the dream-state, which is meant to set the tone for all that follows. . . . .

To my taste this introductory section, including the *Overture* and *Combray,* is the subtlest and truest and most interesting portion of the whole novel. It is highly original, often quaint and exquisite, and it is adroit as a preparation for what follows; best of all, it is comparatively short.

For the rest the substance of the novel, so far as it has any,

[6] "Non! non pas! Çà me ratera mon Jockey."

* *The American Review,* April 1933.

is the doings of the people of the two ways, the aristocratic circles of the Guermantes Way and the Bourgeoisie circle of *Swann's Way* . . . . ending with an assembly at the Princesse de Guermantes's, in *The Past Recaptured,* where we see the old standards of snobbishness broken down and the two streams of society mingled together in a débâcle of all standards whatsoever. . . . .

The nearest approach to a full-length portrait is the grotesque figure of the Baron de Charlus (a Guermantes), ravaged and in the end pitifully broken by his anomalous passions. The nearest approaches to *consecutive* narration are the story of Swann's wooing of Odette and the story of Marcel's love for Albertine. But in neither of these two stories are there any events such as make the staple of the ordinary novel. Swann's experience resolves into the fluctuating emotions of a man who is consciously making a fool of himself, and Marcel's love, when it once gets started, scarcely moves out of a flux and reflux of jealous suspicions that extend through seven hundred and fifty seven pages. And the portrait as well as the stories are simply drowned in a billowing ocean of reflections on every aspect of life. It is in fact this stream of ideas, chiefly psychological, led on and on by an unpredictable association, this, rather than the sporadic events, that forms the matter of the book; and our critical estimation of Proust will depend largely on our judgment of the soundness or unsoundness of his psychology. For myself I may say that I find these reflections in part surprisingly fine and fresh, in part tediously commonplace, in part vitiated by a fundamentally inadequate conception of human nature, in part sheer nonsense. The amazing thing is that any writer could keep up the process so continuously and so long. When all is said, it is a prodigy of the creative will and intellect; and I suspect that many readers' wonder at the immensity of the achievement passes into admiration for its quality. . . . .

The fact is that of the two ways open to the creative imagination Proust knows but one, and has pursued it with a persistence and sagacity and intrepidity which have earned for him something like prophetic repute among those of his generation who are treading with less certainty the same road to the same goal. It is not a wide renown, or, if wide, is a renown largely of mystification. To the generality of men, bound over to a succession of little unending tasks, and content in the respites of toil to snatch at any diversion of pleasure or to sit in somnolent expectation—to these the world of Proust, if known at all, must be a pure bewilderment, and the drift of his moral psychology must be like the shimmering of gossamer filaments blown from their attachment. . . . .

. . . . our present concern, except indirectly, is not with philosophy or religion, but with art, and more particularly with the art of fiction. And since, whether for good or for ill, the theme of the novel from the beginning has been predominantly love, we are to see in what different ways the imagination lays hold of this theme in its search for a world of reality.

Now it must be observed that what we call love is a highly complicated phenomenon. . . . .

. . . . physical desire and the sentiment of love and the recognition of social obligations in love do not necessarily coincide, or may coincide in various patterns. But it needs some reflection, perhaps, to see just how the two ways of fiction are defined by the attitude of the writer towards this complicated phenomenon, according as he looks for the significant reality in its core of physical urgency or in its envelope of sentimental and ethical associations. On the one way the novelist, while not denying, or even minimizing, the basic fact of sex, tends to keep it in the background as in itself an unmalleable force, common to men and animals and unimportant in the differentiation of man from man. What rather interests him is the sense of beauty that arises out of the brute fact as a flower springs from the earth, and that flourishes only with a certain reticence as to its source, just as the flower must not carry the soil on its blossom. But that is only the beginning of the divergence. The final parting of the ways comes with recognition of the ethical associations attached to love. Though he may not deal openly with the matter as would a professed moralist, though indeed as an artist he is bound more or less to deal with it indirectly, nevertheless the family and the structure of society are for him the important fact, the more important as his art rises in seriousness; and the personal sentiment of love in his imaginative world acquires dignity just in proportion as it can be carried on into this ethical sphere. The significant reality for him lies here for the reason that these associations have a validity above the happiness of the individual, being fixed by eternal principles of right and wrong interwoven into the very texture of human life. The people of his imagination may not know these laws, or, knowing, may disregard them; but he knows. One of the readier sources of poignant emotion at the disposal of the novelist is the breaking of his fictitious persons, through their ignorance or rebellion, against this wall of impersonal facts; but the emotion will rise to the height of true tragedy only when the manipulator of the puppets is himself neither ignorant nor rebellious. . . . .

But suppose on the other hand the novelist, and with him probably his circle of readers, has lost the sense of ethical reality and in the social laws sees only a tradition convention (*nomos,* as the sophists understood it) hampering and abridging the fulfilment of individual desires (physis) to no purpose. He may or may not retain feeling for the sentimental penumbra about the physical fact. Without that feeling he will write as a realist after the fashion of Zola, and his interpretation of life, in so far as it adheres to love as the main theme of the novel, will be of the type of *Nana.* In the other case, the sentiment retained, but detached from its moorings in the higher law (*nomos,* as Socrates understood it), will float off into the sort of "symbolism" in which the imagination becomes only a servant of the flesh, or will further evaporate into the so-called "stream of consciousness," after the manner of Proust, in which thought succeeds thought, and image follows upon image, under no other guidance than the haphazard "association of ideas" revived so unexpectedly from an older discredited psychology. But in either case—and this is a point that should not be obscured by a trick of terminology—the writer, whether realist or symbolist, will belong to the broader school of naturalism, in so far as he eliminates that faculty of responsible selection in the field of consciousness which for the humanist belongs to man only, along with the "nature" common to man and the rest of the animal kingdom. And further it should be noted that both branches of the naturalistic school are alike in this, that they rob human activity of any purpose or ultimate meaning. The only difference is that with the realist the result is likely to be a kind of sullen despair or fierce hatred, showing itself in a deliberate recourse to the ugly and bestial as the ultimate truth of things, and producing a curious but bastard imitation of genuine tragedy, whereas with the symbolist the illusion and utter futility of life will reproduce itself in an art ever more and more fantastically unreal.

Certainly illusion, with its attendant train of desolate awakenings, is the underground of Proust's sentimental and naturalistic picture of life, as all his readers will admit, his admirers as readily as his detractors. . . . .

Humanity as portrayed in Proust's imagination is without aim, without joy, without peace, without outlook of any sort; his people have no occupation save to think about themselves, and in *le néant* beyond the phantasmagoria of unsatisfied and forever insatiable desires the only reality for them is the grinning figure of Fear. The author himself knew the malignity of that face; and the look of it gradually paralysed all power of normal association. His last days alternated between a feverish repulsion of society and a no less panic craving for companionship. . . . .

Nevertheless—and this is one of the paradoxes of modern taste—a growing circle of enthusiasts, mostly very young, pretend to read such works with avidity and suck some kind of pride out of the pretension. Why, one asks. And the answer, if one may believe them, is definite enough: their delight is not in the thing represented—and indeed life itself, they say, in any veracious account can give joy to no one—but rather in the act itself of representing. That is, they delight in Proust's art as something utterly detached from life, and as producing a reality of its own. . . . .

If there is pleasure to be derived from Proust—a pleasure beyond that in the mere adroitness of imitation—it is because his novel is a criticism of life as didactic as any that Matthew Arnold would demand, though a criticism pointing in a very different direction. And it may be added that Proust himself knew this perfectly well.

The magic of Vinteuil's sextet is in fact very much a prolongation of life, as Proust carefully informs us, and its spell is inseparable from enchantments out of the past. As Marcel listens, there comes back to him slowly, like a vast bulk gradually looming up through clouds of mist, that fatal scene at Montjouvain. . . . .

We are entitled to ask the meaning of this paradoxical position of a writer who boasts of his art as in no sense a prolongation of life and in the same breath shows it to be rooted in one of the most concrete of animal passions. First of all we are justified, I think, in taking it as confirmation of the view that the ways of the symbolist and the realist in fiction are merely accidental diversions on the main road of naturalism. But for an explanation of the peculiar straddling achieved by Proust we are pointed back to that horror of the void which confronts the self-liberated soul. As a symbolist he sees the solid fabric of life constantly dissolving into sentiment; and sentiment for him is only another name for the stream of sensations floating up from some dark centre of the subconscious under the sway of accidental associations, ungoverned by the will, controlled by no faculty of selection, never solidifying into action. One thing within this field of sentiment might seem to lend order to these chaotic sequences, imposing upon them a semblance of static calm by linking the sensation that has been with the ever newly arising sensation—memory. A good deal has been written about Proust's philosophy of memory, which in the main he borrowed from Bergson; and the very titles of his work as a whole, *Remembrance of Things Past,* and of the last section of it in particular, *The Past Recaptured,* show how seriously he himself took this element of sentimental experience. Undoubtedly also one of the striking features of his art is the skill, amounting to genius, with which he describes the chain of recollections evoked by some trivial event or sudden observation. But in the end memory, too, becomes a factor of despair; it cannot re-create what is gone, or give present reality to what was unreal in the past, or counteract the corrosions of time. . . . .

This vaunted philosophy of memory is no more than a "recoil in horror" from what Proust elsewhere calls the "fragmentary and gradual death that interpolates itself throughout the whole course of our life," our reliance upon it only a part of the futile "plaint of those most humble elements of the personality which are about to disappear," forever swallowed up in the vast backward and abysm of time. It is all vain. The great fear remains. The symbolist's hope of dispelling illusion by a thinner illusion, or of attaining solidity by rolling vapour upon vapour, is itself an illusion of adolescence, a fantastic dream like Ixion's of embracing heaven in a cloud, from which the awakening is into a hell of self-pursuing torture:

Volvitur Ixion et se sequiturque fugitque.

The life of Proust himself, the lives of the romantics through the past century, are evidence.

The whole content of Marcel's memory is coloured, as we know, by that early scene at Montjouvain; and this is indicative of the way in which Proust mingles realism with symbolism in his treatment of the fundamental—certainly at least for him fundamental—theme of fiction. Debarred by his naturalistic limitations from finding anything real in the ethical sanctions of love he is driven in his search for reality down through the superimposed layers of sentiment to the basic fact of animal desire. And we can follow the descent step by step. He cannot stop with that attraction between a man and any chosen woman, which is the simplest form of the passion we call "love," since this enhancement of the individual object desired is the illusory work of the imagination. As he says: "This love of ours, in so far as it is love for one particular creature, is not perhaps a very real thing." . . . . And so he reaches down to the lust of the invert as coming nearest to the fact of pure physical pleasure uncontaminated by sentiment.

Proust's attitude towards this topic is curious and, it must be admitted, not consistent. On the one hand it evidently arouses in him an instinctive feeling of indignation, connected with a residue of traditional morality from which he has not entirely liberated himself. It is even here and there castigated as a vice—whatever a vice may be to a professed amoralist—and he has not reached the stage of frank justification held by a Gide. He often speaks of it as a left-over from an outworn civilization, and as a curse by which a few abnormal persons are plagued. . . . .

It is perhaps the ambiguity attached to homosexuality as at once "natural" and "unnatural" that drives the naturalist in Proust a step lower in his search for the ultimate fact. For there is yet another instinct which not only isolates anomalous desire from any sentimental waste in moral obligations, but concentrates the individual upon himself by the sadistic doubling of lust with cruelty, and wrings out the last possibility of physical sensation in the masochistic union of pleasure with pain. So we reach the rock bottom of "nature," the end of the way which is not that of the humanist. The starting point for Proust's interpretation of life was the scene at Montjouvain. The conclusion is the *Temple de l'Impudeur* maintained in Paris during the war. . . . .

Between the realistic brutality of Montjouvain and the Temple lies the vast expanse of Proust's symbolism. . . . .

As for the other than the Proustian way which we have tracked to the bitter end, I cannot clinch what I have been trying to say better than by closing with a few words on Mr. Edmund Wilson's study of our author in *Axel's Castle*. . . . . There is a sort of finality in Mr. Wilson's setting of the Proustian symbolism at that particular point in its progress towards "the systematic nonsense called Dadaism," where "the metaphysic implicit" in this form of art unites consciously with the explicit metaphysic of relativism. . . . .

49. *The Coming Struggle for Power**

JOHN STRACHEY

. . . . PROUST, D. H. Lawrence, and Mr. Aldous Huxley. In a sense, no three writers could have less in common. Yet all three reflect in a kind of agony the characteristics of the epoch in which they live. . . . . Each of these three modern writers has shared in the tragic view.

. . . . In so far as they are great writers, they share in the tragic tradition of the race. But do we not all feel that each of

* Modern Library, Inc., 1935.

them is only partly a great writer? They are men possessing talents not inferior to the representative writers of other times. And yet, somehow, is there not a question-mark to be put after their names? Is there not something doubtful, something mixed, about their achievement? And does not this doubt, on closer inspection, derive from the very nature of the material on which they have had to work? For every writer, no matter how much he likes to deceive himself on this matter, can only work on the material which the life of his time presents to him. If, as in the case of the three writers in question, their work consists in a commentary, either in the form of the novel, or still more directly in the form of essays, on the actual social intercourse of their times, there can surely be no argument about this contention.

Of the three writers, Proust has achieved the most complete work. Yet it was just in his case that the social necessities of the time and place of his life played the most important role. For Proust's enormous work, besides being so much else, is quite undeniably the odyssey of snobbery. It is, moreover, in one aspect the final proof of the absolutely necessary and praiseworthy character of snobbery in a class society; it is the justification of raising the impulse to social success to the level of one of the great elemental passions of humanity. To a French Bourgeois who died in the third decade of the twentieth century, snobbery was, Proust demonstrates, an elementary duty.

. . . . And if, in the end, the whole exploration proved to have been vain, if when the ultimate arcana had been reached its inmates proved to be not the magically refined and delightful persons of imagination, ... that did not mean that any better results could have been obtained by devoting one's life to any other purpose. . . . . By devoting it to the social passion he had at any rate penetrated to what was, presumably, the highest and most cultivated point in the society of the most profoundly civilized nation on earth.

Thus the discovery that this refinement and cultivation was all a sham, did, at any rate, assure him that nowhere else was there anything better. The note of lamentation which rises throughout the concluding phases of Proust's work is a lamentation for a society which is on the road to dissolution. One recalls that passage in *The Past Recaptured* in which Proust meets again the characters of his work after the interval of the war. He has the momentary illusion that the experience may have improved them. He discovers that, on the contrary, it has made them all worse not better, narrower, more selfish, less humane. Proust, in truth, sang a long agonised requiem mass over the highest expression of human life of which French bourgeois society under the Third Republic had been capable. . . . .

No contrast could seem more profound, nor could prove more superficial, than the contrast between Proust and the English novelist, D. H. Lawrence. Lawrence was the one copious and vital writer which England has produced since the war: the one man who still wrote as if he knew that it was worth while to write. He suffered, however, both personally and as a writer, to the most intense degree from the nature of his environment.

. . . . We find that Lawrence's fancy ran in the same direction as Proust's. Lawrence also, if not in his own person then in the world of his fantasy, climbed the social heights of existing society, to see if by chance something living might be at the top. And Lawrence also comes back with the report that there is nothing. The half-Jewish French bourgeois and the Notts miner both made the same pilgrimage: they both went "Swann's Way" and "Guermantes Way." And, no doubt, they were in a sense quite right. If one rejects politics; if one rejects, like the philosophers, the proposal to change life; if one seeks only to explain it, then truly the best thing that one can do is to seek out what is highest, and so presumably best, in the old society. But both Proust and Lawrence had the misfortune to see through their social ideal. Indeed, it was unavoidable. They were born out of due time: too early to have abandoned the social ideals which still existed, too late to find those ideals in a condition of preservation which could satisfy them. . . . .

Between Mr. Aldous Huxley and Lawrence there is a great contrast, far more profound than that between Lawrence and Proust. . . . .

It is appropriate that it should be a Huxley, a member of one of those principal English middle-class families, which formed and still form, one of the main pillars of the British capitalist system, who would most consciously describe its closing period. And what a description it is! In a series of novels and essays, Mr. Huxley has sent the long, delicate, probing fingers of his analysis into every corner of the life of capitalist society. His findings are always the same. Go where you like, "do what you will," you will never escape from the smell of ordure and decay. . . . .

The other great figure of contemporary letters is Mr. James Joyce. Mr. Joyce is undoubtedly a great poet, whose gifts would be accounted precious in this or any other age. Mr. Joyce's work remains, and will I imagine always remain, memorable. It will mark as aptly the end of that vast literature in English which was the chief achievement of the English-speaking men of the last five centuries, as Proust's novel marks the end of the corresponding French tradition. . . . . He has succeeded for the time, at any rate, and in one particular respect, in reasserting the old high claim of literature to be the prime method of enriching our knowledge of the external world. In this sense, Mr. Joyce, in spite of the extreme Byzantinisms of his later works, is less of an end and more of a beginning than Proust. But if his work is a beginning as well as an end, it is the beginning of something which has little or nothing to do with the culture of the last five hundred years of Europe.

Remembrance of Things Past and *Ulysses* stand like massive boulders marking the end of a long tradition, blocking the old road, and pointing, not very certainly, in some new direction. If it is possible that there can be another major work in the old tradition, in the classical literature of the capitalist class, it must come from America.

50. *The Decade of Illusion**

MAURICE SACHS

. . . . THE WORLD began to understand what riches a life had ceased to bestow when the family of Marcel Proust opened the little apartment of the rue Hamelin that those of Paris who had known and loved him might join in looking on him for the last time. Man Ray was given the authorization to photograph Proust. The white sheet covered him to the chin, where the beard had grown. He was resting at last after nine years of work writing *Remembrance of Things Past.* The news of his death was shocking as lightning, striking the very earth from under our feet; many people —young men especially—who had never come near him wept and prayed as if a brother had been taken from them.

Whatever the appearance of life has been, man receives the death he deserves. . . . . The great glory of "Monsieur France" melted away before death; the work of Proust, on the other hand, grew with his absence. His disappearance from the realm of the living brought him the recompense for which he had hoped. The emotion it produced in a group at first limited reminds me of those great tides of tears which rose in the

* Alfred A. Knopf, New York, 1933. Also Paris, 1918–1928.

masses when Clemenceau and Briand died, those movements of the heart which speak a truth.

The death of Proust followed closely that of Jacques Bizet, his friend of childhood . . . .

He [Jacques Bizet] had a mind decidedly Proustian, not through contact with Proust, for they saw each other but little after the writer had left the Verdurins for the Guermantes, but by reason of a vocabulary completely nourished with humour, that same humour on which the Proustian sense of the comic is based. Later I discovered in *Remembrance of Things Past* a thousand expressions which were familiar, and which were equally based on certain Proustian turns of phrase. For example, the comparison of a cake which the cook made with a sculpture which Michelangelo might have executed for Julius II was "very Bizet." It was the spirit of an epoch and a class. Jacques Bizet and Marcel Proust each had his deepest ties among the cultured bourgeoisie of Paris; they both were marked by it, but one of them made it glorious.

Proust and Bizet were equally attached to Robert Dreyfus, a friend of their childhood. They gave him their affection; he built their altars. For one he wrote a book of memoirs, to the other he dedicated the walls of his study, working thus to remember one under the brotherly dictation of the other. In their death he is their living hyphen. . . . .

"In France," said André Maurois, "a young man asks me to teach him the secrets of the Proustian style; at Princeton they question me on the moral importance of the work of Proust." In all American universities, it seems, one worries first about the moral reasons of written works. Which certainly would be the last consideration of a young Frenchman. . . . .

One day, when Wassermann [intimate friend of France, who called him always his adopted son] was leaving Paris and making his adieux to Anatole France, he asked for something to read on the voyage. France said, "Here, my friend. Life is short; Proust is long. Take this." And Wassermann carried off the rare treasure [the first edition of *Within a Budding Grove,* with a dedication to France]. . . . .

Pierre Abraham has now consecrated himself to criticism. The work he is preparing is monumental; what he has already published is of an importance indicating the weight of the entire work. His volume on Proust seems to me the best which has been published. . . . .

Léon Daudet, writer, physician, politician, and party man, is the son of Alphonse Daudet. He is a man of strong temperament and brilliant speech; he loves to laugh well, drink well, eat well, feel well, and have order in politics. As a critical writer he is among the surest; what he thinks, what he says of the creators of his time is of truly remarkable justice and virility of judgment. Notably it was to his pen that we owe the first article of approbation for Proust, and to him, in large measure, it was due that Proust was given the Goncourt prize for *Within a Budding Grove*. . . . .

It happened that Proust, Gide and Matisse, whose works have an unalterable solidity and whose names are already carved in the earth for the present and for posterity, have never created about themselves that delicious enchantment which produces a mirage. Either by temperament or from love of undiluted truth, nothing in their lives seemed to reveal their superiority to the common run of men. Perhaps that is why they were only recognized late. As they approached their fortieth year . . . . Proust was just beginning *Remembrance of Things Past,* Gide had not published *Si le Grain ne meurt,* Matisse was barely known. Those who fail to web themselves with miracles walk slow-footed amid the confusion of the mass of spectators. Their work, however, is no less grand: Proust is as great as Stendhal, Gide as J.-J. Rousseau, Matisse as Cézanne. But in default of a visible mirage they must needs take themselves to a secret hermitage where the soul, screened from curious eyes, creates amid the bitter pains of childbirth: one in the rue Hamelin, another at Villa Montmorency, another at Nice—those spots which will one day be goals of ardent pilgrimages and which their admirers hungry for mystery will surround with sacred respect. . . . .

[In the house where Jean Cocteau was born and lived many years, a stairway curled majestically around a monumental lamp-post, and at each landing stood a fringed pouf for the comfort of visitors.] . . . . Very often Marcel Proust rested on these thoughtfully placed rectangular seats as he climbed the stairs, either waiting to visit Mme. de Chevigné [Mme. de Guermantes], who lived there, or more tired still from his climb to the fourth floor, where Cocteau lived. For many moments he sat thus, catching his breath. And often since, I have seen the admirers of Proust slowly making the pilgrimage of that sombre stairway and, like him, resting on the fringed benches. . . . .

51. *André Gide, His Life and His Work**

LEON PIERRE-QUINT

HENRI BÉRAUD could not understand why the works either of Gide or Proust or Valéry, all of which bored him to death, should sell so readily, particularly abroad. He believed therefore that Jean Giraudoux, director of propaganda at the Ministry of Foreign Affairs and a friend of the N.R.F., must be favoring this [group] house at the expense of others. . . . .

The wave of religion carried off contributors to the N.R.F.: Jean Cocteau, to whom Maritain opened his arms, the poets Reverdy and Max Jacob, and Gabriel Marcel, the metaphysician. Finally Jacques Rivière, who on his return from Germany had at first gone under to a new profane influence, that of Proust, died in 1925, "miraculously saved," according to Madame Rivière. . . . .

It is the story of his own life that he (Gide) tells in *Si le Grain ne meurt.*—You can put down everything—Proust had told him—but never say "I." . . . .

Gide has no interest in Proust's characters because for him

* Alfred A. Knopf, New York, 1933. Originally, Paris, 1932.

moral conflict alone gives people their reality. "The characters of Marcel Proust, who do not suffer from moral disquietude, make upon Gide, in spite of the wonderful way in which they are handled, the impression of being merely puppets." . . . .

It is remarkable that two of the greatest French contemporary writers should both have seen in the study of the unconscious the means of illuminating the depths of the human soul. Thus regarded, each of them seems to be Bergsonian, although Proust came to Bergson very late, and I suspect Gide of having paid but scant attention to his work. One may say, therefore, of each of them, that he did not really come under Bergson's influence, but rather took possession of the ideas that were floating "in the air" of his period and adapted them to the purposes of his own genius; Proust searching in the unconscious for whatever reality and lastingness there might be in love and art, Gide compelling himself to seek there the point of departure for an acceptable morality. . . . .

The ephemeral outbreak of frenzy in certain circles during the post-war period, the influence of psychiatry, and, in literature, the works of Proust and of Gide have brought a considerable section of the public to regard inversion no longer as a vice, but rather as a sort of fatal disease. Thenceforward the writer may mention "sodomites," provided that he regards them as the children of an accursed race and depicts them as the victims of their own desires and of society, which hunts them down. Society loves to sympathise with its victims (hence the success of books on convict-prisons). For this reason Proust's dolorous accents in *Sodom and Gomorrah* made the subject acceptable. And here there is an indication of the progress of public opinion: inversion has lost its character for immorality and is entering the domain of pathology. . . . .

When *Sodom and Gomorrah* appeared, Gide did not recognise this love in the tragic and repulsive Proustian pictures. In the course of a friendly conversation with the author, he reproached him with having made his picture of Sodom too black, and Proust, with his customary amiability, immediately declared that in his travesty of young people in *Budding Grove* he had exhausted all the lively colors on his palette: grace, charm, youth.

How is it possible that there should be such a difference of outlook? Is the inversion of which Gide speaks something quite different from that described by Proust? One shows us unhappy victims of obsession; the other some of the finest human types. Yet if we remain within our own period, in Paris itself, if we visit one of the resorts where inverts habitually gather together, in the promenade of some music hall, for example, it is Proust's descriptions which seem the nearest to reality.

52. *Twelve Jews**

PETER QUENNELL

FEW WRITERS, of any race or any period, have within so short a time added so rich, so diverse, so densely populated a tract of intellectual territory to the imaginative commonwealth of the Western hemisphere as did Marcel Proust by the publication of his epic novel. Its frontiers are conterminous with those of Europe: it embraces the whole —at least, a very large section—of urbanised, sophisticated modern life, and its personages, each of them typical yet individual, every one of them drawn with extraordinary verve, have their counterparts in most European cities. Talking of Charlus, of Swann, of Madame Verdurin and "le petit noyau,"

* Rich & Cowan, London, 1934.

we find it difficult to speak of them as of fictitious characters. . . . . They have worked their way into the consciousness of the twentieth century as did Balzac's characters into the fabric of the nineteenth; the fact that they are less romantic and more trivial—but then, their triviality is very often truly tremendous —does not reflect so much on the novelist as on his background.

Marcel Proust is sometimes judged by the life he described. According to some critics—not always the most penetrating— he was the cartographer, himself decadent, of a decadent landscape, the anthropologist who with a great deal of unnecessary care recorded the tribal customs of the Cities of the Plain; which, say the critics, are best left undescribed. Such criticism is only applicable, if at all, to the later volumes of Proust's enormous and extremely complex life-work; only in its closing chapters, where his stylistic and creative power has begun to flag, do we recognise the trace of spiritual malady and feel that he is obsessed by, rather than legitimately interested in, the various themes that it was his purpose to unfold. *Remembrance of Things Past* is not a product of decadent genius, for decadence implies limitations, a lack of breadth and poise, both qualities without which so long and absorbing a novel could never have existed. The "humanity" for which critics are inclined to bleat—as though "humanity" were in some way consistent with "wholesomeness"—is implicit in the very exuberance of the entire plan.

. . . . The experiences that give our lives value—that lend them their peculiar tone and colour—are seldom experiences that would find a place in the pages of an orthodox biography. Manias, dreams, purely subjective occurrences for which no form of words can be discovered, take an important share in the construction of the least imaginative human minds. Shadow and substance are wildly confused; one of Proust's greatest assets as a student of character was his refusal to allow the substance, *qua* substance, a more important place in his narrative scheme than those mere nothings that a "sensible" man is inclined to dismiss. Caprice may be as momentous as ambition, a vague velleity as influential as a reasoned desire; since the novelist is dealing with irrational creatures, whose wills are swayed by something and by nothing, who dream and plot and cogitate and brood, he cannot afford to take up the line of superior reasonableness.

Intellectual prejudice must be put aside. There is a touch of the teacher or preacher in almost every nineteenth-century novelist and historian. Proust replaced the standpoint of the moralist by that of the aesthete and by the calm dispassionate curiosity of the modern scientific worker. Somewhat formidable, no doubt, this habit of collecting and collating. Balzac is often depicted in contemporary caricatures as a Rabelaisian giant, surrounded by homunculi, either stuck on pins or imprisoned in glass jars. But then Balzac was a Romantic and a snob; while Proust's romanticism and snobbery were of a frigid, half-mocking kind, always qualified by the inward smile that one imagines must now and then have crossed Disraeli's face, as with lavish Oriental gestures he bowed himself out of the presence of his sovereign mistress, Gloriana of Osborne and the Highlands . . . .

Disraeli gave England the Suez Canal; just as important a gift to France in another sphere was the tract of territory—the line of intellectual communication—represented by Proust's gigantic book. . . . .

. . . . Since time is implicit in [*Remembrance of Things Past*], ... Proust did not feel the need of a definite chronological framework. Time flows on, a stream full of eddies and back-currents, and, like a kingfisher, the narrator's imagination glances obliquely to and fro across its broad, discoloured expanse, lighting up now Combray and his parent's house, now Paris and the *salon* of the Verdurins, now the romantic dusk of Odette's drawing-room.

Peter Quennell

We do not ourselves come to maturity in any regular or systematic fashion. We grow, as Proust's novel grows, by fits and starts, in sudden and unexpected leaps. Or, perhaps, it might be more accurate to say that, although we are continually changing, we are only aware of the changes that have overtaken us in flashes of rare illumination. . . . .

. . . . Proust, of course, was half French, and the half of him that was not French seems but to have made him more French still. No nationalist, in the aggressive sense of the word, he was deeply and romantically patriotic, with a passion for French history, the names of French towns and villages, the architecture of French cathedrals, and the rustic *patois* that he heard on a servant's lips. . . . .

. . . . Proust, with his very marked homosexual interests and the natural elusiveness that characterised everything he did, though his protagonists desire and possess a large variety of women, lifts his account of these adventures on to a plane where the physical transaction itself becomes relatively unimportant. Indeed, there is an ambiguity surrounding the figure of Albertine, who appears at moments to be less girl than boy, a hint of perversity or impotence underlying the temperament of her lover, an air of mystery enshrouding the entire relationship, that persuades a reader—as Proust, no doubt, intended that it should—to devote his whole attention to its poetic, or subjective, aspect. Proust's method is to exalt the attraction itself at the expense of the human personality round which it centres. He spares no pains to break up such attractions into their poetic, romantic, or allegorical constituents, ...

This knack of extracting from human beings a poetic or symbolical significance that transcends and obscures their human personality, Proust did not confine to his analysis of love. His aptitude for arranging his characters in some symbolical, even mythological, pattern seems, now and then, too elaborately developed, his vision unnecessarily comprehensive. He saw everything, every detail, all at once. Society appeared before his eyes like a mammoth Hindu edifice, one of those towering pyramidal structures, where every coign, every ledge, is thickly peopled with astonishing and grotesque symbolism. He must throw his outline around the whole; he must weave his scrutiny among the crabbedest fretwork of its balustrades. Not content with literary impressionism, he determined to reproduce the entire fabric; and it was thus, with the reckless disregard of a man in whom inspiration had become illumination, that he would permit his parentheses to hurry on till they had brimmed the page and were pouring, rapid and intricate, down the next; that he wrote often clumsily, sometimes hideously. . . . . Here a naturalist might have failed, tumbling suffocated beneath the tremendous weight of his material. That Proust, by temperament, was so little of a naturalist, had after all, so slight a regard for realism, proved the ultimate salvation of his book. He had none of that reverence for raw fact . . . . which had been the undoing of Zola and the Goncourts and is curiously echoed to-day in the work of Mr. James Joyce, an old-fashioned realist, roughly turned inside out. Like the Goncourts, he was an inveterate observer; he belonged to the tribe of literary scientists, but his observations were always subsidiary. Not a fact, not a personal or social peculiarity did he unearth, but, in cleansing and burnishing it, he gave it the colour of his own mind.

No writer is apparently more diffuse; few are actually more consistent. His method of preparing for the entrance of a new character by allowing us, as it were, first of all to see the character's shadow projected from behind the scenes and hear his or her voice off, has been likened to that of the great Japanese woman novelist, Lady Murasaki. Proust seldom mislays a character; even "la femme de chambre de Madame Putbus," who never appears but whose mercenary favours the narrator had once planned to enjoy, is referred to again and again in a comic undertone. . . . .

Peter Quennell

. . . . During the night that preceded his death, he was busy dictating an addition to the splendid passage in which he had described the last days of Bergotte, the novelist, using his own symptoms as material. . . . . He . . . . died, with the courage and obstinacy of his race, amid thoughts of the work that had become more important to himself and to the world at large than the life on which it battened. Genius is usually a kind of parasite; microscopic and unprotected when it first enters a human organism, it may develop—in Proust's case, it did develop—till it has engrossed every function of body and mind. All that it leaves of its victims is a walking wraith, or a husky voice in the dim recesses of a cork-lined room.

. . . . The culminating passage, one of the finest he ever constructed, is also one of the most important if we are to understand his book in the spirit in which it was written. Proust's system has an affinity, perhaps not wholly deceptive, with that of Einstein. Like the modern physicist, Proust makes time his fourth dimension; he, too, has disrupted the Euclidean three-dimensional universe—in literature corresponding to the practice of realism—by the new and disturbing element he has introduced. . . . .

. . . . Notice, by the way, how significant is the interval that separates Proust from the attitude of his nineteenth-century predecessors. Where now is the sense of human dignity that, for its own sake, made a man's tragic or commonplace life-history worth telling? Human beings and their passions have only a subjective, or relative, importance. Man has no destiny save to extract from the hurly-burly of his sensations their quintessential, or "timeless," element, for in the flux of changing and dream-like phenomena, this alone, Proust announces, is real and unchanging. Instead of the doctrine of perfectibility—the view of Man as a progressive, ambitious animal—we find a recognition of his poetic and symbolic value.

53. *The Mystic of Memory**

F. L. Lucas

Was it wise, this wisdom that could never take
Joy in the moment for the moment's sake?
That with eyes backward bent ploughed on in pain
The field of life, and reaped but ghostly grain;
Till of earth's myriads he was left alone,
Friendship a folly, love a frenzy grown?
In the gaunt twilight of a lonely land
So might some broken, strange-scrawled column stand;
Or that one bitter pillar, backward turned
To gaze where Sodom and Gomorrah burned . . . .
Who strives with spirits, wrestles for a fall,
And him that calls the dead, the dead shall call.
Vain our deluding arts; all, all in vain
We kiss the pale lips we have raised again.
The more we break, the more we feel Time's power,
Who most have lost the best-remembered hour;
Whose searching hearts find nowhere lasting ease,
Whether in Wittenberg or Méséglise.

"Water-Jelly"—that was the verdict on Proust of D. H. Lawrence. "Ploughing a field with knitting-needles"—that was the verdict of George Moore. It was not often, one imagines, that these two writers found themselves agreeing. And the literary young?—do they read Proust today? Not a great deal, is my impression. They are too busy keeping up to date to find time for a novel in sixteen volumes as much as six years old. Again Proust, though in some ways morbid and *maladif,* is highly intelligent and highly cultivated; probably it is hard for him to compete with writers who seem less hampered in either respect, like Joyce or Lawrence. And again

* From *Studies in French and English,* Cassel & Co., Ltd., London and Toronto, 1934.

Proust is not a manual for Communists. He can never have had anything in common with the modern type of proletarian Galahad who scribbles verse to inform an awed world that he is "learning to shoot." Proust does not flatter the Faubourg Saint-Germain; but of "the workers" he is hardly aware, and shows not a flicker of interest in Karl Marx. Indeed he is individualistic to the verge of obsession. . . . . Today Proust remains a name to quote, but is he read now except by those who read him before? The literary death-rate of our age is terrible.

And yet this book remains very typical of our age; which cannot much pride itself on its good sense, or its artistic nobility; but is excellent at science, and may hereafter be remembered mainly for its advances in physics and in psychology. In psychology no novelist has ever shown a more scientific interest than Proust, with his passion for analysing and classifying the workings of the mind, unconscious as well as conscious. He remained, indeed, not a scientist, but an artist. His general theory of human nature seems to me as fantastic as his particular observations are admirable. But the scientific ambition is there. "Wherever I sought great laws," he writes bitterly at the end, "they labeled me 'detail pursuer.' "[1]

Further, this book is typical of the art, as well as the science, of our age. Perhaps because it *is* the art of a scientific age, the outstanding quality of our literature is its cleverness. We succeed best at biography, at novels, and at journalism. An enemy might say that the first two of these had now become branches of the third. At all events, the praise that rises most often to our lips today is not "How magnificent!" or "How tragic!" but "How clever!" The works of Mr. Aldous Huxley are an excellent example. Now Proust is, I think, at his best a master of character and description; but not more than Balzac. He is also a poet in prose; but not more than Chateaubriand or Flaubert. What astounds his reader again and again is rather his

[1] "Là où je cherchais les grandes lois, on m'appelait 'fouilleur de détails.' "

Mephistophelean and Machiavellian acuteness. It is not, I think, his most valuable quality; but it is his most striking one. He keeps the intelligence strained to the uttermost, as Johnson found with the conversation of Burke. Indeed to read him is in some ways like listening to the conversation of a genius who (unlike most of them) should remain a genius in conversation. It recalls to me the first intoxication, in undergraduate days, of Cambridge talk—a rapture, alas, departed. Stendhal seems naive in comparison, Proust's reader feels the delight of the short-sighted person on whom spectacles suddenly bestow a world of magic definition and brilliance, where all was haze before. One could clap one's hands with pleasure. I have sometimes wondered if to have to pass an examination on this book would not be a better education, and test of education, than most courses at Universities. No one has ever carried to such an extreme the precept of Delphi, of Socrates, or Montaigne: "Know thyself."

And yet did he?

To many the philosophy of Proust seems the hearth and central flame of this book, which is itself the story of his acquisition of that philosophy, and his realisation that to unfold it he must write this book. So does this subtle serpent come full circle, tail in mouth. In itself, one may doubt if his view of life is really so important. It does, however, serve its artistic purpose. It gives his work background, a backbone, a unity. It plays a more essential part in him than in most novelists . . . .

It is strange that both he and his one equal in stature in contemporary England, Hardy, should have shared this obsession with the passage of time this haunted preoccupation with the irrecoverable past . . . .

Memory and Art are at one—

> In that high vision where the heart at rest
> Beholds itself at last possess the unpossessed.

Art can immortalise what Memory reveals only like a lightning-flash; but these are the two gates of Reality.

So life became for Proust an alternation of experience and suffering with recollection and analysis. "Our passions sketch our books, the resting interval writes them."[2] And even if he had not written, the three ultimate things in the world for him would still have been the pain of experience, the ecstatic moments of memory, and the perpetual task of analysis and understanding. The end of Life is, first Truth, then Death. Of the many souls within him, two, he predicted, would be among the last to perish, as his life ebbed away—one, the voice which cried even in his sickroom, "It's fine today!"; the other, the analysing, classifying observer, whose supreme pleasure lay in discerning some new element in common between two states of mind.

. . . . All is dust and ashes—except to remember, to understand, and to create.

Almost all philosophies seem very odd; but few odder than Proust's. It is a string for his pearls; but does its author really deserve our awed respect as a philosopher; even if he was related by marriage to Bergson? . . . . He is inconsistent. . . . . He is capable, in his muddled idealism, of saying on one page that only ideas exist—"everything is in the mind";[3] and on the next that, though Germanophils turned a deaf ear to Belgian atrocities, "and yet they were very real."[4] He may theorise with such sceptical disillusion that modern critics, overjoyed as usual to drive some wedge of unreality between life and literature, can describe his work as showing "complete indifference to moral values or human justices." And yet so far is this from the truth that not only do we find in it a fanatical insistence on the *devoir* of the artist, but *bonté* is one of the words

[2] "Ce sont nos passions qui esquissent nos livres, le repos d'intervalle qui les écrit."

[3] "tout est dans l'esprit."

[4] "pourtant elles étaient réelles."

that he uses with deepest feelings: "that kindness, that moral distinction which Mother had learned from my grandmother to consider above everything else in life—doubtless it is not common sense which is 'that which we find most of in the world,' but kindness. In the most distant spots, the most forsaken places, one marvels to see it bloom spontaneously, like in a secret valley a poppy, similar to those of the world, though it has never seen them, never known anything but the wind now and then ruffling its solitary red hood."[5] It was the poet in him who wrote that; not the philosopher. Proust was surely wiser than his creed. Certainly one may be allowed to wonder a little at the inconsistency which can dedicate to *mon incomparable ami,* Léon Daudet, part of a work which describes friendship itself as not merely futile, but *funeste.*

However, the new and original part of Proust's view of things is not his disillusion—that is ancient enough—nor yet his sense of the eternal appeal of *la princesse lointaine* or the consoling power of beauty—these too are commonplaces. . . . . The only novelty lies in the special value Proust attaches to his mystical moments of *spontaneous* recollection; and in the close analogy he draws between these and the vision of the artist. No one, so far as I know, has suggested this before; though Wordsworth and others have groped round it, they did not distinguish between the two kinds of memory. Yet the suggestion that such moments of recollection are somehow a triumph over time, an escape from transience, is surely more a figure of speech than a reality; due, it may be, to some psychological peculiarity which gave such moments for Proust the abnormal intensity of the mystic's communion with the Abso-

[5] "cette bonté, cette distinction morale que maman avait appris de ma grand' mère à tenir pour supérieures à tout dans la vie — sans doute ce n'est pas le bon sens qui est 'la chose du monde la plus répandue,' c'est la bonté. Dans les coines les plus lointains, les plus perdus, on s'émerveille de la voir fleurir d'elle-même, comme dans un vallon écarté un coquelicot pareil à ceux du reste du monde, lui qui ne les a jamais vus, et n'a jamais connu que le vent qui fait frissonner parfois son rouge chaperon solitaire."

lute. But even with him such moments passed and Time claimed his thrall again. Proust's was a very Pyrrhic victory. This "Quest of Vanished Time," in a word, seems to me valuable for quite other qualities than its view of life. Ironically enough, had Proust understood himself better, he might have been less obsessed with the duty of self-understanding. For his philosophy, as so often, seems largely explicable by the physical and psychological peculiarities of the philosopher. .... His mysticism of memory, ... seems to me one more example of the sanity of Goethe's maxim: "Mysticism—unripe philosophy, unripe poetry." ....

Yet perhaps this scientific novel of a scientific age, with its search for *les grandes lois,* is after all a lesson of the vanity, for the artist, of trying to encroach as an amateur on science. The answer to so many of Proust's general problems is to be found not in Proust, but in Freud. The qualities that make this novel good remain the same as have made older novels good—its powers of dramatic episode and description, its character-drawing, its poetry, its personality, its style. It is not a new philosophic revelation. It remains fiction, though it annexes the interest and the charm of other literary forms as well—of autobiography in the style of Montaigne and Rousseau, of *pensées* like those of La Rochefoucauld and La Bruyère, of prose-poetry like Chateaubriand's. Surely this is enough. Need we also acclaim Proust as a philosopher?

Of the form, again, and the construction of this novel we hear as much as of its philosophy—too much. .... But one may prefer forms of construction whose excellence does not need explaining. Proust's whole work, like many of his single sentences, seems to me in danger of bursting from all he tries to pack into it. It tripled its length between 1913 and his death, nine years later. It was unfinished because he died; it might have remained so, if he had lived.

.... If we seek classical comparisons, there seems to me far more in common between Proust's picture of society and the mixture of mordant psychology and poetic pessimism with which Tacitus has recorded the decadence of the old nobility of Rome, while on their ruin like ferocious thistles in their purple there towered a new race of upstarts. Tacitus, Saint-Simon, Proust—each has left his record of the brutality and baseness under the magnificence of aristocracy in decline; just as the same spectacle inspired Racine to create for the stage in *Andromaque* or *Britannicus* characters who are like were-wolves in satin. . . . .

In Proust, indeed, France has added one more to her numerous *penseurs,* not to her few philosophers. He has the quick perception of a woman, not the organising logic of the builders of systems. . . . .

. . . . he lays his finger on the disease of our age, which will soon be too hurried to dream at all, except for the purpose of being analysed out of the neuroses its own frenzied haste engenders; and soon fly so fast as to leave behind, not only the waves of sound, but poetry itself. That seems to me the essential wisdom of Proust, among other things in him that are hardly sane. Had he only been able to keep his poetic imagination more living still, he would not, perhaps, have needed distance or misery to keep love alive in him; nor have seen only dull prose in whatever his hands could embrace.

Perhaps this failure was partly because he neglected so the other half of life—the physical half that obsessed D. H. Lawrence, just as Proust was obsessed by the analysing intellect. Had health not been denied him, had he kept more sanity about the physical side of existence, he might have reached a less despairing view both of life and love. . . . .

Perhaps there is something a little Teutonic, or Judaic, in the melancholy metaphysics of Proust—as there is a German heaviness about many of his sentences, especially when philosophy breaks in; so that they stagger to their close, groaning beneath their burden of provisoes and qualifications and alternatives, ... Yet even Proust's most crowded and interminable periods preserve a kind of monstrous energy and variety, like those motley processions of faces that pass before one on a moving staircase on the Underground. Here is no Jacob's Ladder reaching to the stars and trodden by seraphic shapes; yet it vibrates with a vast complexity and power. And at other moments his style will suddenly drop its weight of thought and go gliding on its way with a melancholy grace like that Mariana of the South whom Marcel watched in childhood by the Vivonne— . . . .

Not as a gospel, then, nor yet as a novel (*Madame Bovary,* for example, seems to me a far more perfect work of art), but as a vast combination of confessions, *pensées,* and poetry, this book can be one of the most moulding experiences in life for those who read it. It remains typically French in its combination of vivid originality with loyalty to tradition and intelligence. A German would have made it too metaphysical and hysterical; an Italian, too rhetorical; a Russian too mystical and mad. Had it been written in England, the law would doubtless have suppressed what it has, with typical English illogicality, winked at in translation. There have been times since the War when our interests have clashed with those of our neighbour; when we have resented what seemed the shortsighted injustice of her policy; but when we come back from the miseries of statecraft to the world of letters and consider what in literature our age has produced to compare with this work, then the most civilised thing in Christendom seems still, as for now three centuries, the genius of France. . . . .

1935

54. *In Search of Proust**

HAVELOCK ELLIS

. . . . AFTER A separating interval of over a century it is possible, with an effort, to realise what Rousseau was like and what, for good or evil, he effected in the world. . . . . There are various great and definite achievements to be placed to his credit or discredit . . . . he has changed the spiritual and emotional atmosphere of our Western world. . . . . This does not mean that he was absolutely original; many others were moving in the same direction. But it was Rousseau who, by some natural personal quality, effected the general change. . . . .

That can only be done by an abnormal man who is, almost inevitably, an imperfect man, under-developed on one side if over-developed on another. It is only such a man who is forced to approach life from a new angle. There may possibly be millions so forced. But when it happens that a man thus made comes along in an age peculiarly fitted to respond to the vision from this new angle, and uniquely gifted with the power to express it, he will win for himself a place among those immortals who created the world.

I come to Proust.

* These extracts from Havelock Ellis: *From Rousseau to Proust* (New York and Boston, 1935), are used by permission of the publishers, Houghton Mifflin Company.

Havelock Ellis

. . . . I suspect in Proust—with whatever hesitation I may still feel over the problem—something of that same type of genius which Rousseau illustrated. Not by any means that Proust displayed it in so splendid and overpowering a degree. The revelation itself was less overwhelming, and, moreover, not of a nature to appeal at first to more than a limited section of human beings.

Yet it may have been of the same nature in this essential respect that here a man was born into the world who saw and felt in it something that had not been seen and felt before, or at all events not seen and felt in so convincing a way that the world itself became conscious of the revelation. We see evidence of this in the fact that there was at first an almost complete blindness to what Proust brought; even the publishers who later were glad to accept his work at first rejected it. New books and essays about Proust are now constantly pouring out from the press.

If further I am asked to state explicitly what I mean by suggesting that Proust has brought a new vision of the world, it may suffice for the present to bring forward one small example from his work. It is indeed possibly an example to which he himself attached significance, since he published it before-hand in *La Nouvelle Revue Française* as "La Regarder Dormir." The comparison of the two versions, it may incidentally be remarked, is of considerable interest, for it helps us in the study of Proust's literary technique. We find him transposing passages, making little additions or omissions, and changing expressions, nearly always for the better, more simple and more direct, as when the simile of "un être analogue à un végétal" becomes "une plante." More curious is the change in the name of the sleeping girl, who is also the chief heroïne of the whole narrative, from Albertine to Gisèle. It may be recalled that Gisèle was one of Albertine's girl companions at Balbec. I gather from the photographic reproduction of pages of Proust's manuscript by Pierre Abraham that "Albertine" is the name there used, and why it was changed for magazine publication remains obscure.[1]

Rousseau lived and responded—incoherently it may indeed often have been—in a world with which he was in actual contact and by it often buffeted. Proust lived in a *camera obscura,* he was occupied with an immense world of reflections he had accumulated from afar. When a friend quoted to him the saying of Gourmont, "One only writes well what one had not lived," he jumped up, exclaiming: "That is the whole of my work!" . . . .

It used sometimes to be said that Proust's conception of character had put the art of his predecessors in fiction out of date. He conceived a figure in the round, in all its vital complexity, while their representations are flat and superficial; he himself told Bois that he had tried to establish a three-dimensional psychology, and some critics have accepted this view, or we might say that he tried to effect in fiction something of what Cezanne strove after in painting. . . . . Feuillerat's exploration of Proust's manuscripts . . . . shows that Proust's opinion of his characters tended to change progressively as his work advanced. So that the new dimensional character is not so much a deliberate method of the artist as simply an added complexity accidental to his changing view. We need not throw aside Stendhal and Flaubert because we also have Proust, any more than we need throw aside Pascal because we also have Rousseau.

. . . . "Every social condition has its interest," Proust wrote in an article in the *Figaro,* "and the artist may perhaps feel as

[1] The final result of Proust's constant and unceasing elaboration of his work until the last minute when it left his hands is not satisfactory when we examine into details, while careless printers and negligent proof-reading have added to the errors made by Proust in setting down contradictory statements concerning his characters and forgetting what he had previously written. A number of such errors were brought together by E. Marsh, "The Text of Marcel Proust," *London Mercury,* May 1923. Every reader can easily add to them.

curious to show the ways of a queen as of a dressmaker." He felt the seduction of the people of the world, but his final judgment of them was severe; he was never their dupe. "What idiots they are!" we are told he often exclaimed, as the outcome of this malicious sympathy. Yet there is the devil in it all!

That, however, is but another way of saying that the key to Proust's personality is of pathological nature. To turn ferociously against Proust the man may be on the surface natural and justifiable. But it is only so when we assume that we are concerned with a normal man, of ordinary healthy constitution, leading the average human life of his social class. We are concerned with a man who fulfills none of these conditions. Nor will heredity suffice to explain him. Rousseau's heredity we can study; it is full of illumination on Rousseau the man, though his genius remains, as it always will, a mystery. But the Proustian heredity most naturally leads us by no means to Marcel, but to his younger brother Robert, following in his father's footsteps, and attaining to distinction in his profession. In Marcel we have to recognize an exasperated sensibility which is morbid in origin, and we cannot find the key by approaching it in a mood of moral vituperation, but rather of tenderness. Even Albert Feuillerat, in one of the most penetrating and accomplished studies of Proust's genius, concludes that the principal element in the special combination of conditions which make Proust's work original is of pathological nature. . . .[2]

It may seem to some rather extravagant to couple Proust

[2] Some writers have emphasized an influence of Bergson on Proust. But Proust himself, while declaring that he would have no objection to calling his novel Bergsonian if it really were so, denied that it was. "My work is dominated," he said to Bois in 1913, "by a distinction which not only does not figure in Bergson's philosophy, but is even inconsistent with it. For me voluntary memory, which is specially memory of the intelligence and the eyes, only brings us unfaithful images from the past, while an odour, a taste, recurring again under quite different circumstances, awakes the past in spite of ourselves, and we feel how different it was from what we thought it to be, when depicted by voluntary memory, as by a painter using wrong colours." But in general philosophic outlook Proust was more influenced by Bergson than he here admits.

with so immensely significant a figure as Rousseau, though it is not here suggested for the first time.[3]

Certainly from the moral point of view—I mean, of course, in their relation to social life—they are not even on the same plane. Proust was consciously above all an artist. He was concerned, as he said to Bois, with a quality of vision, the revelation of the particular universe, within the individual, which other individuals fail to see. "The pleasure that the artist gives is that of enabling us to know another universe." Rousseau was a great artist in literature, and he realised that, as indeed Proust has said, style is not mere adornment, but the very stuff of the medium in which the artist works, but he was not primarily a conscious artist and was contemptuous of *gens d'esprit.* The fountain from within which he released brought a new vision, but it was primarily an impulse to action, and one which could stir the masses and alter not only the quality of human sensibility, but the shape of the human world. For the masses of men, who are aesthetically blind, the world remains the same as before Proust appeared. It is the finer spirits for whom it can never again be quite the same. . . . .

. . . . in some respects we may find a real analogy between Rousseau's revelation and Proust's. It is true. There is probably even more than an analogy, a real relationship, in personal temperament and its morbid directions. Duffner in his medical study of Proust places him in the schizoid or schizothymic group, and definitely relates him in this respect to Rousseau. This does not involve insanity; but it represents a psychic temperament which becomes exaggerated in insanity. Bleuler termed it *autism,* a living in oneself, which often involves two widely contrasting aspects of personality. But Rousseau represents this state in a far more decided shape. . . . .

[3] It is noteworthy that, even before Proust's death, the parallel was suggested by Mr. Middleton Murry in the *Quarterly Review,* July, 1922. Proust's work, he declares, marks the arrival of a new sensibility to which the only parallel is Rousseau's *Confessions.*

We see the schizoid resemblance with Proust, but on the same foundation we also see the wide difference. They were both copious correspondents. But if nothing remained of Proust but his letters (in that case, it is true, they would never have remained!), a touch of contempt would have clung, even if sometimes smilingly, to Proust's memory. If nothing remained of Rousseau but his letters, he would still have been recognised as one of the greatest figures of his century, clearly revealed without any disguise. . . . .

The great masters of literature—like Rabelais and Montaigne and Shakespeare and Landor and Huysmans and Proust and Joyce—have often possessed within themselves a plastic force by which, for good or for evil, they were impelled to mould language afresh, to invent new words, to spell old words afresh, to bend language into new constructions, and to make it possible to express what had never been expressed before. . . . .

It is worthwhile to quote, from the reminiscences of his friend Reynaldo Hahn, a small example of Proust's method of direct observation. They were walking together in the country garden of a friend to whose house, it happened, they had both been invited, though at that time Hahn knew little or nothing of Proust's literary interests.

"Would you mind," asked Proust in his childishly gentle and rather sad voice, "if I stay behind a moment? I want to look again at those little rose trees." I left him. At a turn in the path I glanced behind. Marcel had made his way back to the rose trees. I proceeded to stroll round the mansion, and then found him still at the same spot, gazing fixedly at the roses. His head was bent, his expression grave, his eyes winking, his brows rather frowning, as if by an effort of impassioned concentration, with his left hand pushing his little black moustache between his lips and biting it. I felt that he heard me coming, but did not wish to speak or move. I passed without saying a word. A minute later he called, and rejoined me running, hoping that I was not angry. . . . . How often (Hahn adds) have I later assisted at similar scenes! At such moments Marcel was in total communion with Nature, with art, with life, his whole being concentrated on a transcendent work of penetration, alternating with aspiration, entering, so to say, into a state of trance, reaching to the roots of things and discerning what none could see. . . . .

In seeking to define "style" to Bois, Proust himself put it as "a quality of vision, the revelation of the particular universe which each of us sees and others fail to see. The pleasure the artist gives us is that of enabling us to know another universe. . . . .

55. *Memories of Proust**

MARIE SCHEIKÉVITCH

IT WAS IN 1905 that I saw Marcel Proust for the first time, at one of Madeleine Lemaire's musical evenings. . . . . at the other end of the studio, I noticed in a group of people a very pale young man with admirable eyes. Over his whole person was imprinted a graceful weariness; his hands, long and exquisite, moved in pleasingly harmonious gestures. Now and again one folded itself back under his chin to support it, or else was placed in front of his mouth to hide his laughter, the sparkling eyes alone betraying his mirth. He was a voluble talker. His eyes continually wandered about without appearing to fix their attention anywhere, but they were so penetrating that it was evident one was confronting a pitiless observer.

Marcel Proust's voice had several ranges of tone, and from

* The selections from Marie Scheikévitch: *Time Past* (New York and Boston, 1935), are used by permission of the publishers, Houghton Mifflin Company.

being almost confidential could swell out ringingly, or at other moments fade away into whispers. He expressed himself by means of allusions; an extreme politeness and a longing to show himself affectionate breathed through all his remarks. He compelled attention from his hearers, and rewarded them always by flashes of wit which flared up at the very moment he appeared most modest and detached, as if having lost all interest in what he was saying. . . . . I noticed also the care he took to express himself with precision, coming back over details, choosing unexpected comparisons, quoting writers, and now and again interspersing his discourse with a stanza of verse. His conversation displayed a rich eloquence, a wide and original culture; to each person he approached he no doubt said unusual things, for the interest he aroused was most noticeable.

When he listened to music, his eyes, so precisely observant when he talked, at once looked far away; he no longer moved; his head, slightly thrown back, appeared overburdened by the mass of black hair framing it with darkness. He could bend his limbs about and intermingle them with the ease of a child; his wrists were double-jointed; his legs coiled around each other as do tropical creepers.

I discussed him with several of his friends, who told me many different things, but all agreed on one point; he was like no one else. It must in truth be stated that numerous were those who did not believe in his genius. I read his essay on Ruskin and his first book, *Les Plaisirs et les Jours,* and felt a keen interest in the minuteness of his analyses, the compactness of his details converging to the same effect, and the subjectivity with which he surveyed various positions. But I was greatly surprised to hear that he had taken up Ruskin's work in order to translate it, though he hardly knew English. Ruskin's style is rich, supple, daring in striking similes. Proust took scrupulous care over this work. Our friends, Madeleine and Leon Yeatman, saw much of him about this time; at every moment he rushed to them to verify a detail and make sure he allowed no mistake to slip into his translation. . . . .

When, in 1900, Ruskin passed away at eighty-one, at Brantwood, near the lake of Coniston, Proust, brooding over the author he so much admired, re-read the page where Ruskin speaks of a little man whose statue is to be found on one of the façades of Rouen Cathedral. He wished at once to go to Rouen. One fine morning, therefore, he took an early train accompanied by Monsieur and Madame Yeatman, and spent the whole day visiting the Cathedral and other churches in the town. He wanted to find, among the countless sculptures adorning the Portail des Libraires, the small statue which did not measure more than ten centimetres in height. It was Madeleine Yeatman spotted it, greatly to Proust's joy, for he despaired of ever discovering among all these stone denizens the little fellow who had inspired Ruskin with that fine page quoted in *En Mémoire des Eglises Assassinés*. The sacristan who escorted the visitors assured them he had known Ruskin. Proust was delighted and asked numerous questions to which the man replied as far as his memory would help; it seemed to our friends he rather piled it on, in view of Proust's evident interest. At the end of the visit Proust asked his companions if twenty francs were a sufficient tip, a considerable sum in those days. They assured him it was. All three left the Cathedral, but Marcel suddenly broke away to go back, and joining his companions a few moments later: "I have added another louis," he explained. "Think of it, a man who has known Ruskin certainly deserves that!"

One should read, in *Pastiches et Mélanges,* the prodigious description Proust elaborated about this page of Ruskin, inspired by the beauty of Rouen Cathedral and the pathetic, crumbling statuette. . . . . Although I appreciated his remarkable gifts, he was still for me a mere acquaintance. But during the year 1911, Reynaldo Hahn spoke to me about him during one of the weekly luncheons at Madame Caroline Reboux's, meals we had nicknamed "luncheons Thermidor" on account of the succulent lobster which was usually served. . . . . He proposed to make me better acquainted with Proust and begged me to help the fortune of the book. . . . .

I had not long to wait for this meeting, which I had not solicited but had long desired: Proust came to see me. However, ... each time the conversation seemed to approach the subject of his book, by some skilful manoeuvre he avoided speaking about it. I felt greatly embarrassed by the compliments with which his talk was permeated; he kept on overwhelming me with them.

They appeared so exaggerated that, in order to change the subject, I, in my turn, diverted the talk and spoke about Russian literature. Proust immediately pricked up his ears. . . . .

It was a queer sensation I retained from this first visit, where, without telling each other anything of our personal lives, we both had the feeling (Marcel confirmed this later) of perfectly understanding and knowing each other. When he was about to leave, I ventured to say I had read all he had so far published; he looked at me with mistrust, sat down again, and craftily put me a few posers. I understood that I was to pass a sort of exam, and fortunately I managed it, for it was with a kindly smile and the promise to come again that he followed me in the hall. Nevertheless, on the doorstep, he assumed once more that decorous behaviour which had so paralyzed me when he first arrived.

Marcel Proust's alternation between friendliness and remoteness, like warm and then icy water he seemed in turn to shower over his friends, rendered intercourse with him peculiar: sensitiveness, imagination were perhaps at war with a longing to preserve his freedom. The next day I received from him marvellous roses.

That same year I saw him several times, but it was only

during the summer of 1912 that our acquaintance took an affectionate character. I was then at Houlgate spending a holiday with friends, among whom was Calmette, and we often went to the Cabourg Casino. One September evening I was surprised to see Marcel Proust wandering about, lost and staggering under the lights, and wearing, in spite of the heat, a heavy overcoat unfastened so as to reveal a loose dinner-jacket and under it several woolly waistcoats. He had then a beard, which made his face longer than it really was, giving it the appearance of an El Greco. He carried an extraordinary straw hat in his hand; altogether his presence in such a place seemed very weird. Mine was just as strange for another reason. I cheerfully went up to him, for he had not yet noticed me, and took him to Calmette, the editor of *Le Figaro,* who had been the first to welcome Proust's articles in his newspaper and whose obligingness was proverbial. And indeed Calmette, although in much of a hurry to get to the bacarat room, anticipated Proust's request for the publication of *Pastiches.*

"Yes, it is settled," he explained. "I spoke about it to Francis Chevassu for the supplement."

I spent the whole evening with Proust. . . . . Taking advantage of his position as a man by choice unattached, he brought me to confess that, although I pretended to show reluctance for society life, and thought little of it, I yet filled my time with futile occupations. . . . . He urged me to tell him more. . . . .

Marcel Proust listened to me, evidently satisfied at having conquered my reticence; as for myself, feeling his sensitiveness attuned to my mood, I was not dissatisfied. Thus then became established between us an atmosphere of trust often renewed during subsequent talks which later he recalled as "the brilliant and vivid memories of Cabourg." . . . . He now realized that his work interested me, so he spoke about it, though never by openly starting the subject. He pronounced the name of

"Swann" in a most suave way, *"Suane,"* as a sort of secret slipping through his lips. . . . .

There was a curious contrast between his deliberate modesty concerning himself—I would even say humility—and his sarcasms, his pitiless remarks when he portrayed some of our contemporaries; his delineation then became sharp-edged, though he at once wanted to soften it by more kindly remarks, sometimes even of an excessive indulgence. On the following day, when he recalled what he had said previously, he made me promise to forget it, gave me other pictures rather blurred over, yet far more cruel in this veiled form.

These nightly outings allowed him to find contact again with the external world. . . . . A mail always reached him at . . . . [a] late hour, though there were no more deliveries; Proust threw a rapid glance at the envelopes and thrust them into his overcoat pockets; already bursting with boxes of medicines and newspapers unopened.

. . . . No one has ever, orally, made up pastiches with such perfection and fun. So also his *Pastiches,* which *Le Figaro* was about to publish, remain masterpieces in that style, on account of his thorough knowledge of the authors he imitated; these sketches would by themselves vouch for Proust's gifts. When he conjured up any person he wanted to describe to me and whom I did not know, he adopted that person's gestures, tricks, and voice; I then saw appearing in front of me an old lady famous under the Second Empire, or else the very type of the military man of that same period.

Proust did not display the stunning manner of a Jean Cocteau, who also had a genius for imitating people, nor that exclusively belonging to Chaliapine, but a deep understanding which portrayed at the same time character and external appearance, and brought forth member after member to conjure up a whole society. . . . . No longer was he then the Marcel who stammered confused excuses, accused himself of failings of which he was not guilty, or searched sadly for misdeeds he reproached himself with. No, he was now a Marcel sure of himself, and conscious of his prodigious gifts. He displayed them in your honour with a generosity of which he enjoyed the rebound.

Such was his way of ascertaining what documentary treasures he had accumulated; on the top of this, at the same moment, his listener became for him a new subject to study—suddenly he scanned your features with devilish malice: Had you fully understood the meaning of his tale? Straightway, he managed to put you more precisely to the test. With the wariness of a thief, he questioned you and judged you. Sometimes he laid traps, pretending he had forgotten a fact or a name. His scorn burst out if his interlocutors had erred through boasting, or when pretending they knew, had confused matters and been grossly mistaken. He used to tell stories specially concerned with the ignorance of society people, and the self-possession with which they go right off the track amidst their errors. His eyes, so particularly mobile, flashed with malice; he had great difficulty in veiling his laughter which suddenly burst forth, pitiless, in strident notes. . . . .

Proust's memory, always active, was another faculty which increased his chances of suffering; having for long concentrated it on the study of classical authors and the behaviour of his contemporaries, he used it on his own behalf, and kept with meticulous exactness the count of what he considered due to him. . . . . He resorted to subterfuges to test friendships he deeply valued. In one special case he borrowed a fair sum of money simply to win the evidence that this loan, readily granted, was a proof that nothing was altered in the feelings of one of his friends towards him. But, since he always wanted to make his position clear, when he wrote to thank his friend for the loan, he explained his motives. . . . .

During the winter and spring of 1913, Marcel Proust frequently came to see me. We often dined at a restaurant, and several times went again to the Russian Ballets in the company of Jean Cocteau. . . . .

Swann's Way was at last to appear in November. Marcel was busy with the publicity campaign. . . . . I did my share by proposing to Adrien Hébrard that an interview with Marcel Proust should appear in *Le Temps,* and this duly happened on November 12, 1913, the interviewer being Elie Joseph Bois.

This interview is interesting for several reasons: to begin with, it is the first document in which Marcel Proust explains himself freely concerning his work, and gives precious indications to it, as a whole. The very date of the interview enables us to put a stop to discussions which have arisen regarding the way Proust composed his books, and to doubts which have been expressed concerning the existence of a central scheme. . . . .

I have been careful in adding to my personal recollections on this matter by having a recent talk with Monsieur Bois, now editor of *Le Petit Parisien.* This is what he told me.

Monsieur Hébrard summoned him: "Go and see Marcel Proust. He has just written a book to which my attention has been drawn by a person whom I wish to oblige. Go and interview him but I warn you that Proust is a very peculiar being. I choose you among my collaborators because I believe you will be able to understand him. Make an appointment at once."

And thus it was done. When Bois arrived at the Boulevard Haussmann, one afternoon at three o'clock, he was introduced into the young author's study, a dim room lined with cork. In the light of a small lamp, Proust, in his brown dressing-gown, was impressive to anyone who had never seen him before, especially from the brilliance of his eyes which grew more and more animated as he talked about his book.

Bois took notes for long hours, and it was quite late in the evening when he left Proust, carrying away with him a copy of *Swann's Way.* This conversation, during which the author's intentions and the genesis of his books had been so minutely explained, aroused in Bois genuine enthusiasm. He felt obliged to read the book at once and spent the whole night in that occupation. In spite of the density of Proust's style, Bois had read the whole book without fatigue when the morning came, and had even read over again the opening part, which he admired most. Using his notes, he traced the main outlines of his article and took it to Proust to make quite sure he had grasped his meaning. Céleste brought it back to him with a letter containing copious annotations. Proust, although liking it, feared it might appear as but a duplicate of another article due to appear in *Le Figaro*. But it was Bois's interview that commanded attention, and it still carries weight. . . . .

The War, the first bereavements, the general anxiety came to part friends. Every individual had much to endure in his or her own field, and Marcel regretted not to be able to take an active part in this emergency. His distress was intense as he watched the cataclysm, and his sympathy found heartrending accents as he mourned departed friends. I can never forget the tender solicitude he displayed toward me when my brother was killed. It is not that he tried to console me—he knew quite well this could not be done in such a misfortune; but he spoke with such gentleness, such discerning lucidity that his words did not make me feel rebellious as so many others did.

One day Marcel told me how discouraged he felt, as now all literary enterprises lacked interest; I protested and told him how much I had at heart his work and its completion. I showed him my copy of *Swann's Way,* which I had sent to be bound in white vellum and which had just come back. He was much touched. "Very well," he whispered, "since you want to know what became of Odette, lend me your copy and I shall write in it a summary of the remaining parts." . . . .

This narrative, written in my copy of *Swann,* sums up the work published later in the books not yet issued at that time.

The main extracts are taken from *Within a Budding Grove* and *The Sweet Cheat Gone,* the proofs of which he was correcting seven years later. In answer to my question, "What became of Madame Swann?" he borrowed from his manuscript, not only conceived at that date of 1915, but in part written out. One can follow the leading ideas of his work and its whole conception in the extracts quoted in this summary, which is also an answer from beyond the grave given by the author, in view of his death before the complete edition of his work, to critics who argued among themselves, notably Louis de Robert and Benjamin Crémieux, whether Proust had really a guiding plan for his complete work. . . . .

I was one evening dining with friends at [Walter] Berry's when, on looking through his books, I found a small volume bearing the arms of the "Guermantes." This cultured man, who was President of the United States Chamber of Commerce, did not know Marcel Proust. I wanted him to offer this small opuscule to the author of *Swann,* and I suggested they should meet. But there was always a great deal of cunning required to bring about a meeting with Proust. I wrote to Marcel to praise my host's intellect, and promised him a surprise if he came to my home one afternoon at three. This was an hour almost out of the question for a rendezvous with him, for he very seldom agreed to move from home in the afternoon. I do not know whether I proved very eloquent, or whether curiosity got the better of him, but he promised to come before long.

Walter Berry, a sceptic by nature, was pleasantly surprised. From their first meeting there existed between them a bond so mutual and so striking that the three of us did not part company until two in the morning, after having concluded the day by dinner at a restaurant. Marcel, nevertheless, had not agreed to accept the little book, and on his side Berry had refused to take it back. For eight days the book travelled backward and forward between my house, the Boulevard Haussmann, and the Rue Guillaume where Berry lived. At last Marcel kept it and sent to Walter Berry two hundred cigarettes and to me two hundred white roses. . . . .

I do not think that at this period he read copiously; nevertheless, he had a special gift for finding the important passages in any book and memorizing them. How often have I heard him referring to an author (I speak of modern ones), though he confided to me he had only just glanced through that man's book, yet he had marvelously grasped his attitude and his views! He even managed to quote his text. When he studied an individual who might help him to complete a character he was creating, he never hesitated to go direct to him or make him come. His chauffeur Odilon, husband to his maid Céleste, was often asked to go and bring the person he wanted to question. He would explain to Odilon with a smile:

"You are not an interesting subject of study for me, for you always tell me the truth, but there is a person I have seen several times and who interests me greatly. Until now he has only told me lies and he thinks I believe them. I am going to have him come here once more, and I will knock down his scaffolding of lies like a house of cards."

He had a passion for reaching the truth about people, and many a time went to the actual spot where, taking care not to be seen, he could gather first-hand evidence, while later, once more back in his retirement, he continued to ponder over these cases. . . . .

One evening Marcel came for me to dine at a restaurant. I was still very anxious about my young brother, news of whom had not reached me for three weeks. While I was getting ready to go out, the post brought the long-awaited letter and a little parcel from the front. The parcel contained one of those tinder-boxes, then almost unknown, which soldiers were making from fragments of shells and coins; this one was made out of two English pennies. Marcel was enraptured with it.

"Are you fond of me enough to give it to me?"

Delighted that I could prove I was, I replied: "But of course, take it."

During all the evening Marcel would take the tinder-box from his pocket, examining it with much feeling.

"Do you know," he told me suddenly, "you will find it back in my book."

And in fact, in the first volume of *The Past Recaptured,* I read, a long time after: "There were rings and bracelets made from fragments of shells or driving-bands also tinder-boxes fashioned from two English pennies to which a soldier in his dugout had succeeded in giving such a patina that Queen Victoria's profile looked as if chiselled by Pisanello."

The original tinder-box had been preciously kept by Marcel, and he desired Céleste to give it back to me after his death. I confess I was greatly touched when, faithful to his wishes, she brought it to me. We talked together about Marcel's daily way of life. He had never had any fixed hour to ring for her when he got up; any time between eleven in the morning and seven in the evening, though usually about five. She used then to bring to his room a lighted candle for his fumigations with Legras powder, as recommended to asthmatic subjects. The chambermaid brought the powder in saucers and he breathed it for a long time. Then he had his *café au lait* with three crescent rolls, and often this was the only food he took all day. The coffee had to be as strong as essence and it took an hour and a half to prepare three small cups; he liked it boiling hot. Sometimes, when he had to go out, he had a dish sent him from a restaurant—stewed beef or a Russian salad, on rare occasions a small chicken—but, towards the end, he hardly touched anything. In the evening, Céleste placed at his side a tray on which was a cup, a bottle of Evian water, sugar, a kettle, and a box of lime blossoms. He worked in bed, in his nightshirt, with a cardigan of natural Pyrenean wool over it. . . . .

1936

56. *Seven Years' Harvest**

HENRY SEIDEL CANBY

.... CONSIDER THE FICTION and drama, for example, which has by common consent been regarded as the most "significant" and usually as the "best"—from Shaw on through Galsworthy, Thomas Mann, Dos Passos, O'Neill, H. G. Wells, Sinclair Lewis, Ernst Toller, Jules Romains, down to the current books of Malraux, Bunin, and the proletarian novelists and Marxian playwrights. There in varying degrees, the books written belong to social science or psychology as much as to literature, and the personality of the writer has been far more subjected to his need for expressing social ideas than was Milton's to his Puritan theology. Or more potent still, regard the so-called "naturalism" of this period, which is only realism made utilitarian. Novelists particularly (such as Dreiser) have given us pictures of society so painfully objective, so minute and unsparing in detail, that all personal aim seems lost beyond the desire of the writer to sink himself in his subject until all design, all "argument" in the old literary sense of that word, is withdrawn, and we are given nothing

* Farrar & Rinehart, Inc., New York, 1936. Reprinted by permission of the publishers.

but evidence. It is significant that the wish-psychology of the individual, which always strains toward success, if not toward heroism and romance, has had no outlet in this period except in markedly inferior and usually in sentimental work. In its courageous breach of this self-denying ordinance lies the secret perhaps of the triumph of the long-winded *Anthony Adverse.*

Nor do the intensely introspective works of James Joyce and Marcel Proust invalidate my argument. Almost as much as the *Forsyte Saga* they exhibit the creative intellect taking responsibility for society, and making its contribution to a better understanding of the social complex in whose growing complexity we have to live. Nothing could be more different from the intensely individualistic exuberance of Rabelais (who also had social purposes) or the brooding sense of personality in the social satires of Swift. These moderns, perhaps the outstanding individualists in literature of our period, have become, the one sometimes almost unintelligible, the other finespun to the breaking point, in the attempt to make their books diagnoses of the ills of society. . . . .

57. *The Social Attitude of Marcel Proust**

JOHN J. SPAGNOLI

THE READER OF *Remembrance of Things Past,* almost completely hypnotized by the minuteness of Marcel Proust's psychological analysis, is likely to attach only slight importance to his social ideas. That is what most critics have done, while those who have stressed them have done so with some axe to grind.

The first two volumes of the work—*Swann's Way*—only oc-

* Institute of French Studies, Inc., Columbia University, New York, 1936. Reprinted by permission.

casionally lead the reader to believe that Proust gave the social structure any thought. . . . . Not until the reader is well into the second part of the sixteen-volume novel—*Within a Budding Grove*—does he realize that Proust's study of individuals takes into account, quite regularly, not only individual traits (which may or may not be universal) but also traits that the individual derives from the particular society—French society—and from the particular part of society in which he was born or in which he moves. But these latter traits are surrounded by so much else that they are not yet likely to stand out in the reader's mind. Impressed by Proust's analysis of man's everyday experiences, both physical and spiritual, he fails to notice to what extent Proust treats man as a social creature. . . . .

In the first place, Proust has been set down as a thoroughgoing sceptic . . . . but nonetheless a sceptic like Proust may have definite views on certain social manifestations. Those who believe in his scepticism usually wish to convey the idea that he had no definite views at all on organized society.

In the view of another critic of Proust—Joseph Wood Krutch . . . . —we again get the impression that he has no definite views on society because he has no interest in it—a lack of interest due to the life his poor health has compelled him to lead. (It is not true that he was compelled to lead that sort of life. He chose it himself. . . . .) Again we ask whether skepticism of what exists may not be based upon ideas. And may not these ideas be common to the sick and the strong, the recluse and the man of action?

The same critic goes on to say that ". . . . His detachment . . . . is the result of the attitude inevitable in a man who had learned long ago to stand outside the stream of life, to feel himself no part of it, and to compensate for the absence of active or vital impulses by the cultivation of those contemplative pleasures which for most men are secondary at most."

. . . . we refute this typical criticism of Proust's work by pointing out that . . . . the reader will have occasion to see scores of cases in which Proust takes sides, pronounces judgments that are not purely relative, feels himself a part of the stream of life and has active and vital impulses. That he felt detached from the ordinary pursuits of men is true . . . . but what intellectual does not assume detachment in order to perform his labor, which is also, we must not forget, a part of the stream of civilized life?

. . . . It has been pointed out by many critics, the foremost of whom are Curtius, Edmund Wilson, and Krutch, that Proust's work has nothing to do with economic problems. Curtius says that ". . . . The work of Marcel Proust is perhaps the only example, in our capitalistic era, of a great literary creation in which the economic problem is not touched." Mr. Krutch writes: "Critics of his novel have not failed to reproach him with the complete absence of feeling for amelioristic sociology, with something which amounts almost to an unawareness of the fact that movements exist for the promotion of the greatest happiness of the greatest number."

Such a reproach gains force with the spread of the idea of the totalitarian state. The Marxian theory of society, in particular, has acquired such great importance since the Russian Revolution that works of art have been graded more and more according to the part played in them by the struggle between the two large classes of industrial society, the bourgeois or capitalist class and the proletariat. . . . . But even with the omission of the class struggle, an artist may note the detailed and more complex facts of people's lives, especially in their relations with others. That is what Proust has done. By doing so, he has shown what he favors, what he condemns in society. . . . . It is true that Proust was not a crusader, but we must not overlook the fact that, in spite of his predominant esthetic interests, he considered his social views important enough to himself to express them forcefully and dogmatically. . . . .

In his analysis of an individual Proust seems to be constantly aware of the social class to which that individual belongs. Each of his characters too is conscious of belonging to a particular class. The classes are those which all true historians of modern civilization speak of: the nobility, the bourgeoisie, the working-classes. There is here no economic interpretation of history. Proust knows that, though in their economic struggles people may refer to themselves as the employer or the employee, they nevertheless think of themselves as belonging to different social classes as they exist in the historical period. There are definite class traits that cannot be wiped out by the relatively recent division of classes brought about by the industrialization of society. . . . .

For Proust, one of the duties of the novelist is to be conscious of class, if the truth is to be discovered. He must respect class distinctions in portraying a character and "depict each class differently." . . . . Proust, the good student of Professor Darlu, was always interested in ideas, and he absorbed the lesson of Taine and his disciples, if, indeed, he did not sense the spirit of the times which was probably one of class-consciousness, or, to put it more broadly, one of classification.

That Proust saw, felt, and wanted to convey the sharp division between classes is also evidenced by the titles of his works: *Swann's Way* and *Guermantes' Way,* . . . . The former represents the bourgeoisie, the latter the aristocracy. The two were as far apart as the two poles. Proust's consciousness of class led him to believe for a long time that it was impossible for the two ever to meet. . . . . He believed in his early years that classes were rigidly fixed and individuals were forever in the same class but he learns later that society is always in flux. . . . . Family or race or religion may take precedence over and struggle against the large social class to which we belong. Proust shows practically all these material interests in conflict in the Dreyfus case, but for the most part, when dealing with matters of social import, he is concerned with criticizing each of the large classes of which society now takes cognizance: the nobility, the bourgeoisie and the working-classes. If there is anything wrong with society, he implies, the root of the trouble is there in that division and in the attitude of everyone toward that division. Disregarding the economic struggle in his work, he seems to be of the same school of thought as Julien Benda, who believes (V. "Discours à la nation européenne") that the economic struggle can be brought to an end only by the reformation of the moral side of society. That the reform is possible is evident from the fact that the individual may surmount the material interests which Life and the social structure under which he lives impose upon him. There already exist individuals who have renounced all the material interests for the sake of an idea. The force of atavism and of social environment, which Proust has already shown to be inescapable, will then become ineffectual. "The influence of the environment is not as important as is generally believed. . . . . The real influence is that of the intellectual environment. We are what an idea makes us." "The influence attributed to the environment is particularly true of the intellectual environment. . . . ."

The strongest thread of Proust's criticism of society was spun by his treatment of snobbery. . . . .

In view of the fact that no other important novelist has been preoccupied with snobbery,[1] we may very well ask why Proust was so regularly conscious of it as to make the great majority of his characters snobs. He himself has put the label upon them. When he does not apply the term to them, he introduces actions and opinions of theirs for the obvious purpose of showing the

[1] . . . . Saint-Simon, though not a novelist, undoubtedly influenced Proust greatly in the study of snobbery. His influence is more direct than that of Balzac. Furthermore, Bourget had been presenting snobs in his novels during Proust's formative years and Bourget the psychologist, though not the moralist, was the sort of writer that appealed to Proust.

snobbery of the society he was depicting. And often they are the actions and opinions of the narrator himself.

It is likely that Proust was not always, in the course of his life,—especially when he was not in the detached position of the author at work—vividly conscious of snobbishness. That may explain why, even when at work, he seems at times to be unaware of it in the behavior of his narrator, who is really himself. But there may be another explanation. As M. Feuillerat has proved by comparing an old copy of *Within a Budding Grove* and *The Guermantes Way, I,* now existing only in galley-proofs printed in June 1914, with the same works as they appeared in their final form in 1918 and 1920 respectively, Proust composed his novel in two manners. The first was the uncritical method of noting his reminiscences to give as far as possible a picture of his childhood and early youth at Combray, Balbec, and Paris, with the ideas, feelings and emotions he had had at the time of which he was writing. In the second method he became critical. It is likely that at the time of writing even the first part Proust was constantly aware of the amount of snobbishness that had entered into the ideas and feelings he had had in the earlier part of his life but that he thought it best to leave it all in without commenting upon it in order to recreate what he has called the poetic atmosphere of the youth and his ambitions. But by the very fact that he refrained from commenting upon it we may conclude that he either did not consider snobbery a terrible vice or that he actually wanted to show his early snobbery in order to tell the truth and to produce a better effect later when showing his salvation from snobbery by means of his criticism of himself as well as others. . . . .

Gabory states that snobbery is a fault in Proust's work but that it is used as a technical device. If we knew what "technical device" really means here we might discuss this theory intelligently. Part of the snobbery in Proust's work, that of the narrator himself, which is only a small part, might be considered a technical device in the sense that Proust wanted to prepare the contrast we spoke of a few lines above (unless we say that he was applying the naturalistic tradition of documentation).

. . . . It is wise to attempt to define briefly what we mean by a snob before we judge Proust.

We shall take the word to mean not only "one who makes birth or wealth the sole criterion of worth and is cringing to superiors and overbearing with inferiors in position" and "a vulgar pretender to gentility," according to the English definition, but also, according to the French, "one who shows stupid and artificial admiration for everything that is in vogue" . . . .

Proust's ability to understand things profoundly as revealed in his comprehension of the styles of a number of authors—Flaubert, Saint-Simon, Balzac, the Goncourts, etc.,—in his *Pastiches* is sufficient evidence of the intelligence of his admiration of things.

His attempt to keep up with society might seem to be a point against him. Clive Bell reports that Proust took lessons in deportment. He shopped at the Trois-Quartiers because the Comte de Montesquiou-Fezensac shopped there. He fought a duel with Jean-Lorrain, to keep up with the old tradition. He was particular about all the niceties of social life in the matter of clothes, food, wines. His associations with the Ritz in Paris have been reported by many. . . . .

Proust did pretend to gentility. That he was vulgar about it no one will admit. Vulgarity was not one of his traits. He may have been aggressive about getting into genteel society, but he was not vulgar. In his long work we find only an occasional bit of vulgarity, for example, in the speech of the Baron de Charlus, talking about Mme. de Sainte-Euverte. So slight is the lapse that Edith Wharton is quite justified in saying that Proust is never vulgar. Aggressiveness in worldly ambitions may be blameworthy, but then we have no definite proof that his leaving his young friends, in his adolescence, in order to frequent some salon or other was not rather weakness of character, of which there is plenty of evidence in his life. He could not resist his "natural" bent, which was undoubtedly in the direction of snobbery. . . . .

All we have read about Proust . . . . indicates that he never showed himself to be overbearing with inferiors. Everyone reports his liberality toward servants. . . . .

Did Proust make birth or wealth the sole criterion of worth? No. He is emphatically against those whose sole recommendation is money. . . . .

We now come to answer the question whether he was cringing to superiors. The work by Mme de Clermont-Tonnerre (who has been accused of malice toward Proust) gives us an affirmative answer. So do most of his letters to the Comte de Montesquiou in which he caters to the latter's every whim, humbles himself before him and looks up to him as a god. . . . .

There is one important mitigating factor that must be mentioned along with any accusation of his cringing before his superiors: he was not stupid in his cringing; he was intelligent and ironical about it. . . . . Furthermore, the time came when he got tired of cringing, even with a reservation. The death of his parents made him turn away from active participation in the futile life of the society in which he had cringed, and, though he had a pathological fear of solitude, he plunged into it. The cringing period was over before he was thirty-five.

. . . . We must . . . . —in considering whether or not Proust was a snob,—divide his life into two periods, before and after his thirty-fifth year, and we must say of his entire work that with a few exceptions it contains a critical attitude toward snobbery and that the attack upon snobbery becomes intensive and forceful particularly in what he wrote after 1914. . . . .

The form that snobbery usually takes in Proust's work is the attempt to get into smart society, with its accompanying scorn of those in a lower position. . . . . But snobbery is not limited to those who want to get into the salons of the upper classes. It exists even within these classes. There are different levels within the nobility itself. . . . .

. . . . In his manhood, as an experienced man of the world, Proust is very severe toward the upper classes. He finds in the mall the vices that theologians have ever thought of. . . . . Proust believes that the ambition of most people is to rise to the sort of life that the upper classes lead, as if that were the ultimate goal of life. He dissects them in order to show us the sort of intellectual world we live in, as the medical student dissects every part of a body, not merely the brain, to see what it is made of. . . . .

It is true that Proust has not gone far beyond the surface of high society. He does not give details on all phases of the life of any character but himself. . . . . Proust is interested only in the surface of life—except in so far as he considers himself, as an artist—and that his criticism is a criticism of the form society has assumed . . . . his work constitutes a sort of "mémoires" of the time (of the period from 1870 to 1917). He was diligent, however, in his study of the surface of things, in spite of his constant criticism of realism and naturalism. . . . .

Though Proust was impressed with the nobility throughout his life, was always anxious to learn something more about it, pitied those who did not have the "grain of salt" necessary for the appreciation of the stories told about members of the nobility, ... he was never fooled into believing that as a class, because of its high social position, it was superior intellectually to others. He found vanity and conceit to be its prime motives. . . . . He notes that society people are mediocre and believes that if one is conscious of that fact one should give them up in order to realize one's true destiny. In *Remembrance of Things Past* he upbraids the society journals for having "the nerve or the stupidity to call the upper classes the *élite*" and states that "the intellectual merits of a salon and its elegance are in inverse ratio to each other."

The stupidity of society people is even greater than their vanity. That of the Faubourg Saint-Germain is extraordinary and is made worse by their malice. . . . .

The nobles have no intelligence and, therefore, cannot be perfectly noble, for to be so one must use not only the heart but also the intellect. . . . .

It has been maintained in defense of this society—by the Comte de Luppé and others—that the nobles were intelligent enough to see Proust's genius and to invite him for that reason. . . . . Yes, Proust agrees that the upper classes want to meet men of talent, but, though they have them at their tables and in their salons, they do not understand them. . . . .

On the subject of morality Proust lashes the upper classes mercilessly. The lack of money . . . . the corruption of sensual pleasures often lead the aristocracy to a life of expedients, ...

Proust, who was always very generous and helpful to his friends, stresses in his work the selfishness of society people. . . . .

The question of sincerity in life moved him almost as much as it moved André Gide. He mentions it constantly in his correspondence. He was particularly concerned with it during the War. He writes to Lucien Daudet: "I hate . . . . false duties." He realizes that false duties are assumed by everyone during wartime. This same sort of insincerity is part of the aristocrat's make-up. . . . .

. . . . Morally, Proust makes the bourgeoisie superior to the upper classes, but, besides the fact that he is not in agreement with all its moral principles, his lack of enthusiasm for the class keeps him from stressing this phase of its life.

. . . . There is solidarity in Marcel's family at Combray, something patriarchal about it . . . . They have a certain feeling for their religion, ... and certain religious practices like going to mass on Sundays and to the services for the "month of Mary."

In the second part of the work, comprising all the volumes written or revised after 1914, we see a different bourgeoisie, as well as a different society, in which family life or the well-linked family scarcely exists. . . . . All of this bourgeoisie outside of Combray has a different notion of life. It imitates the nobility, wants to live like it, and has all the faults and vices, which, as we have seen, Proust believes are the accompaniment of that sort of life. The bourgeoisie has none of the virtues which the nobility can afford to have, however superficial they may be, however weak they may seem when compared with the vices. . . . .

Yet Proust does not approve of all the ideas of the old bourgeoisie. He does not like its class distinctions, which seemed to be based on the principle of money or income: . . . .

To sum up in a few words, we may say that Proust criticized the old bourgeoisie when it established class distinctions and when it adhered to a morality that subordinated affection to some puritanical principle, and that he was severe in his attitude toward the new bourgeoisie for falling into all the social vices of the nobility. . . . .

Do our own observation and the historical facts related by all historians, even those of the extreme left, invalidate Proust's ideas? Proust, let it be said, without going into commerce, industry, banking or any of the practical affairs of life (except diplomacy, ...) lets us know by an occasional remark that he is not ignorant of the obvious fact that they are run by the bourgeoisie. . . . . Once again he shows the effect of a literary influence. He presents a middle class such as Balzac saw during the Restoration. Historians prove that Balzac's observation was faithful while Proust's was not in this respect. . . . .

. . . . It would be false to maintain that in his picture of French society, which deals mostly with the upper classes,

Proust took no great interest in the lower. . . . . Proust's life having been limited in its scope, the list of proletarian characters is necessarily restricted to the serving class with which he came into contact. . . . .

Early in his work Proust tells us that he is not attracted by the bourgeoisie but that he likes the "mystère" of the lower classes as well as that of a group like the Guermantes. This liking for the common people never suffered the disillusionment to which his liking for the nobility finally came. He had a natural sympathy for the working classes, and he is proud of the fact that they always had confidence in him. . . . . In his work he often pays tribute to the peasants both directly, and indirectly (by praising the Guermantes for their occasional displays of peasant traits, particularly peasant simplicity). He tells us of his liking for the workers. "I had the habit of putting the workers on an equal footing with the *gens du monde.*" "I had never made any distinction between classes. . . . . I had never established any difference between workers, bourgeois and great lords, and I would have taken them all indifferently as friends, with a certain preference for the workers." And the reason why his second choice goes to the lords is that he "knew that they could be expected to be more affable to workers than the bourgeois." During the war he writes Lucien Daudet that the death of the sons of the lower classes causes him more sorrow than that of the sons of the upper classes. He often calls our attention to the bourgeoisie's scorn for the lower classes, and to cases in which the nobility mistreats servants. . . . .

As we have seen, Proust does not like the formation of artificial classes and for that reason objects to the solidarity of the working classes which forces him to put himself into another class to which he does not want to belong, the class of the employers. It is this same dislike for classes that makes him ridicule those workers who by their words and actions show themselves to be anxious to "give themselves class." He seems to be saying: "I'm willing to believe you're an estimable creature, but by trying to make me believe it you're making me doubt it." He doesn't like the "chip-on-the-shoulder" type of self-assertiveness. . . . .

We have seen Proust ridicule the common people in what might be considered offhand as the attainment of the democratic ideal. However, he is really criticizing the ambition and snobbery of the people in their attempt to raise themselves out of the lower strata of society. He believes that this is the contrary of democracy. . . . .

Proust is democratic. He is not afraid of changes to an equalitarian society. For instance, one of the traits he wants in society is politeness. He sees the grace and gentleness that go with the politeness of the society he lives in. He knows that these qualities will be used to defend this society. . . . .

Proust was both a realist and an idealist.

As a realist he observed carefully the world about him and with scientific accuracy noted the details which, according to the latest nineteenth-century thought, enter into the composition of character. This compelled him to treat each of his characters as a social being, belonging to a particular class with distinctive traits which play an important part in his behavior. From such observation of individuals, Proust charted the flux of late nineteenth-century French society and drew general conclusions regarding the different social classes.

However, his observation soon reaches a point where it ceases to be scientific and is colored by his abnormal temperament. Unattached to any social institution, he can criticize every one of them with the intransigeance of an idealist. He is sensitive to all the faults of society and refuses to see any spiritual values in it. He therefore depicts a world in which the upper classes have no intellectual, artistic or moral principles, in which the middle classes are interested only in making money and in rising to the social position of the upper classes, and in which the lower classes have the same social ambition as the others and the greed that springs from such ambition.

Proust's realism made him write like one who believes that there is no possibility of fundamental change in society: the traits which he sees manifesting themselves in a social way are moral traits that will continue to exist no matter what labels may or may not be given to the different strata of society, for these strata will always exist whether we acknowledge or try to ignore them. But in the latter part of his life his idealism often got the upper hand and led him to express the opinion that change is possible. He attributes the faults of society to the senseless class-distinctions which now exist but which need not be permanent, and he hopes that they will be wiped out and that men will by this change cease to esteem and aim for the worthless things they now value highly.

. . . . we must add that Proust had no social sense, if a social sense implies concern for institutions such as the State, the family, the church. His interest in the State is practically null; his interest in the World War, through which he lived, was almost negligible. The church was for him a center of esthetic interest; he saw in its architecture and in its rites the expression of certain forms of beauty. As for the family, he is concerned with it either in the manner of a biologist and naturalist or in so far as it affects his own immediate well-being. Never does he consider it as an institution necessary to society. Though he makes much of family life in a part of his work, it is only from the purely individualistic point of view: . . . . The question of filial duty does not enter his mind; here again the sentimental attachment of child to parent is the only one considered, ... He takes extramarital relations quite casually and even praises those who enter into them provided he finds in them those spiritual qualities we have mentioned above: . . . . Proust never judged them on a sociological basis. His whole theory of love is amoral and a-social. It does not occur to him to argue, as a Gide has done, as radicals do, that the liaisons he observes and describes are compatible with a certain form of society. Like a biologist he considers them natural and inevitable and beyond the ken of social laws. He pities those whom society ostracizes because of the fulfillment of their natural wants, but it does not occur to him to speculate on the power of the will to overcome such wants. . . .

58. *Du Côté de Chez Proust**

LEWIS GALANTIÈRE

DURING THE last half dozen years of Marcel Proust's life one of his closest friends was an American—Walter Berry—(whose) place in the life of Paris was in some respects uncommon. He was born there in 1859, spent most of his life there, and died there in 1927. But though he served as president of the American Chamber of Commerce in Paris, he was in a sense never a member of the American colony. . . . . His presidency of the Commerce group came during the War when, presumably, a man of social distinction was wanted, one who would be helpful at the Foreign Office and could persuade ladies to work on relief committees, rather than a president typical of the Chamber's humbler rank and file. By profession he was a lawyer, but he was not in active practice (he had served as judge on the International Tribunal in Egypt during 1908–1911). By birth he was out of the Mayflower, and his mother was a New York Van Rensselaer. He had an appreciative familiarity with the arts, and his library was magnificent. . . . .

* From *Town and Country*, December 1937; also Black Sun Press, Paris.

Externally, for those who did not know him, his chief distinction was that he was society's pet American—perhaps as Swann was society's pet Jew. Well off, unmarried, handsome, making of worldliness a career and doing it with great grace and a rare generosity. . . . .

. . . . That Proust and Walter Berry should have spent nearly twelve hours together on first meeting suggests certain reflections which do them both honor. Bearing in mind the three sorts of people Proust ordinarily took to, Mr. Berry must have been a man of cultivation and sensibility, since he was neither a gossiping servant in a great house, nor a homosexual. Again, apart from testifying to Proust's personal charm, it reduces the quota of snobbery often attributed to Mr. Berry that he should have awarded so much time to a man who, in 1916, could have been known to him only as a petted favorite of *le gratin*—a rank which, after all, Mr. Berry himself held. . . . .

. . . . There is, I am convinced, an almost general misapprehension concerning the hyperbole he [Proust] employed to express his admiration and affection for certain people. Madame Scheikévitch (an intimate friend, though I still take issue with her) feels that his letters to Montesquiou and Berry "can in no way heighten Proust's reputation." In a rather stilted translation she is made to say, "With great humility, often a mere pretense, he could lavish excessively flattering compliments upon his correspondents." But the case seems to me less simple than this. For one thing, when Proust wrote to Mr. Berry in June, 1922, ". . . . you who are probably the being whom I most love in the world," he was not writing what we may call flattery; the words were either true or false. For another, Proust was capable of genuine humility in the presence of the performance of a task or the manifestation of a gift impossible to himself. Then, also, Proust had yearned all his life to be liked by others, and it is this yearning, this habit of making himself agreeable, that takes on the aspect of flattery in his letters. Finally, something that has never been sufficiently recognized: both in his novel and in his letters Proust gave expression to a deep sense of fun. He did not at all mind pulling a fellow's leg, and if you read him properly you can see that he often did it with great daring. One can imagine him writing to Mr. Berry (or anybody else) and saying to himself as he wrote, "That'll fetch him! This, now, is exactly how the dear fellow secretly fancies himself . . . . no, it would be even better expressed like this . . . ." I see no harm in this little game played by the invalid in his chamber; and I have yet to read or hear that any recipient of Proust's most elaborately complimentary letters disdained them, or was pained by them. It is only third persons who have the moral strength to rise above them.

59. *Proust and Santayana—The Aesthetic Way of Life**

VAN METER AMES

. . . . PROUST SHOWS THAT the interweaving pathways of association have naturally a structure not different from the organization characterizing art. Since artistic form is an arrangement of pleasing repetition, to trace in retrospect pleasure-giving recurrences will shape a work of art. Every kind of art supplies the counterpart of a past in its formal relationships, and to enjoy them is like indulging in reminiscence, so that for Proust to recall his past was not for him to forget the importance of form, but to find ready at hand

* Willett, Clark & Co., 1937.

forms worked out and worn smooth by the course of his own life.

He has been accused of inability to control his material only by readers too short-winded to follow him through. In addition to the form he found in life, he deliberately devised integration and equilibrium, so that the reader who continues gradually realizes that beneath the fine texture of Proust's novel is a powerful articulation; that interesting as the details are in themselves there is more interest in their reference; that great as his achievement would remain if it were merely the autobiography it first appears to be, it is infinitely greater when seen to have the architectonic that has always ribbed and vaulted a consummate work of art. Admiring the tensile strength of this vast structure, the reader may even feel that it is too tightly riveted; the wonder of seeing joined together things that had been kept asunder may verge on the suspicion that it has been overdone. In the last volumes the various themes are caught up and blended until the conclusion rolls in with the force and finality of an orchestra coasting to the close of a symphony. . . . .

Proust wishes to avoid factitious symmetry, but seems obliged to exaggerate unity in his novel to show that unity in life cannot be exaggerated. He wants the ultimate unity that Balzac discovered among pieces needing only to be brought together; not an artificial, forced unity, but the kind that is not seen at first, "hence vital and not logical, which has not shut out variety and frozen execution" (*The Captive,* I, 219) . . . . Proust had unraveled something of himself at every step of his development, and could not rest until he had gathered up the skein of his past to wind it close in the lap of his consciousness. . . . .

In imaginative remembrance and artistic re-creation of the past the pain and triviality of life acquired the value of art: they ceased to be sordid to become exalting, to be shaken by a tremor of significance that redeemed evil—not to make it good but purifyingly bad, as it could be only in imagination. What enjoyment Proust had formerly found in life had come to him chiefly from works of art, and rare moments like the experience of the three trees, in which existence, taking on the spell of art, had tinctured his sea of troubles with drops of redeeming blood. So he vowed to pour his whole past into art, what was already beautiful along with what was not. Having observed that subject matter was indifferent to a painter who could make a masterpiece out of a shack or out of a cathedral already a work of art, Proust took the stupidity and pettiness, the vice, folly and cruelty of his friends, as well as their noble qualities; he took the perversity and vanity of his own life, the desperate loneliness of it; he took the anguish of his mind and body, with the moments of bliss, and through the alchemy of art left nothing but beauty.

His life had fallen far short of art until he became an artist. Only then did his early misery (and occasional joy) become a lost paradise to be regained through the remembrance of things past. He transmuted his life without recourse to mythology or religion, except for the sake of metaphor; and he resorted to figures of speech not to bedeck his memoirs but because only through allegory and allusion could he express the emotion he felt when anything floated back to him across the vista of the years. Change, the destroyer, when overtaken by the wings of imagination, became like the illusion of movement in an arabesque, ever returning in an eternal pattern. . . . .

. . . . Like any artist, Proust worked with the materials familiar to him; and the way he wove in everything he saw, regardless of what it was, shows that subject matter was indifferent to him as long as he could fit it in through similarity or contrast, to heighten an effect he already had in mind, or to make another that he had not thought of before.

The good he won from existence he might have achieved in

the Middle Ages or in ancient Greece, if he could have been himself; for what he valued was his own way of seeing and associating things. Yet alien as he was to the age he lived in, his orchid-like consciousness could have flowered only in the hot-house atmosphere of modern aestheticism, glassed in by the class distinctions which fascinated him, planted in soil enriched by all previous culture, and watered by the inspiration of recent or contemporary civilization. Without Greek art and mythology; without the smoldering memory of Sodom and Gomorrah; without medieval monuments and ideologies already archaic; without Venice; without Saint-Simon, Racine, Balzac, Dostoievsky and Ruskin—without Bergson—Proust's mode of seeing and feeling would have been impossible; nor could his sensibility have preceded modern music and painting. He is inconceivable without his personal and cultural past, the recovery of which was his art.

Art for him was not merely emotional fireworks, not simply complicated play, but the most earnest concern of man, the only one that could save him from futility. He was so pessimistic about existence in general and enthusiastic about art in particular that he was unwilling to call art the best part of life—it was too good for life. Among all the blind alleys he saw, art was the only avenue leading through to the open country of hope. Anything not art, or not redeemed by a touch of art, was death—though he called it life. Merely to be alive was already to be dead; to embrace art was to escape life and to triumph over death.

But though he often asserted this faith in art, he had his doubts. "Was there in art a deeper reality in which our true personality finds an expression that the activities of life do not give?" Perhaps art was not worth sacrificing for, perhaps it was not "something from beyond life, not sharing its vanity and nothingness . . . ." (*The Captive,* I, 270). He was afraid that the originality of great artists, instead of being the reflection of a reality more than human, might be only the result of industry and technical cleverness.

In thinking about the death of Bergotte and in meditating on Vinteuil's *Septet,* Proust swung back to the feeling that in art was a "formula eternally true, forever fecund with an unknown joy, a mystic hope." He sensed "the strange call which henceforth I should never cease to hear, as the promise and proof that something else existed, attainable through art . . . . besides the void which I had found in all my pleasures and even in love, and that if my life had seemed vain, at least it had not exhausted everything" (*The Captive,* II, 82). This may be taken as his final view, since it appears in the volume he was working on at the last. In fact he is said to have rewritten the passage about Bergotte's death as his own approached, and he could not bring himself to believe that Bergotte was gone forever. Somehow his achievement must save him even after the freezing of the planet.

In discussing his mystical interpretation of art, Proust said that we seem to enter this life with a burden of obligations contracted in a previous existence, and that this explains the urge to art (*The Captive,* I, 255, 256). He would not say that art saves man by giving stimulus and outlet to his imagination, an opportunity for him to integrate himself through contemplation of form and rhythm, and a chance to feel equal to the world through finding his problems solved symbolically. He would not admit that art provides simply an intensification of consciousness. This would not do for Proust, at least when he believed art to be an intimation of immortality. He interpreted the feeling of deliverance communicated by art as a token of another world, though to a psychologist this exaltation of art might be just Proust's way of saying how much it exalted him. He felt that the imaginative, metaphorical character of art was essential to it because only by breaking from everyday appearance could art adumbrate the transcendent truth which he believed to be its burden. For him art had a supernatural sanction as categorical as Kant's imperative, though it commanded artistic activity rather than obedience to an abstract moral law.

Proust's attitude was Platonic and mystical and cannot be shared by anyone who regards art as a natural part of natural existence, a phenomenon subject to physiological, psychological and sociological explanation like other human activities. But his assertion of a divine promise and summons in art may be taken as a poetic expression of the value of art. Feeling it to be vastly more important than anything else, he seized upon the traditional means of communicating supreme emotion. Following the poets who have followed Plato, he fell back upon reminiscence of another world to explain the spell of art, though his individualism led him to think of each artist as having descended from a unique eternity of his own. Regardless of how literally Proust believed it, or how much he prized it, if personal survival retained great attraction for many of his readers, then by linking art with immortality he could count on evoking sympathy for his emotion toward art. But he seems too sincere deliberately to have used such a device merely for effect. And at times he confessed misgivings about the mystical interpretation. In the final volumes (though they apparently are not the last he worked on) he did not count on personal immortality but faced death as the destruction of the individual, whose work might survive fifty years before it also would disappear.

Despite his idea that art was something more than life, he sometimes played with the notion that life could be refined and stylized to the pitch of art. For him art was music, painting, architecture, sculpture, theater, literature, and only through courtesy, humor or metaphor did the other activities of man, which he lumped together as "life," appear to him artistic, though in varying degrees they might approach the value of art. . . . . For him the deft overcoming of difficulty alone was not art, but only suggestive of it, because one of the elements in it. Equally short of art, though analogous to it, were forms and rhythms observed in nature, or in a face, or in the involuntary aspects of behavior—all of which appealed to him as if appearing in art—though here . . . . it was the imaginative "as if" added by the author that raised the experience to the power of art. When he saw the artistic process where no art would have been but for his own participation; and when he saw an artistic result where no artist had been at work but himself: he did not find art in life; he superimposed art on life.

But in the end (at the end of the book if not of the author's life) along with the disappearance of other distinctions that had seemed important, even the difference between life and art had to go, for he found them coinciding as surely as he saw a *rapprochement* between the bourgeoisie and the aristocracy. . . . .

To Proust a mere aesthete was not only cut off from life, but failed to appreciate art. He ridiculed and pitied the "celibates of art" who "have the unhappiness of the virginal and the lazy, and whom fecundity in work would cure." Their artistic enjoyment is sterile because they do not make the effort to realize profound personal impressions. "But laughable as these amateurs are, they are not altogether to be disdained. They are nature's first attempts in trying to create the artist" (*The Past Recaptured,* II, 43, 44). . . . .

He deprecated the mere aesthete, yet seems to have regarded artistic creation as the means of reaching the deepest appreciation. His joy in the aesthetic attitude, induced chiefly by art and inspiring him to be an artist, lay in the release that Schopenhauer called relief from the Will. For both men salvation lay in shifting from the role of participant to that of appreciative onlooker; and both found this transference facilitated not only by the enjoyment of art but through reminiscence, which Proust practically identified with his own art. . . . .

Schopenhauer differed from Proust in attributing the bliss of contemplation to the suppression of self. In the Proustian version of the contemplative attitude, its mystical culmination is not the quietus but the apotheosis of self with all its private, personal values. His art was devoted to preventing the transcendence of personality.

It is not contradictory that the "eternal man" in him, rising above pain and vanity, should incite the man of letters and be aided by him. Through writing Proust clung most tenaciously to the external essences which alone mattered in the flux of things. He did not prostitute his unworldly vision to worldly ambition. He was ambitious, but only to write; and he wrote to save his soul. He wanted to write supremely well, and rejoiced in every indication that he was becoming a great writer, because for him nothing else was worth doing, and because when he wrote well everything he was aware of had value, everything was redeemed. . . . .

. . . . the romanticism of Proust is classic, because he was never satisfied with his memories until he had given them the sharpness of original impressions and the structure of ultimate art. Nor did he achieve this through make-believe, but through arduous attention to qualities which seemed to him objective and to have a claim upon him. Hence he has something of the "great variety" and certainly the "precision of characterization" that Mr. Santayana has admired in Shakespeare. If *The Sense of Beauty* argues that "progress lies in the direction of discrimination and precision, not in that of formless emotion and reverie," *The Remembrance of Things Past* has proved that emotion and reverie, when they are discriminated, become inexhaustible sources of form. . . . .

In *The Sense of Beauty* "expression is the quality acquired by objects through association." Proust would agree with this, but his work shows this to be no less the definition of form than of expression. Mr. Santayana is not ready, like Croce, to accept the identification of form and expression implicit in Proust, but does admit that expression (association) "can give images the same hold upon our attention which might be secured by a fortunate form or splendid material."

This is one reason why Mr. Santayana took the time to read nearly all of Proust's novel, and liked it. "You might think some of his analyses tedious, but when you have had the very same perceptions yourself you are fascinated with the minuteness of his account." He added: "I was interested to find toward the last that he also had the idea of essences. It is impossible that he should have got it from me, but he had hit on the same thing."

If it was the same thing, then Mr. Santayana indirectly, at least, admitted relations in essences, for relations are the quintessence of essence for Proust. Yet Proust thinks of essences as somehow rising above the relativity and change in which they are discovered—as shadowing forth an eternal reality behind all process. How such a reality is related to the events of earthly existence is not clear in either of these men, but neither has any philosopher from Plato to Whitehead been able to solve this problem without appeal to mystical insight. . . . .

Proust and Santayana belong, with Schopenhauer, to the great tradition that puts contemplation above action. . . . .

. . . . The appropriate fulfillment of Proust's work was its being read by Santayana. At the same time it is the artist's work which gives the aesthete his most precious experience. It is characteristic of Santayana that he should have enjoyed Proust. . . . .

. . . . His (Proust's) *forte* was metaphor, which, to Aristotle, was the mark of genius. . . . .

1938

60. *Marcel Proust**

GEORGES LEMAITRE

.... IT IS BY NO MEANS easy to classify the work of Marcel Proust. At first reading it seems like a semi-autobiographical novel; .... the plot does not present any vivid and striking features. .... In spite of this, there is a gripping fascination about the whole work. .... In fact the novel is of minor importance, and the real merit of Proust is to be found in his exhaustive and living picture of French high society in the course of the past half century; in his unbelievably penetrating investigation of almost unknown corners of the human mind; in his original conception of beauty and art; and, last but not least, in his strange, new vision of Time. In all these fields, descriptive of society, psychology, aesthetics, philosophy,—though he may have been influenced by Saint-Simon, by Ruskin, by Bergson—Proust formed his own personal and thoroughly original views. ....

The study and minute description of the special characteristics of French high society from 1890 to about 1920 may not seem at first to be a matter of engrossing interest. It was a highly sophisticated and artificial community, which, apart

* From *Four French Novelists,* Oxford University Press, New York, 1938.

from a certain temporary brilliance, did not produce anything of real value. It is dead and gone by now, and there is not the slightest chance of its revival even in a remotely similar form. Nevertheless, in studying the circumstances of the development of that particular group, Proust discovered and brought to light the general, almost universal laws governing the formation, growth, and decay of any social group in any place and at any time. . . . .

The haste with which Proust wrote his last volumes may account for minor inconsistencies in the portrayal of a few of his characters; but generally the variations and unexpected transformations in the characters are the consequence of changes brought by Time . . . . Time transforms people in our eyes for two reasons: first because new and unsuspected sides of their character are presented to us; and, secondly, because the character itself is subjected to an uninterrupted process of inward transformation and flux. . . . .

. . . . If the motion of life is to be registered at all, it must be by an art as mobile and fluid as life itself. In this respect, Proust has attempted the almost impossible—and succeeded. . . . .

Classical psychology for a long time concentrated on the obvious and clear phenomena of the conscious mind. Intelligence was analysed and for centuries reason was made to account for nearly all our thoughts. Today the subconscious is an object of almost popular interest, but it was not so when Proust began observing people and things. The success of his writings was even to a large extent responsible for drawing the public attention to some of the most obscure, yet powerful potentialities of our nature. Proust held that all that we feel deeply, is practically beyond our understanding and control. As depth of feeling takes us down into the subconscious, we find its laws and manifestations frequently interfere and clash with the decisions of our conscious will-power. To discover some of those all-important and little known laws was one of the great interests of Proust's life; the results of his enquiries are among the most engrossing attractions of his books.

In order to be able to reach as far as possible into the depths of our subconscious life, Proust, whenever he can, will linger on the threshold of our conscious mental activity, during the uncertain moments when we are falling asleep, in the weary hours of persistent insomnia, or in the vision-haunted days when we are abed with fever. He will even, though more rarely, try to explore the mysterious world of dreams. In every case, his careful observation of the slightest and most elusive impressions, felt by almost each of us, though few are really aware of them, reads like the record of an illuminating revelation.

It is in his observations of everyday life, however, that Proust displays his most amazing virtuosity. He is not much interested in the actual meaning of what people say, nor in their ostensible motives, nor the obvious consequences of what they do. But he is intensely eager to catch exactly the particular manner in which they speak or act. . . . . An unexpected gesture will often betray the real man. The mask does not fit closely all the time; a sudden move or a smile will lift it for a second and allow Proust to get a glimpse of the face beneath. Then Proust will meditate long and earnestly on what he has been able momentarily to see. Such an occurrence may seem entirely unimportant, and in itself very often is; but this is the only way we have of getting at the truth. The so-called important things in life may mean nothing at all, but a world of revelation sometimes unsuspected lies in trifles.

Proust therefore deliberately keeps out of his books the great turns of events, the catastrophes, in which most novel writers revel. . . . .

Proust seems to have received some of his most vivid impressions of beauty in the contemplation of flowers. Throughout his writings, and particularly in the first and earlier part, he composes again and again, like musical themes, entrancing evocations of floral harmonies. . . . .

But the real revelation of beauty was to come to him from still simpler objects, and in stranger circumstances. . . . .

. . . . Art is nothing but the result of original contact between the artist's personality and the world, and the fixing of the derived impressions by means of shapes, colour, sounds, or words, as the case may be—in painting, music, literature, and so on. As Proust himself noticed, the original sensation, when grasped by chance, tends to manifest and express itself spontaneously—in words in the case of a writer. . . . .

So the conclusion is reached that there is at least one sure way to reach happiness; after obtaining an original and thoroughly personal perception of some fragment of the world, to express it through the medium of a definite work of art.

How did Proust come to form such a theory? Ruskin may have influenced him to some extent. Bergson held a very similar doctrine. But quite probably it was in contact with artists and works of art that he found himself and discovered his own creed. . . . .

But it is above all in music that Proust found inspiration. Proust was a young and receptive adolescent when, about 1885, after a long, dull interlude, there began a real renaissance of musical taste in France. At that time Wagner, who at first had been practically ostracized by the Parisians for nationalistic reasons, was now definitely sponsored by enthusiastic French admirers; and in his train came the magic throng of all great German masters. When Proust took his first steps into society, he entered groups where good music was held to be one of the essentials of life . . . . Proust himself was endowed with an uncommon, inborn feeling for music. Even ordinary noises had for him a musical value. . . . .

Among Proust's favourite composers, Wagner for long held

the foremost place. Proust seems to have been thoroughly filled with his music and to have lived, especially when he was young, in a sort of mystic, Wagnerian atmosphere. To César Franck, who may be said to have brought a little of the Latin love of order and clarity into the powerful Wagnerian turmoil, and to Fauré, Franck's pupil, Proust had probably the closest personal affinity. Beethoven he admired greatly; but it was only in later years, when his enthusiasm for Wagner had taken a somewhat less exalted tone, that his predilection for Beethoven came to the fore. Of course he knew and loved the Symphonies of Beethoven; but it was the string quartets of this composer which seem to have had a special attraction for him. Nor were Chopin and Schumann without their influence. Proust's tastes naturally followed the trend of the cultural period to which he belonged; yet his appreciation of music showed no trace of affectation. The adulation of the virtuosi, a failing rather common among "society" music-lovers, was utterly foreign to his nature. He loved music, not for any technical display, but for the meaning which it may hold. . . . .

To Proust music was above all the revelation of a reality beyond the reach of intelligence. It is the best way we can find to penetrate the husk of conventional and impersonal conceptions about people and things and to discover our genuine, original impressions. It brings into conscious being the deeply concealed realities of the soul. Music is an artistic fixation of the deepest and most inexpressible of our feelings. As such it is closely related to the experience which Marcel had in connexion with the steeples of Martinville or the trees of Balbec; but with something more added to it. A feeling of fulfilment comes from the discovery of the truth that lies at the very core of our being and from its complete and adequate expression. This expression is an absolute realization of one's personality and brings about a supreme and unsurpassable happiness. . . . .

So Marcel Proust, in his quest for happiness, after having

been disappointed in his social ambitions and his sentimental expectations, finds at last the rock on which to build his life: that is, art. . . . . The pure, indestructible bliss of artistic creation is the reward of a long, slow, and sometimes weary search. In this search, though the goal was now clear to him, Proust still had to find his own way, and the way was to be shown to him in the course of time by Time itself. . . . .

Proust has several conceptions of time—which are not contradictory but are merely different views of the same reality. These divergences may give the impression that his ideas are more complicated than they really are. Sometimes he considers Time as an enemy, eager to destroy everything that is dear and precious to us, perpetually changing each one of us into another being. It kills our affections, subtly undermines our health, slowly but surely ruins our minds, turns pretty maidens into decrepit old hags. A great part—perhaps the greatest part—of Proust's writings is intended to show the havoc wrought in and around us by Time; and he succeeded amazingly not only in suggesting to the reader, but in making him actually feel, the universal decay invincibly creeping over everything and everybody with a kind of epic and horrible power. This conception of Time is a reflection of Proust's own experience. His whole life was a fight against Time—an endless struggle to last out a few more moments in spite of tremendous physical odds. He felt, especially in the latter part of his existence, more than ever threatened by the danger of having his thread of life cut short before he could express all that he had to say. Then the idea of Time became like a haunting nightmare and all his writings of that period bear the stamp of the ever-present, hostile obsession.

At other times, however, especially in the early part of his life, and mostly in the first version of his writings, Proust considers Time from a completely different angle. This conception of Time is closely related to the Bergsonian idea of duration. Time is not an abstract and theoretical vacuum; it is a reality filled with our own emotions and feelings. Since our present state of being is always to a very large extent conditioned by what we have been in the past, since our thoughts and passions of today are nothing but the development of our thoughts and passions of yesterday, the past is not completely abolished and dead. . . . .

. . . . But this treasure lies buried in our subconscious mind. It is as if it were enclosed in sealed jars, and even with all our intelligence we cannot reach it. Time past is Time as good as lost to us.

If only we could somehow rediscover the treasure and recapture the time that is past—and lost to us! If we could have one of these jars, open it and breathe again that wonderful, intoxicating perfume! We have seen that, according to Proust, a supreme pleasure may be derived from contact with unalloyed reality and in perpetuating, through the medium of an art, the original impression obtained thereby. Impressions that are genuinely pure and unadulterated come but rarely, however; intelligence is ready to interpret every present sensation to suit its own practical purposes and to rob that sensation of its sentimental content. But what of the sensations experienced in the past? Here is an inexhaustible mine for art, if we could only reach it. . . . .

. . . . And indeed meditation brought Marcel the answer to the enigma, together with a sense of the full meaning of his vocation in life.

Resurrection of the past in the wake of an accidental, involuntary physical sensation is the keystone of Proust's conception of life and art. It combines past and present in a miraculous unity. It brings back from the past a rainbow of rich and varied impressions. These past impressions have been, as it were, purified, decanted, by the influence of Time in our subconscious mind. . . . .

. . . . these impressions, alive but deeply concealed within us, are conjured up out of our subconscious mind by a physical sensation which is overwhelmingly present. The present sensation adds something of its own reality to the old impressions thus brought to light. Without this association, the recollection of the past would be like a dream, a mere phantom, having no solidity nor strength. But its close connexion with a sensation that we positively feel imparts to it a compelling actuality.

So Proust discovered a reality more wonderful than reality itself. Everyday reality is forcibly present, but is often adulterated by an intellectual elaboration which does not give our imagination a full chance of coming into play. The recreated reality retains unspoilt all the glamour of the past and even magnifies it, while it holds all the strength and savour of the most obvious present. . . . .

Proust . . . . goes one step farther and plunges into metaphysics. Past and present have in fact been grasped as a complete whole, indissolubly mixed together—as a single tremendous experience. But then, according to our normal conception of Time, past, present, and future are clearly separated and cannot possibly overlap one another. Yet we feel that in defiance of all the laws generally accepted as governing our world, past and present on rare occasions do actually meet and unite. And what is that state in which past and present are one, if not Eternity? So, with Proust, we transcend our common human experience and penetrate, as it were, into a superterrestrial realm. . . . .

. . . . Proust's task is perfectly clear to him. He will fulfil himself by perpetuating in a work of art the tremendous discovery he has made—he will incorporate it in a book. These flashes of eternity will become the precious substance of his creation. He soon realized, however, that on account of their dazzling brilliance and their comparatively rare occurrence, they were not sufficient in themselves to constitute the whole matter of a literary work. At best, they could be used like brilliant jewels studding a less conspicuous surface. Then Proust thought of the mass of information he had collected regarding the main preoccupations of his early life: love, and society, and the great laws of morality and psychology that he had discovered, when he was applying all the power of his intellect to the search for that unknown principle which eluded the intelligence but which was finally revealed to him through the medium of some accidental sensation. . . . .

. . . . All the notes he had taken—all the adventures he had had, great or small, thrilling or dull—were the elements of a work which had gradually been taking shape in his mind all through his life. . . . . Hence the strange and singular character of the book: it is at once a collection of memories and an account of how and why the book was written. And as Proust's life experiences draw to a close, the book which has been produced under our very eyes, so to speak, finds its justification and its excuse—and is finished. . . . ."

*61. Portraits of a Lifetime**

J. E. Blanche

Marcel Proust used to say that the poet's function consisted in extracting the essence of his feelings in the form of metaphor, so as to free them from the contingencies of the time element. I do not aim so high; but the artist, Proust asserted, did not invent, he discovered—for art dwells in hidden correspondence. The universe in its darkling manner longs to enter into touch with us. By what magic

* Coward-McCann, Inc., New York, 1938.

did Proust, the modern Prospero, in his cave evoke the spirits of earth and air and fire? According to him, we have the power to break the enchantment holding things within bonds, to raise them to our consciousness and to prevent their sinking irrevocably into nothingness. This urgent struggle with forgetfulness, this frenzied and ceaseless effort to attain a timeless absolute, is the fundamental theme of *Time Past* and of *Time Recaptured*.

Here I am putting together materials, sticking scraps on to sheets. In order to build his own universe, Proust, the sick man, cut himself off without regret. But I shudder when I think of the subject I have undertaken so late in life to write and which, despite my age, I cannot look upon impartially. When I reread pages that are like a rapid sketch, like the notes with which travellers used to fill their scrapbooks before photography was invented, I fear that some of the pages hold too many names of doubtful interest, that they will assume the aspect of films taken long ago, depicting everyday events which have but an ephemeral interest. But Proust has written, "Art is not the fruit of a conscious choice, it is born of the union of a religious idea with the love of things." This love, I think, I have not lost.

62. *Enjoyment of Literature**

JOHN COWPER POWYS

LIKE THE MASTERPIECES of all great novelists Marcel Proust's *Remembrance of Things Past* is a whole world in itself, a world into which you can pass, in

* Simon and Schuster, 1938.

which you can dwell, in which you can continually be discovering new avenues, new vistas, new horizons. . . . .

When one thinks of the work of James Joyce, our *other* famous modern, and considers what enormous erudition, philological experimentation, and symbolic architecture he labours under, one feels as if Proust's great shelf of volumes were created by the easiest method of all possible literary methods—the *rambling autobiographical essay!*

Having once "established" his characters, he seems only, without bothering about plot, to let them live and love and hate and die at the uninterfered-with pleasure of chance and fate; and this appears to make his job so easy that one almost begrudges him his success. . . . .

. . . . the beauty of Proust's masterpiece is that while it hits off with such exquisite malice all the fine shades of middle-class snobbishness and upper-class arrogance, and discloses with such subtle sympathy all the humorous refinements of old family-retainers, its *real theme,* its inmost essence, has to do with the most evasive element in our secret personal life, namely with those obscure feelings of delicious ecstasy which are as hard to arrest or analyse in their swift passage as it is hard to explain why such small, slight, trivial, and casual chances are the cause of their rising up out of the depths.

These rare individual ecstasies are to Proust—or at least to that prophetic soul in Proust embodied in his hero—precisely what the same experiences were to Wordsworth, that is to say, authentic "intimations of immortality"; and it is impossible to think of any great novel that proves this daring proposition, and this very definite proposition, so effectively as Proust does. Neither Goethe in *Wilhelm Meister* nor Romain Rolland in *Jean-Christophe* conveys to us such a clear-cut unmistakable "message" as to the nature of the human soul and its relation to the Eternal as Proust does in *Remembrance of Things Past.*

In other words while catching so vividly one after another

the insect-flights, the plant-loves, the aquarium-gestures of human society's snobbishness and perversity, the book begins and ends with those "obstinate questionings," so congenital with the Hebrew spirit, as to the relation between the individual soul, incarnated in time, and *that* which lies beyond time. . . . .

The curious thing about these sensuous "intimations of immortality" in Proust is that *they come by chance* and that they are connected with irrelevant and perfectly trivial occasions. Here, as in other things, we note in our author a complete lack—as if he were colour-blind or had no ear for music—of that particular nerve in the human soul which is the cause of so much nobility of character as well as of so much sickening hypocrisy, and which we name by the ambiguous word "spirituality."

There is nothing "spiritual" in Proust; and this it is that gives such formidable authority to his aesthetic and philosophic generalizations. What indeed we have come to feel, and not without justice, is that an "intimation of immortality" based upon the effect on our soul of a *petite madeleine* dipped in lime-petal tea is of more actual and living weight than all the mental arguments of the Platonic Socrates!

The second dominant *motif* of a book that is surely the most important work of fiction of our time is the gradual clarification and definition of the hero's first principles of art. These are also summed up in the final volume of *The Past Recaptured,* and they condense themselves into a convincing proof of the *subjectivity* of all great art as against the noisy and aggressive heresy, so tempting, so plausible, so obvious, that beauty, like truth, has an objective reality in the cosmos, before which the business of each artist is to reduce his personal imagination to a blank.

Thus we find this great work of Proust, as it takes its place beside all these other masterpieces of human genius, reaffirming the doctrine implicit in Homer and the Hebrew Prophets as well as in Rabelais and Shakespeare and Goethe that man's redemption lies in the character of the individual and not in mechanized efficiency.

What might be called the third *motif* of the work is the problem of erotic jealousy. To emphasize this particular theme Proust has recourse to the inspired device of projecting into the first place in the book two protagonists who hold much the same symbolic relation to each other as do Daedalus and Bloom in Joyce's *Ulysses.*

But Proust's young man has a more personal resemblance to his friend Swann than Daedalus ever had to Bloom; and it is wonderful to note—considering the complicated "streams" of so many different "consciousnesses," for which, as his tale moves forward, he has to dig channels and lead them like currents of various temperature and density round and about each other in the sub-aqueous world of his own mind—how free from any *real* obscurity Proust's art is.

It has many resemblances to the art of Henry James; but I think it can be said—certainly as far as individual paragraphs are concerned, and even in some cases, remembering *The Sacred Fount,* in the final disentangling—to be clearer than that great master's method! . . . .

So vibrant are . . . . [the] chords of jealousy throughout this book and so furiously, one might almost say from an Anglo-Celtic point of view so comically devoid of all impulses of magnanimity towards the objects of their desire, that one begins to sigh for that more indulgent, more generous, less analytical touch of—well! say of the sonnets of Shakespeare, a touch which can still be found in the poetry of as young a poet as our Dorsetshire Kenneth Hopkins: . . . .

But Proust's microscopic analysis of "each patterned circumstance of love" is only equalled by the devastating realism with which he traces, step by step, its pitiful disillusionment and final perishing; for Proustian love certainly *does* "alter when it alteration finds."

Here again, in this universal dissolution under the sliding away of the golden sands, one pauses to ask oneself whether time, even time itself, cannot sometimes be tricked?

But one thing is certain, the whole subject of Proust's great book is the battle of man's soul with what Hardy calls the "delving imps" of time.

Time is the antagonist of this book; and the timeless—revealed in art and revealed in these rare outbursts of the self that is eternal—is the protagonist. But this deeper theme in the book is half-concealed by the wavering consistence of the element that embodies it, just as the vital centre of a jelly-fish is surrounded by the floating substance of its transparent body.

And this gelatinous element that rises and falls with the fitful undulations of the tide of our life is the element of our secret sense of superiority to one another—in other words, the element of snobbishness.

Now in Proust's book this snobbishness is primarily *social,* and only secondarily intellectual and aesthetic; whereas in the psychic chemistry of many impassioned readers of Proust the social variety of this universal ingredient plays a subordinate part, while its kindred emotions, such as cultural, moral, and even professional snobbishness, are revealed to the most cursory introspection. . . . .

. . . . the truth is there are uncommonly few great writers, though there must have been many portrait-painters, who have had the privilege of living cheek-by-jowl with the beau monde as Proust did; and we may note that among the novelists who *have* described such circles, such as Thackeray, Disraeli, and Henry James, and some would add Balzac and Tolstoy, there is nothing to approach the microscopic analysis—at once aesthetic and scientific—of Proust's investigations in these glass houses of his botanical garden. . . . .

Few Proust-lovers will disagree with me when I maintain that as a painter of the Great World's dependents, or perhaps I should rather use the heraldic word and say "supporters," he is unsurpassed, except—and with what a difference of emphasis!—by our own Sir Walter Scott. . . . .

Proust's way of analysing all that St. Paul declares to be "a shame so much as to speak of" strikes my mind as the best possible way in which a writer *can* deal with these things, unless of course, either for his own pleasure, or the pleasure of temperaments akin to his own, he wants to be provocative. . . . .

The truth is that directly you touch any human sex-nerve, whether it be normal or abnormal, and both are in nature, you touch a nerve *that can only be understood from inside*. . . . .

But if I find lapses in Proust's handling of "the most dangerous of human nerves," I am reduced to astonished awe at his perfect insight into the heart of a selfish aristocrat. We need never, I think, have known such persons ourselves to feel the delicious shock of absolute truth in what he reveals about them. . . . .

In regard to Proust's *method* of writing, his most remarkable device, or perhaps we should say discovery, is the imaginative bringing together of ideas, or essences, or images that in objective reality are scattered through many various levels and dimensions, but can be fused together by our power of feeling things, not in their isolation, like instruments of torture in a museum, or like nectarines in cotton-wool, but in their living, breathing, fluctuating environment, permeated by the airs and sounds and smells about them, and by our own complicated feelings with regard to them.

But the art of fusing together these scattered essences, moral, emotional, psychological, sensual, and all treated, for the whole process implies both sensibility and analysis, with what might be called *aesthetic science,* is no easy achievement. It entails, if the style is to represent the dissolving horizons into which the ripples of these psychic-sensuous "events" vanish, a certain stretching out of sentences and paragraphs, yes! and even of pages, to a length before which all but inveterate Proustians are forced to cry, "Hold, enough!"

The truth is there are two urges in this great writer; and not all of us can sympathize equally with both. Thorough-going Proustians, like thorough-going Wordsworthians, are rare birds.

In one of these urges the scientific element predominates—though the science is Proustian science—while in the other the aesthetic element, which lies closer to the author's private philosophy, leaps up to monopolize the field. . . . .

It is interesting in any case to note how in the vast canvas of *Remembrance of Things Past* the Proustian "science" often gives the Proustian "aesthetic" a little more than it can carry off. This is curious, considering his steady faith in subjective as against objective methods of art.

In the hands of Dorothy M. Richardson and in those of James Joyce the art of the novel makes use of what I believe May Sinclair was the first to call the "stream of consciousness." Now strictly speaking, this is *not* the method of Proust; for while we are told what the hero thinks or what Swann thinks we are told this rather by the author than either by the "I" of the story or by Charles Swann.

In fact, Proust permits himself to do to the limit the very thing that is anathema to the artist-type of author; that is, to intersperse his fiction with what is not so much a "stream of consciousness" as a stream of Proustian commentaries upon consciousness! . . . .

But the grand secret of Proust, that sacred "message," which I as a good Lollard of literature so obstinately seek for, has to do with that *madeleine* dipped in tea and with the two or three other occasions of the same revelation, until the culminating one at the end rounds off the book.

And to what does this really amount? Surely to the conclusion, daring and startling as it is, that the mood in which we arrive at the kind of ecstasy described by Proust and without which, he admits, many people go through their entire life, is not a mood connected with what we call "beauty," nor with what we call "truth," nor with what we call "love." It is a mood, or let me say *a moment,* when we are made rapturously happy by what Wordsworth calls "the pleasure which there is in life itself." . . . .

Speaking with respectful nicety, it might justly be called the Miracle of the Mass in the natural world. It is something that *happens by chance;* and could occur to a selfish person, a criminal person, to a devilish person, just as easily as to a saint.

. . . . if we regard Marcel Proust and James Joyce as the two most formidable writers of the present epoch, it is interesting to note that while the Irishman treats all his characters except Stephen as a titanic Gulliver of satire and parody who is enjoying a burlesque show of Lilliputians with a mixture of disgusted relish and relishing disgust, Proust keeps up his serpentine progress through the hearts, nerves, and brains of all his people with an intensity of analysis so exquisite, so finespun, so *levelling,* that instead of feeling the mixture of puzzled and respectful awe that we feel in the presence of Joyce and even of his *alter ego* Stephen, we are prepared to argue with him in our own minds, so real have his people become to us, and expostulate with him as to his treatment of them, as if all he had done was just to introduce us to them, and that formality once safely over we could take our own view of their proceedings and their fate. . . . .

Our present generation in the literature of Europe and America have no men of genius that even approach Proust and Joyce. I am old enough now to have lived through three great literary dictatorships. When I was at college Dostoievsky and Nietzsche were the rulers of our spirit. When I first visited

America Anatole France and Thomas Hardy were our masters. But all the way through the decade that is now closing the more serious book lovers among us, I mean those who are concerned with real original genius and not with mere skilful craftsmanship, have turned perforce, whether we go deeply into their work or not, to Proust and Joyce. . . . .

1939

63. *The Cosmological Eye**

HENRY MILLER

IN SELECTING Proust and Joyce I have chosen the two literary figures who seem to me most representative of our time. Whatever has happened in literature since Dostoievski has happened on the other side of death. Lawrence apart, we are no longer dealing with living men, men for whom the Word is a living thing. . . . .

Despite all that may be said against him, as an artist, or as a man, he still remains the most alive, the most vitalizing of recent writers. Proust had to die in order even to commence his great work; Joyce, though still alive, seems even more dead than Proust ever was. Lawrence on the other hand, is still with us: his death, in fact, is a mockery of the living. Lawrence killed himself in the effort to burst the bonds of living death. . . . . With Proust and Joyce there was no struggle: they emerged, took a glance about, and fell back again into the darkness whence they come. Born creative, they elected to identify themselves with the historical movement . . . . It is against the stagnant flux in which we are now drifting that Lawrence

* New Directions, Norfolk, Conn., 1939.

appears brilliantly alive. Proust and Joyce, needless to say, appear more representative: they reflect the times. We see in them no revolt: it is surrender, suicide, and the more poignant since it springs from creative sources.

It is in the examination, then, of these two contemporaries of Lawrence that we see the process all too clearly. In Proust the full flower of psychologism—confession, self-analysis, arrest of living, making of art the final justification, but thereby divorcing art from life. An intestinal conflict in which the artist is immolated. The great retrospective curve back towards the womb: suspension in death, living death, for the purposes of dissection. Pause to question, but no questions forthcoming, the faculty having atrophied. A worship of art for its own sake—not for man. Art, in other words, regarded as a means of salvation, as a redemption from suffering, as a compensation for the terror of living. Art a substitute for life. The literature of flight, of escape, of a neurosis so brilliant that it almost makes one doubt the efficacy of health. Until one casts a glance at that "neurosis of health" of which Nietzsche sings in *The Birth of Tragedy*.

In Joyce the soul deterioration may be traced even more definitely, for if Proust may be said to have provided the tomb of art, in Joyce we can witness the full process of decomposition. . . . .

In these two exponents of modernity we see the flowering of the Hamlet-Faust myth, that unscotchable snake in the entrails which, for the Greeks, was represented by the Oedipus myth, and for the whole Aryan race by the myth of Prometheus. In Joyce not only is the withered Homeric myth reduced to ashes, but even the Hamlet myth, which had come to supreme expression in Shakespeare, even this vital myth, I say, is pulverized. In Joyce we see the incapacity of the modern man even to doubt: it is the simulacrum of doubt, not its substance, that he gives us. With Proust there is a higher appreciation of doubt, of the inability to act. Proust is more capable of presenting the metaphysical aspect of things, partly because of a tradition so firmly anchored in the Mediterranean culture, and partly because his own schizoid temperament enabled him to examine objectively the evolution of a vital problem from its metaphysical to its psychological aspect. The progression from nerves to insanity, from a tragic confrontation of the duality in man to a pathologic split in the personality, is mirrored in the transition from Proust to Joyce. Where Proust held himself suspended over life in a cataleptic trance, weighing, dissecting, and eventually corroded by the very scepticism he had employed, Joyce had already plunged into the abyss. In Proust there is still a questioning of values; with Joyce there is a denial of all values. With Proust the schizophrenic aspect of his work is not so much the cause as the result of his world-view. With Joyce there is no world-view. Man returns to the primordial elements; he is washed away in a cosmological flux. Parts of him may be thrown up on foreign shores, in alien climes, in some future time. But the whole man, the vital, spiritual ensemble, is dissolved. This is the dissolution of the body and soul, a sort of cellular immortality in which life survives chemically.

Proust, in his classic retreat from life, is the very symbol of the modern artist—the sick giant who locks himself up in a cork-lined cell to take his brains apart. He is the incarnation of that last and fatal disease: the disease of the mind. In *Ulysses* Joyce gives us the complete identification of the artist with the tomb in which he buries himself . . . . Joyce takes Dublin with its worn-out types; Proust takes the microscopic world of the Faubourg St. Germain, symbol of a dead past. The one wears us out because he spreads himself over such an enormous artificial canvas; the other wears us out by magnifying his thumb-nail fossil beyond all sensory recognition. The one uses the city as a universe, the other as an atom. The curtain never falls. Meanwhile the world of living men and women is huddling in the wings clamoring for the stage. . . . .

As Gillet has well said—*Work in Progress* represents "a picture of the flowing reminiscences, of the vain desires and confused wishes which wander in our sleepy, loosened soul, which comprises the crepuscular life of thought. . . . ." But who is interested in this language of night? *Ulysses* was obscure enough. But *Work in Progress* . . . . ? Of Proust at least we may say that his myopia served to render his work exciting, stimulating: it was like seeing the world through the eyes of a horse, or a fly. Joyce's deformity of vision, on the other hand, is depressing, crippling, dwarfing: it is a defect of the soul, and not an artistic, metaphysical device. . . . .

It is interesting to observe in the works of Proust and Joyce, and of Lawrence as well, how the milieu from which they sprang determined the choice of the protagonist as well as the nature of the disease against which they fought. Joyce, springing from the priest class, makes Bloom, his "average" man or double, the supreme object of ridicule. Proust, springing from the cultured middle-class, though himself living only on the fringe of society, tolerated, as it were, makes Charlus, his king figure, a bitter object of ridicule. And Lawrence, springing from the common classes, makes the type Mellors, who appears in a variety of ideal roles, but usually as the man of the soil, his hope of the future—treating him, however, no less unsparingly. All three have idealized in the person of the hero those qualities which they felt themselves to lack supremely. . . . .

Charlus . . . . is a colossal figure, and Proust has handled him in colossal fashion. As symbol of the dying world of caste, ideals, manners, etc., Charlus was selected, whether with thought or not, from the forefront of the enemy's ranks. Proust, we know, was outside that world which he has so minutely described. . . . . Always shy, timid, awkward, embarrassed. Always a bit ridiculous. A sort of cultivated Chaplin! And, characteristically, this world which he so ardently desired to join he ended by despising. It is a repetition of the Jew's eternal fight with an alien world. . . . . But if it is typical of the mechanism of the Jew, it is no less typical of the artist. And, true artist that he was, thoroughly sincere, Proust chose the best example of that alien world for his hero, Charlus. Did he not, in part, become like that hero himself later on, in his unnatural effort to become assimilated? For Charlus, though he had his counterpart in reality quite as famous as the fictive creation, Charlus is, nevertheless, the image of the later Proust. He is, indeed, the image of a whole world of aesthetes who have now incorporated under the banner of homo-sexualism.

The beautiful figure of the grandmother, and of the mother, the sane, touching, moral atmosphere of the household, so pure and integrated, so thoroughly Jewish, stands opposed to the glamorous, the romantic, alien world of the Gentile which attracts and corrodes. It stands out in sharp contrast to the milieu from which Joyce sprang. Where Joyce leaned on the Catholic Church and its traditional masters of exegesis, thoroughly vitiated by the arid intellectualism of his case, we have in Proust the austere atmosphere of the Jewish home contaminated by a hostile culture, the most strongly rooted culture left in the Western world—French Hellenism. We have an uneasiness, a maladjustment, a war in the spiritual realm which, projected in the novel, continued throughout his life. Proust was touched only superficially by French culture. His art is eminently un-French. We have only to think of his devout admiration for Ruskin. Ruskin! of all men!

And so, in describing the decay of his little world, this microcosm which was for him *the* world, in depicting the disintegration of his hero, Charlus, Proust sets before us the collapse of the outer and the inner world. The battleground of love, which began normally enough with Gilberte, becomes transferred, as in the world today, to that plane of depolarized love wherein the sexes fuse, the world where doubt and jealousy, thrown out of their normal axes, play diabolical roles. Where in Joyce's world a thoroughly normal obscenity slops over into a slimy, glaucous fluid in which life sticks, in Proust's world vice, perversion, loss of sex breaks out like a pox and corrodes everything. . . . .

. . . . After writing the last volume, with its memorable treatise on art, Proust goes back to his death-bed to revise the pages on Albertine. This episode is the core and climax of his great work. It forms the arch of that Inferno into which the mature Proust descended. For if, retiring ever deeper into the labyrinth, Proust had cast a glance back at that which he left behind, he must have seen there in the figure of woman that image of himself in which all life was mirrored. It was an image which tantalized him, an image which lied to him from every reflection, because he had penetrated to an underworld in which there were nothing but shadows and distortions. The world he had walked out on was the masculine world in process of dissolution. With Albertine as the clue, with this single thread in his hand which, despite all the anguish and sorrow of knowledge he refuses to let slip, he feels his way along the hollows of the nerves, through a vast, subterranean world of remembered sensations in which he hears the pumping of the heart but knows not whence it comes, or what it is.

It has been said that Hamlet is the incarnation of doubt, and Othello the incarnation of jealousy, and so they may be, but— the episode of Albertine, reached after an interval of several centuries of deterioration, seems to me a dramaturgic study of doubt and jealousy so infinitely more vast and complex than either Hamlet or Othello that the Shakespearean dramas, by comparison, resemble the feeble sketches which later are to assume the dimensions of a great fresco. . . . .

Herein lies the importance of Proust's epic work, for here in the Albertine episode we have the problem of love and jealousy depicted in Gargantuan fashion, the malady become all-inclusive, turning in on itself through the inversion of sex. The great Shakespearean dramas were but the announcement of a disease which had just begun to run its staggering course; in Shakespeare's time it had not yet eaten into every layer of life, it could still be made the subject of heroic drama. There was man and there was the disease, and the conflict was the material for drama. But now the toxin is in the blood. For such as us, who have been eaten away by the virus, the great dramatic themes of Shakespeare are but swashbuckling oratory and pasteboard sets. Their impression is nil. We have become inoculated. And it is in Proust that we can sense the deterioration of the heroic, the cessation of conflict, the surrender, the thing become itself. . . . .

Between Stavrogin and Charlus, however, there is an enormous gulf. It is the difference between Dostoievski and Proust, or if you like, the difference between the man of God whose hero is himself and the modern man for whom not even God can be a hero. All of Dostoievski's work is pregnant with conflict, heroic conflict. . . . .

. . . . Proust, imagining himself to be making of his life a book, of his suffering a poem, exhibits through his microscopic and caustic analysis of man and society the plight of the modern artist for whom there is no faith, no meaning, no life. His work is the most triumphant monument to disillusionment that has ever been erected. . . . .

At the root of it was his inability, confessed and repeatedly glorified, to cope with reality—the constant plaint of the modern man. As a matter of fact, his life was a living death, and it is for this reason that his case interests us. For, intensely aware of his predicament, he has given us a record of the age in which he found himself imprisoned. . . . .

. . . . Sad as it is to contemplate the grandeur and nobility of these pages, moving as it is to observe that a great work had been built up out of suffering and disease, it is also tonic to realize that in these same passages there had been dealt the death-blow to that school of realism which, pretending to be dead, had resuscitated itself under the guise of psychologism. After all Proust was concerned with a view of life; his work has meaning and content, his characters do live, however distorted they are made to seem by his laboratory method of dissection and analysis. Proust was pre-eminently a man of the 19th century, with all the tastes, the ideology, and the respect for the powers of the conscious mind which dominated the men of that epoch. His work now seems like the labor of a man who has revealed to us the absolute limits of such a mind.

The breakdown which, in the realm of painting, gave rise to the school of Impressionism is evident also in Proust's literary method. The process of examining the medium itself, of subjecting the external world to the microscopic analysis, thereby creating a new perspective and hence the illusion of a new world, has its counterpart in Proust's technique. Weary of realism and naturalism, as were the painters, or rather finding the existent picture of reality unsatisfying, unreal, owing to the explorations of the physicists, Proust strove, through the elaborate diffraction of incident and character, to displace the psychologic realism of the day. His attitude is coincident with the emergence of the new analytical psychology. Throughout those veritably ecstatic passages in the last volume of his work—the passages on the function of art and the role of the artist—Proust finally achieves a clarity of vision which presages the finish of his own method and the birth of a wholly new kind of artist. Just as the physicists, in their exploration of the material nature of the universe, arrived at the brink of a new and mysterious realm, so Proust, pushing his powers of analysis to the utmost limits, arrived at that frontier between dream and reality which henceforth will be the domain of the truly creative artists.

64. *Books and You**

SOMERSET MAUGHAM

.... FINALLY, I must remind you that our own time has produced in Marcel Proust a novelist who can stand comparison with the greatest. His work has been so well translated that I am inclined to think it .... loses nothing in its English dress. He wrote one novel only, but that in fifteen volumes. When first they were made known to an astonished world, they were praised out of all reason. I myself wrote that I preferred being bored by Proust to being amused by any other writer. A second reading has made most of us assume a more sensible attitude. He is often repetitive, his self-analyses grow wearisome, and his obsession with the tedious emotion of jealousy fatigues in the long run even his most willing readers; but his defects are more than compensated by his merits. He is a great and original writer. He has subtlety, creative power and psychological insight; but I think the future will hail him above all as a wonderful humorist. So I recommend you to start at the beginning of this copious novel, read till you are bored, skip and start reading again; but to take care to miss nothing of Madame Verdurin or the Baron de Charlus. They are the richest creations of the comic fancy our time has seen.

65. *Reflections on the Role of Music and of Some Musicians in the Works of Marcel Proust**

René de Messieres

Above all, music has one property which strengthens and justifies in advance the very essence of the *Past Recaptured*: music exists only in and by duration; it is the brilliant proof that Time is not limited to destruction alone, but also preserves and creates. A note is not an isolated value; it is the bridge between the note which it follows and the one it introduces; a musical phrase has no individual unity except insofar as its first elements survive in us in order to determine the relative value of those phrases to follow.

This characteristic gains the utmost importance with the insistent return of certain musical themes, or leitmotifs. A motif is typified by the fact that to the particular charm of the musical phrase is added the new significance and, as one might say, the spiritual consistency which are given it by its previous repetitions.

Certainly every one is aware of the importance of this spiritual consistency in Proust, of this "dimension of time"; "The flowers which I see for the first time do not seem real flowers to me."

* By permission of the author. Translated by Miss Edith Johansen.

It is undoubtedly with the intention of completely utilizing this psychological effect that Proust borrows actual motifs from musical technique—the motif of the bell-towers of Combray, motif of the "petite madeleine," motif of the little phrase of Vinteuil. This latter acquires increasing prestige through its incessant repetition; and after having been, for Swann, the "national anthem of his love," every time it reappears it recalls even as a certain theme from *Tristan,* the symbol of unhappy love and of something which surpasses it. . . . .

An excellent example of these "variations on a motif" and one which extends over a good part of the work, is the little group of Balbec, the garland of budding young girls. They pass before our eyes, symbol of youth, of carefreeness, light, inseparable, the grace notes in a luminous trill. Then they take flight only to return once more, ever more insistent, holding the hero's attention more and more fixedly; the appearance of each of the girls—one might say her tonality—varies unceasingly: now one, now another takes the foreground in a sudden burst, until finally Albertine eclipses all the others, becomes the dominant in a sort of musical bridge which resolves the graceful and dancing scherzo of the garland and prepares the way for the tragic andante, theme of love and despair.

From a still more general point of view, we might say that the plan of the entire work is conceived according to the lines of musical structure; many points now considered absurd or obscure would be clarified if one would admit this fact. The first pages, which discourage so many impatient readers, appear as an overture wherein one finds exposed, or at least subtly interwoven, all the principal motifs of the work, victoriously freed from all chronological worry, following a privilege usually reserved for the world of dreams[1]—or of music. . . . .

It is indeed thus, step by step, that Proust's work develops

[1] "When a man is asleep, he has in a circle around him the chain of the hours, the sequence of the years, the order of the heavenly host." (*Swann's Way,* 3).

and we need not fear making the comparison more precise and saying that its development recalls the sonata form.

Thus in Proust's works, two themes are interwoven and opposed to each other: the theme of a Time which destroys against the theme of a Time which preserves and creates; the second theme finally dominates throughout the last volume, indefatigably gaining strength during the triumphant "coda," until the entire work reaches the climax on the dominant chord, on the word Time. . . . .

A study of Proust's ideas about the characteristics of a musical language might lead us to presume that he had little liking for a music which aims purely at the picturesque, at the imitative, such as Rameau or Saint-Saëns found so diverting, a music which is an offspring of language, which is intelligible and obvious, imitating a clap of thunder to announce a storm, or the song of birds to indicate a forest. He prefers a music which is expressive, which transposes an emotion or a sensation by means of a more distant, more profound analogy, the secret kept between the musician and his initiates. If for example a phrase from the septet of Vinteuil calls forth the idea of morning or of a cock's crow, it is not because this phrase imitates the cock's crow, but because it offers the musical equivalent, a joyous effervescence of the melodic curve.

Nevertheless we must never forget that Proust is not a theorician, that he feels bound to logic neither by duty nor by desire, that he lets himself be guided by his authentic impressions, or to a lesser degree, by the opinions of those around him (or the desire of reacting against these); and finally, in the course of the long period which represents the ripening and the composition of his work, his tastes undoubtedly underwent changes.

From earliest childhood he received a rather varied musical education. In spite of the reservations we have made, his "Portraits of Musicians" in the *Plaisirs et les Jours* give witness to a delicate knowledge and appreciation of Gluck, Mozart, Schumann and Chopin. He continued to enjoy them, as he reveals in his correspondence, and even in detached allusions throughout the *Remembrance of Things Past.* Yet Chopin alone holds a place that is at all notable: more than once the narrator takes up the defense of the old Marquise de Cambremer, an admirer of Chopin, against those who would deprecate such an old-fashioned taste.

. . . . There is . . . . [another] direct and important reason for the probable influence of Wagner's music on the works of Proust: the unbroken continuity of the former. Wagner's first audiences were struck (as a whole unfavorably) by this characteristic, and in spite of the superficiality of such impressions, they express a reaction which we can readily understand:

> From the overture to the last note of the score, said one of the earliest critics of *Tannhäuser,* the composer's little phrase rolls on and on, like macaroni, which strings along and never breaks. One is supposed to swallow this thing in one gulp and still not choke.[2]

and another critic:

> It's like reading in one fell swoop a book that has neither commas nor periods.[3]

This is almost word for word the same expression which the early readers of Proust used to describe him. Of course that does not mean that this continuity is identical in the two cases. But in both of them, the principles of distinction, instead of being conventional or expected ("airs" from operas, "chapters" from books) are organic, vital, and therefore disconcerting to our mechanized intelligence, rich in meaning only for those who are willing to attune themselves to them. Proust made the admirable effort to recognize in Wagner (and we in turn can recognize in Proust) this principle of unity and of division in the use of those motifs whose significance we indicated in our opening pages:

[2] *Figaro,* November 6, 1859.

[3] Auber, author of the *Domino Noir.*

> I began to perceive how much reality there is in the work of Wagner, when I saw in my mind's eye those insistent, fleeting themes which visit an act, withdraw only to return and sometimes distant, drowsy, almost detached, are at other moments, while remaining vague, so pressing and so near, so internal, so organic, so visceral that one would call them the resumption not so much of a musical motif as of an attack of neuralgia.[4]

Certainly Wagner did not invent the motif, but he made of it a wider, more complex and more internal application than any other composer, just as one might say of Proust's literary motif.

. . . . through the acutely sensitive avatars of the Duchesse de Guermantes and her final humiliation, there still persists what might be called the Guermantes motif, the myth of the priceless bird, rosy and golden, which in the last pages is to settle down even on Gilberte, just as in Wagner the motif of the sword or of the Grail may pass from person to person. And thus, through the psychological contradiction or even the changes of personality, there breathes the poetic, musical unity of the hero. . . . .

In spite of Proust's numerous and laudatory references to Wagner's music, his admiration is not blind nor indiscriminating. He is quick to find the uninspired measures of the first works—*Lohengrin* or *Tannhäuser*. It would not be incongruous to make a comparison between one of the essential ideas of Proust's and the theme of the *Meistersinger*: the struggle between vibrant poetry and critical intelligence. But comparison does not mean influence, nor even conscious relationship. He speaks rather little of the Tetralogy; but he was undoubtedly thinking of it when he acclaimed, not without awe, Wagner's "vulcanian ability," his powers of creation.

At bottom, the true Wagner is embodied for him in *Tristan* and in *Parsifal*. These are the operas which he names time and time again as examples of perfect beauty. Here, length is no

[4] *The Captive*, p. 210.

longer synonymous with diffusion, weightiness, but rather with insinuation, insistence—it creates a new value in depth, imposes upon emotion or dream more reality, through joining it more closely to a physical, throbbing rhythm. And one may apply all these things to Proust's style as well.

The central theme of *Tristan*—one might say its only musical phrase—is based on the idea with which Proust was eternally obsessed: the despairing attempts of two people to find each other, attempts which cease to be hopeless only with death. The love song finds here, in its intensity and in its misery, a sort of purity which sets it above, or at least outside all moral considerations.

Parsifal is an even more precise symbol of the line followed by Proust: the conquest of all that is superior in him and in the universe, a revealing, inescapable evocation, through a purification not so much moral as metaphysical, mystical. . . . .

We should not be astonished . . . . to find Proust irritated by those who, through stupidity of taste or through snobbery condemn Wagner under the banner of the anti-melodist theories. . . . .

Liberated from all prejudices, more anxious for a musical continuity of life than for theories, Proust is able to combine with his admiration for Wagner an equally great interest in Debussy.

He had some very personal reasons for this latter interest, because among his friends are to be counted some of the most fervent attendants upon Debussy's rising star. Proust's good friend, the violinist Ysaye, was one of the organizers of the String Quartet; Robert de Montesquiou once thought of having *Pelléas* presented at his home; Robert de Flers was one of the first to introduce Debussy to the public. However, these random influences are less important than the profounder relationships. In a page impregnated with fantasy, Proust reveals the special value of the pleasures he experienced from Debussy's work, and indicated in what family of musicians he classes him. . . . .[5]

However great may be Proust's obligation to Wagner, as far as the general construction of his work is concerned or the role of the motif, a great number of his pages remind us on the other hand of Debussy's style—flexibility, unobtrusive unity, crystal-like but by no means binding half tones. . . . .

We must now examine one other musician, who occupies an infinitely greater place in the work than all the others together—who is as real as the others for any reader of Proust, and yet whose name will appear in no musical dictionary . . . . "a Bach, a Wagner, a Vinteuil. . . . ." We must now speak of Vinteuil.

It would be wrong to say that Vinteuil is "music." The two works which Proust attributes to him—a Sonata and a Septet—are analysed with such precision that it is possible to ascertain a definite style in them. It would be much more exact to say that Proust, as he has so often done, created his musician by synthesizing all the musicians whom he preferred. To understand this, we must study the respective importance of the elements which enter into this synthesis, an importance which may easily have varied with time. And besides, Proust does not combine in Vinteuil all the musicians who have interested him. We would look in vain, for example, for any trace of Debussy.

On the contrary, it is in no way absurd to look for suggestions of Wagner in Vinteuil. The way in which the motif is prepared in the two works which Proust describes, the way it is announced as though from a distance; the very treatment of that motif, and above all, its insistent repetition; a certain manner of creating expectation and of fulfilling this expectation—all that is typical of Wagner.

On the other hand, the personality of Vinteuil, modest,

[5] *The Captive,* pp. 152–53.

timid, a little awkward, introspective and satisfied with his enclosed existence—is exactly the contrary of Wagner, who cannot help revealing himself in his musical style, whose power surges through his purest and most delicate measures. Also, none of the works of Vinteuil which Proust analyzes, or even cites, is in any way theatrical, one of the greatest characteristics of Wagner; and this difference must modify even the conceptions of the role of music. The work of Wagner which has the closest connection is probably *Tristan,* which reminds one somewhat of an extended sonata. But there is little need of conjecturing, when Proust himself frankly gives us the formula:

> As I played the passage, and for all that in it Vinteuil had been trying to express a fancy which would have been wholly foreign to Wagner, I could not help murmuring: "Tristan," with the smile of an old friend of the family, discovering a trace of the grandfather in an intonation, a gesture of the grandson who had never set eyes on him. And as the friend then examines a photograph which enables him to estimate the likeness, so, in front of Vinteuil's sonata, I set up on the music rest the score of *Tristan.*[6]

If we would find a great musician who in certain aspects is related to Wagner, and who is yet distinguished from him, it seems to me that we must turn to César Franck. Not only was his work the great revelation of the years spanning Proust's youth—more than that, Franck was the idol of the same group which consecrated itself to the diffusion of Wagner, the group of Vincent d'Indy. The latter liked to point out the approximations between the two masters (chance encounters rather than premeditated imitations), and emphasized particularly the large and varied use which Franck made of the motif.

Without making too much of biographical similarities, without making of Franck a "key" for Vinteuil, we can yet assert that as a whole he presents the same moral physiognomy, the same curve of existence: timid, dissimulating, his brilliance

[6] *The Captive,* p. 209.

hidden under a bourgeois bonhommie, poorly adapted to the life of his century, Franck, just as Vinteuil, gave piano lessons to win his daily bread, and his pupils never suspected the least connection between their master and the composer whose glory was gradually rising. (Exactly as the aunts of Proust refused to believe that their piano teacher could possibly have any relationship to the illustrious Vinteuil.)

Franck's glory was not so wholly posthumous as was Vinteuil's. However, one must not forget that his Symphony was played only once during his lifetime, and that his masterpiece, *Rédemption,* long remained unknown. But it is mainly the moral elevation, the religious fervour, the spiritual disquietude rising finally to complete serenity, the absence of sensual anxiety, which may serve as elements of comparison.

Franck left one sonata for piano and violin, remarkable for the rare equilibrium between the two instruments. The introduction of the piano into the first movement is not unanalogous to the description of the sonata of Vinteuil.

> It had been a source of keen pleasure when, below the narrow ribbon of the violin part, delicate, unyielding, substantial and governing the whole, he had suddenly perceived, where it was trying to surge upwards in a flowing tide of sound, the mass of the piano-part.[7]

Nor is it impossible to find at the end of the third movement and in the fourth movement of the same sonata an impression akin to that which Proust would describe to us in the discussion of the famous "little phrase."

We are consciously using vague terms, for it would be imprudent to believe in too comfortable a solution. A more precise analysis of the little phrase would undoubtedly show us that it is in part pure creation inspired by complex memories; it represents a style more than a work, and of this style Franck is a great, but certainly not the only exponent. Many other musicians in France remained faithful to the singing and well-

[7] *Swann's Way,* p. 268.

defined melodic line, to the discreet use of motifs. Proust himself exhorts us to remember this: "We must not forget that the sonata for piano and violin of Fauré is anterior to that of Franck's."

This care for chronology shows not only what importance he attached to the two works, but also in what esteem he held Fauré. And it was with the latter alone that Proust had direct relationships (unless one would consider Reynaldo Hahn purely as a musician.) One of the biggest entertainments that Proust gave, one of those which Montesquiou supervised, was given for a recital of Fauré; and we can read in his letters that Fauré was often a guest in his house. Less profound, less anguished than Franck, knowing none of his mystic flights of fancy, Fauré is also more balanced, more delicate. This might mean that his "influence," undoubtedly present in Vinteuil's Sonata, is much less probable in the Septet.

And indeed, this latter is presented to us as a much more complex work, more tormented, bolder. Although of a magnificent sureness of composition, it surprises the narrator at first, and even displeases him for the very reasons which will later make it more precious. The analysis seems to reveal an evolution in the course of which Proust's taste became more sure, more demanding, more avid for tragic grandeur. There is no longer any question of the nervous, delicate, somewhat slender elegance of Fauré. On the contrary, such works of Franck as *Rédemption* or the *Symphony* would certainly not feel overwhelmed by the terms which Proust uses to describe the Septet—a triumphal and complete masterpiece.

Nothing can keep us from thinking of the quartet or of the finale of the Franck Symphony as we read the following:

> This phrase broke up, was transformed, like the little phrase in the sonata, and became the mysterious appeal of the start. A phrase of a plaintive kind rose in opposition to it. . . . . Presently the two motives were wrestling together. . . . . In the end the joyous motive was left triumphant; it was no longer an almost anxious appeal addressed to an

empty sky, it was an ineffable joy which seemed to come from Paradise. . . . . I might be sure that this new tone of joy, this appeal to a super-terrestrial joy, was a thing I would never forget.[8]

A super-terrestrial joy which liberates him from the ordinary, prosaic joys, just as the ineffable sadness of the "little phrase" had delivered Swann from his terrestrial sorrows, which had tortured and humiliated him.

. . . . of those sorrows which were now become his own, without his having any hope of being, ever, delivered from them, it seemed to say to him, as once it had said of his happiness: "What does all that matter; it is all nothing."[9]

And certainly that does not alienate us from the music of Franck; but it seems to me that there is a still more definite indication of Beethoven. For it is towards him, the giant of music, that Proust's admiration was to be more exclusively concentrated, accordingly as his suffering and his genius grew and were purified.[10]

. . . . We know at the end of his life Proust never tired of hearing the last quartets, notably the fifteenth, and had them played at his home at great expense. And it seems impossible not to recognize the super-human boldness of these last quartets in the final style of Vinteuil:

The glowing septet differed singularly from the candid sonata: the timid question to which the little phrase replied, form the breathless supplication to find the fulfillment of the strange promise that had resounded, so harsh, so supernatural, so brief, setting athrob the still, inert crimson of the morning sky.[11]

It is the same term of harshness, but a pleasing harsh-

[8] *The Captive,* p. 352.

[9] *Swann's Way,* p. 352.

[10] There is nothing surprising in this association of the two names: "Through César Franck and his school, it is in France almost exclusively that one can find preserved the Beethoven tradition of the variation," says Vincent d'Indy in his *Cours de Composition musicale;* and in his César Franck, he draws a fine associative analysis of Franck's quartet and the later quartets of Beethoven.

[11] *The Captive,* p. 344.

ness, that Charlus is to use in describing Beethoven's fifteenth quartet.

But it is above all the emergent figure of Vinteuil, his creative fire, his victory over despair, which evoke the titanic and legendary figure of the older Beethoven, whom no one would have suspected to exist in the Vinteuil of the first volumes:

> This Vinteuil, whom I had known so timid and sad . . . . The joy that such chords had aroused in him, the increase of strength that it had given him wherewith to discover others led the listener on also from one discovery to another, or rather it was the composer himself who guided him, deriving from the colors that he had invented, a wild joy which gave him the strength to discover, to fling himself upon the others which they seemed to evoke, enraptured, quivering, as though from the shock of an electric spark, when the sublime came spontaneously to life at the clang of the brass, panting, drunken, maddened, dizzy, while he painted his great musical fresco, like Michelangelo strapped to his scaffold and dashing, from his supine position, tumultuous brush-like strokes upon the ceiling of the Sistine Chapel.[12]

Such a delirium of volcanic creation makes us think of the Beethoven of the great symphonies, and particularly of the ninth, the anthem to joy, the hymn of deliverance. For that is to be the ultimate symbol of the musician for Proust; he who delivers, he who, according to the words of Beethoven, knows ". . . . how to dominate suffering so that he may console himself better for that suffering."[13] Proust might well take those words into consideration, he who has told us that the supreme goal of art is to make us "consider the people who make us suffer so that we may attain their divine form."

Divine form of creatures and things! Divine form of their own weaknesses. It is on this summit that Proust and Beethoven join. On this summit music fulfills the mystic promise that Proust demanded of it at the outset.

A promise of immortality? Who can say?[14] Rather—and this is of even greater value, for on the plane to which Proust

[12] *The Captive,* p. 344.

[13] Quoted by Benoist-Méchin, *op. cit.*

[14] See Benoist-Méchin, *op. cit.*

would raise us, there is no more meaning to the words death and immortality—a promise of salvation.

Promise of salvation, one might say, on so many levels, and undoubtedly in so many stages; salvation, through the discovery of our individual soul; through the hope of discarding our every-day self; through the revelation of a magic language, at once free and restricted, which transmits without betraying the "differences"; salvation through clarification, the justification of the processes of art which Proust, left to himself, would perhaps never have dared to push to their limits; and above all, salvation through the attainment of a serenity, a purity which is truly the divine, attained the hic and nunc, here on this earth and from this time forward.

There is at least a part of Proust's debt to his increasingly extended, increasingly binding contact with music.

But does this suffice to explain his entire work?

He himself would warn us against such an exaggeration: "That phrase may indeed have been able to symbolize a call, but it could not have created talents and made of Swann the writer he never was."[15]

We are far from solving the enigma of Proust.

66. *Introduction to Proust**

DERRICK LEON

Remembrance of Things Past . . . . is by no means a faultless book. Undoubtedly it is too long: not only hundreds of words but hundreds of pages too long. . . . . By excessive diffusion, the original form of the

[15] *The Past Recaptured,* p. 204.

* Kegan Paul Trench Trubner & Co., Ltd., London, 1940.

novel was subjected to a terrific strain; and by altering the scale without sufficiently reinforcing the actual structure, its shape became so obscured that for a long time it seemed to be meandering and insignificant.

. . . . The fact that he died before he was able to correct and revise the last three parts of his novel was as great a tragedy for his work as it was for the author. *The Sweet Cheat Gone* and *The Past Recaptured,* in particular, are marred by an occasional sketchiness and uncertainty that is far less apparent in any of the previous volumes; and despite the immense labour that it must have cost his literary executors—Jacques Rivière and Robert Proust—to prepare his manuscript for the press, errors so astonishing remain in the text that they give the impression that the development of the book was never fully planned.

In *The Sweet Cheat Gone,* for example, there is a passage stating that Saint-Loup is to keep his wife continuously supplied with offspring, when in the succeeding volume he leaves but one daughter; just as it is stated that Gilberte is eventually to become the Duchesse de Guermantes, an event which certainly never happens during the course of our acquaintance with her, and is, presumably, some error left from the original version, in which, of course, her husband could not have been killed in the War.

Similarly, in *The Past Recaptured,* there are other passages which herald future developments that are never realized: there are identical phrases employed to describe the physical results of the same vice shared by Legrandin and Saint-Loup: Oriane de Guermantes is supplied with the completely new name of Marie-Sosthènes, and even in the remarkable dissertation upon time there are curious obscurities and redundancies, to the extent that in some cases the same passage has been inserted twice, with the variation of but a few words, and only a few pages between each version.

Moreover, the method by which the whole book was amplified has created a certain sense of unreality regarding several of the most important details. As a considerable part of the first and third chapters of *The Past Recaptured* must have been completed round about 1912, and the long chapter dealing with the War not until several years later, we find many of the major characters at the Princesse de Guermantes' party, despite the evidences of age announced, still remarkably young after the lapse of time which has intervened since their last appearance. We know that the "little clan" was in full swing, and that Swann was in love with an Odette no longer in her first youth, before Marcel's birth. So that even allowing that the latter is intended to be a few years younger than Proust himself—he could not be much more, since we know that he is a young man entering society at the beginning of the Dreyfus case—this means that the "mistress" is still giving huge crushes, and Mme de Forcheville taking lovers, when both these ladies must be nearly seventy. But if this is barely credible, hardly more so is the external aspect of the deeply intimate life which Marcel leads with Albertine beneath his parents' roof, while his mother is called away conveniently to Combray to nurse a relative who remains ill for an unconscionably long time, and his father disappears from the narrative altogether.[1] Even as early as the first volume of *Within a Budding Grove* there are vague and inexplicable inconsistencies, as when Marcel's grandmother seems to live, now permanently with his parents, and now in a separate establishment of her own; and in the hotel at Balbec Marcel reads of Albertine's arrival with her parents, when subsequently she appears to be an orphan more or less in the care of her aunt, Mme Bontemps.

In addition, throughout the whole of the work there are to be found long and redundant passages which could add little

[1] It is almost certain that Proust's affair with "Albertine," whoever she was, terminated shortly before the war. Many long passages would therefore have been interpolated later which explains, though it does not excuse, this strange uncertainty.

of value to any novel. The famous introduction to *Sodom and Gomorrah,* is, although a remarkable innovation, indispensable to the development of the work, and a treatise of great power and understanding. But it is difficult to find any adequate justification for the lengthy expositions of military tactics, or Brichot's endless dissertations upon the meaning of the place-names about Balbec. The sum of many such digressions, when it does little to advance the portrayal of character or the development of the action, merely serves to weaken the cumulative effect of a work which was composed with the most detailed and passionate care. Yet despite all its diffuseness, it is amazing how the subtle and persistent interlocking of episodes never weakens. Not only is the moment when Albertine announces to Marcel her knowledge of Mlle Vinteuil prepared for thousands of pages before, when as child, he looks through the window of Montjouvain; and the climax in *The Sweet Cheat Gone,* when he receives Gilberte's telegram and imagines that it comes from Albertine, anticipated already in the early days of *Within a Budding Grove,* when Gilberte writes to him for the first time, and, owing to her ornate and pretentious calligraphy, he finds the utmost difficulty in deciphering her signature; but nearly every fresh episode in the book at once develops some past theme, and simultaneously introduces a new one. With what ingenious skill the introduction to *Sodom and Gomorrah* is foreshadowed in the conversation about the fertilization of her plant at Mme de Guermantes' dinner party, or M. de Vagoubert is first discussed by M. de Norpois, and the full significance of certain implications demonstrated only much later, when he is shown at the Princesse de Guermantes' in conversation with M. de Charlus.

. . . . There are so many minor characters . . . . that the very inclusion of their names merely increases the reader's difficulty in registering such others, whose number is already vast, as perform a very necessary part in the development of the exposition. Yet others recur under different names, such as Mme d'Orvillers and the Princesse de Nassau; both of these ladies, if not actually the same, being so similar as to serve little or no purpose by their dual representation.

Indeed, the greatest weaknesses of the book are the expression of precisely the same qualities that contrived to produce its extraordinary power, and are consequently inseparable from it. For Proust was so determined to give everything that he possessed, so determined to express himself with ultimate freedom and completeness, so determined that nothing that might add to the value of his work should be omitted, that he could not restrain himself from saying everything too frequently, too persistently and too much. . . . .

Similarly it may be quite reasonably asserted that too many of Proust's characters turn out to be inverted. Whereas no legitimate objection can be taken to the choice of this phenomenon as literary material, and his treatment of the subject is, in every sense, beyond reproach, it adds nothing to the value of his contribution that he has made this weakness so ubiquitous.

. . . . drama, with Proust, is concerned far more deeply with inner realization and illumination than with any external action. Many of the most important events in the book take place as in a play, off stage, and are sketched in quite roughly in a few lines, as, in the theatre, a minor character may divulge a major tragedy in a short speech. This is not to say that Proust cannot write dramatically in the accepted sense—for the scene in which Mme Verdurin incites Morel to quarrel with M. de Charlus has a naked power and a pathos that is almost Shakespearian—but that, for him, the most intense drama lies in the sudden juxtaposition of two impressions which, simultaneously compared, produce a powerful emotional realization of the persistent but unperceived changes which have taken place between them. . . . .

These moments of concealed drama, which depend for their

value not upon any external action but upon the sudden realization of change, occur at irregular intervals throughout the book, repeated with increasing frequency until, in *The Past Recaptured,* they form the basis of all the author's philosophical conclusions, and their plaint reaches the fervour of a prophetic monody. . . . .

. . . . *Remembrance of Things Past* is no more a pure novel than it is pure autobiography, pure psychology or pure philosophy. Incorporating every aspect of the author's physical, emotional and intellectual life, it portrays probably a more vivid and a more comprehensive picture of a growing and developing consciousness and personality than any other novel that has yet appeared.

Its method of detached objectivity, even when it appears to be most subjective, is applied as much to the unfolding of Marcel's inner life as it is to the description of the life about him. For realism, to Proust, meant an exact reconstruction of the inner essence, rather than of the outer aspect, of his authentic impressions. It is for this reason that he deliberately substitutes for a photographic reproduction a form of representation that most truly permits him to describe accurately his most valued perceptions. Unlike Elstir, the quintessence of the impressionist school of painting, he rarely seeks to describe the outward aspect of things as they appear to the eyes rather than to the intelligence. Nor ever once, like Balzac, does he assemble with minute accuracy the interior of a room. But by recreating the beam of sunlight that spilled upon the floor, the scent of lilac in the air, or the musty smell of old books, he can convey a sense of vividness and depth that any amount of detailed description is powerless to evoke. . . . .

His style, despite all the compexity of those interminable sentences, deeply influenced by his admiration and appreciation of the prose of Ruskin,—"that mighty and majestic prose . . . . so fervid and so fiery coloured in its noble eloquence, so rich in its elaborate symphonic music, so sure and certain, at its best, in subtle choice of word and epithet"—is a triumph of flexibility and expressive skill. Clear, curt and suave when he is ironic, it can be brilliantly acid, tenderly poetic; sombrely powerful or lyrical with the most gentle and most moving beauty. . . . . Enriched by his remarkable and comprehensive culture, by his deep love and understanding of classical literature, of music and of painting, the whole work displays a wealth of similes derived with an equal aptness and facility from biology, from physics, from botany, from medicine, or from mathematics, that never ceases to astonish and delight.

As for the characteristic and elliptical form of the sentences themselves, despite their occasional obscurity, the habit of assimilating them without difficulty is very soon acquired. And while undoubtedly Proust will always remain caviare to the general, the great sensitiveness and variety of his prose is alone sufficient to keep his name alive so long as a civilization remains that can appreciate an exceptional culture, and value literature as an art. But style, with Proust, as with all the great writers, is never more than the means to an end, and at no time, as for example, with the Henry James with whom he has so much in common, does it overstep its position in the narrative to violate the laws of character. All Proust's people speak in their own way with their own phrases, or with the phrases of their respective sets, and never in the involuted and complicated phrases of the author.

In conclusion, it must be emphasized how inconspicuous, almost irrelevant indeed, Proust's faults become in comparison with the superb success and ingenuity with which so many supplementary themes are continually interwoven and continuously developed until they are combined at last in the incomparable final chapter. This alone would make it impossible to deny Proust's right to claim his place amongst the greatest novelists of the world. . . . .

Derrick Leon

To those who seek in the novel a form of diversion or an opiate such as is offered by the cinema or the radio, Proust has nothing to say. But to those others for whom literature, as every other branch of art, of science, or philosophy and of religion, is a recognized approach towards understanding the mystery and beauty of the world, his work will afford a quite extraordinary amount of suggestive and interesting material. . . . . No other novelist has ever been so little concerned with entertainment or distraction. His work contains humour, poetry, drama, passion and tragedy: all the irony, the triviality, the beauty and the disillusion of human life. But nowhere does he make the slightest concession to imagination.

At a first attempt, the prospect of toiling through the seven[2] long parts of *Remembrance of Things Past* may appear to be formidable and even distasteful. But once set ourselves to do so, and, when we have reached the end, it is probable that our most powerful sensation will be that never again—at least until many years are past and we can re-read the book with something of our original appreciation and excitement—shall we find any novel that compares with it in its impressive wealth of insight and understanding. Its verisimilitude and its veracity are amazing. In this lies its greatest strength. For, in the words of Ruskin, "Wheresoever the search after truth begins, there life begins"; of Goethe, "The first and last thing required of genius is the love of truth."

[2] As they are now divided.

67. *Invitation to Learning**

CAIRNS: Marcel Proust uses the story of the disintegration of French aristocratic society as a background on which to record his impressions of psychology, manners, customs, love and, particularly, art and time. Mr. Maurois, would you agree that that is the theme of the novel?

MAUROIS: Perhaps the theme could be expressed in one sentence of Proust himself: "Time, as it flows, is so much time wasted and nothing can ever be truly possessed save under the aspect of eternity which is also the aspect of art."

VAN DOREN: Perhaps it is such a feeling that inspires certain persons like Saint-Simon or Pepys to keep diaries. I have always thought so. For them it must have seemed that time would continue to flow, and everything with it be swept away, unless they imprisoned it in their books. . . . .

TATE: Mr. Maurois, don't you think that it is interesting that Proust, in power and technique one of the most advanced novelists, should partly return to a very old form of the old novel? His novel is partly a very elaborate personal record.

MAUROIS: Oh, yes, certainly. And you have, included in the

* Unrehearsed broadcast by the Columbia Broadcasting System, with Mr. André Maurois as a guest, quoted by permission of Random House, publishers.

book, a short novel which is exactly a classical novel of the old type.

CAIRNS: You mean the section, "Swann in Love"?

MAUROIS: Yes, the second part of *Swann's Way,* so different from all the rest of Proust's work. . . . .

CAIRNS: . . . . You will recall that, as a young man, Proust had two major ambitions—love and society. He wanted to be received in French society; he wanted to have a great love affair. But later on in life he concluded that those two ambitions were not worth while, and for them he substituted his interest in time and art. He ceased to pursue love and society for themselves, but stormed them indirectly through the instruments of time and art.

MAUROIS: Exactly. Love and society became for him themes for his art. The true artist always ends in giving up real life in order to see it better, and from outside.

TATE: Mr. Maurois, don't you think that Proust looked upon the society of his time differently from, for example, Thackeray in his time? The social framework may be disintegrating, but that isn't Proust's main interest, is it? Isn't it rather the individual consciousnessness, the secret life of the characters? Don't you think generally that literature tends to be interested in such private experience when the social framework begins to break up? Private experience becomes very important, whereas it wasn't so important perhaps in the age of Racine. Life was much more social.

MAUROIS: Yes, except, of course, that, even in the seventeenth century, you also had men like Pascal or La Rochefoucauld who were very much interested in analyzing the feelings of the individual.

VAN DOREN: And Saint-Simon's *Mémoires.*

TATE: Yes, but I was thinking of the novel as a sort of public form of literature, comparable nowadays to the drama of the seventeenth century. Perhaps the kind of experience we have cannot be conveyed in the drama. And isn't it significant that our great writers tend to be novelists?

VAN DOREN: I don't see why we shouldn't take Proust at his word when he tells us that this book came into existence because, at a certain moment of his life, something happened over which he had no control, and which made him remember his past. Do you happen to know . . . . the autobiography of W. H. Hudson, the English writer? . . . . He begins by telling a story something like Proust's. Suddenly—this was in his old age—the whole of his past appeared, as clear as if it were on a map, as if he looked at it from a mountain top.

MAUROIS: Well, Chateaubriand had the same experience. He tells us, in the *Mémoires d'Outre-Tombe,* how, because he had heard a skylark, he suddenly recaptured all his youth, and the atmosphere of Combourg which was to him what Combray was to Proust.

VAN DOREN: One of Proust's points surely is that we do not control our memory evenly. It plays tricks on us. Sometimes it gives us a great deal; sometimes nothing.

CAIRNS: That is one of the points he makes about memory, but I think he is more complex than that. He has a well-formulated theory of time. He regards time as an enemy and he also regards it as a friend. It is an enemy in the sense that it destroys the values that he observes in the external world. It is a friend because, through a strange process that he devised, he was able to use it to recapture the past.

TATE: Although Marcel Proust solved this problem in a special way of great originality, isn't he really concerned with the oldest meaning of art—to capture from the wreckage of the past something of permanent significance?

CAIRNS: Oh, I think so. I think it goes back at least to the discussion in Plato's *Symposium* of the thirst for immortality.

MAUROIS: Proust thinks that there are two sorts of memories. The first is at work when you reconstruct a thing just by reason. The second is the intuitive memory which starts working suddenly because you heard a skylark, like Chateaubriand, or drank a cup of tea, like Proust, and because this one sensation resuscitated the whole experience. Proust's theory is that intuitive memory is the only true memory.

VAN DOREN: Yes, through a sort of mystical experience.

CAIRNS: He wanted an involuntary memory—some way of conjuring up experiences otherwise than through reason. His finest experiences came through involuntary memory; but because they were involuntary he could not control them. That was a source of unhappiness to him.

VAN DOREN: He was a great psychologist, just as Saint Augustine was a great psychologist, and his best pages are on memory and time.

TATE: Wouldn't it be interesting to compare Proust to Saint Augustine, who, in the fourth century, wrote the greatest imaginative analysis of memory before Proust? Saint Augustine is a Christian moralist, and is concerned with the moral control of this seething life beneath consciousness. Proust wanted to subject it to a different control, which we call artistic control, for lack of a better word. Proust wanted to bring it to the surface; it became the most powerful thing in us. Saint Augustine was interested in suppressing it.

CAIRNS: But I think Saint Augustine was just as much of an artist as Proust. And I think they both made the same point: that you recapture the past through imagination and not through intellect. . . . .

TATE: Mr. Maurois, is it true that in *Swann's Way* it is all memory of this second kind? For example, the section that you mentioned a moment ago, "Swann in Love," was, you said, a small classical novel. Isn't that a deliberate act of imagination, rather than memory?

MAUROIS: Oh, no. Certainly not. As we have already said, that second part is not typically Proustian.

TATE: In the beginning of the novel and at the end, we see the boy narrator, and those two parts of the book frame the middle part, which isn't actual memory.

VAN DOREN: As a matter of fact, it happened before he was born.

TATE: Now doesn't that bring us around to Proust's technique as a novelist? It seems to me one of the most interesting techniques ever devised.

MAUROIS: But again I think we find this technique only in the first and third part, whereas the second part could be the work of any great novelist. Dickens might have done it.

TATE: Or Tolstoy might have done it.

MAUROIS: But, of course, not so humorously. . . . .

CAIRNS: Proust said that all he wanted was a single moment of relief from chronological time. . . . . Time is the central theme, and all else is subordinate. There is a further point on which I would like your opinion, Mr. Maurois. Has Proust brought a new sensibility into French literature, a sensibility comparable to that of Montaigne or to that of Rousseau? Proust to me seems closer to Montaigne than to Rousseau from the point of view of sensibility.

MAUROIS: He certainly would be closer to Montaigne than to Rousseau, but I think he is original. He brings us something quite new. I pronounced the name of Bergson. I think we should come back to him. You see, Proust is really the novelist of the beginning of the twentieth century, as Bergson was its philosopher.

CAIRNS: Would you like to state what you understand to be new in Proust's contribution?

MAUROIS: Well, first of all, he sees life much more in detail than anyone before him. To Proust a minute is just as important as two years to any other novelist, and he spends as many pages to describe this one minute as anyone who writes a novel about a complete love story.

CAIRNS: He found the tremendous power of the detail. That is something that other novelists had not observed before him.

MAUROIS: That's one thing. Then another thing is that he had an idea of the relativity of sentiment, much more accurate an idea than anyone before him had. Of course, Stendhal could see that too, but Proust much better.

VAN DOREN: He must have seen human life in a very complicated pattern. Everyone notices as he reads this book the many ironies which arise out of the fact that no one individual is ever completely known by the individuals who associate with him, by the various groups among whom he passes. I take that to be true of life. No one is ever fully known by anyone. Proust reminds us of this more clearly than any other novelist does.

CAIRNS: I could not help but be struck by a parallel in Plutarch when I reread *Swann's Way* this week. You will recall that Plutarch said that he was not interested in what the men he described had done, so much as he was interested in the very minute aspects of their lives, such as an involuntary gesture or a mere glance into the eyes. He thought that revealed much more about the great men of whom he was writing than the mere record of their deeds or the books they had written, and I felt that Proust had somewhat the same technique, that it was the involuntary gesture of a particular man that revealed to Proust the hidden secrets of the man rather than the day-to-day life of the man. . . . . I take it that Proust himself figures pretty largely in the novel. You knew Proust personally, did you not, Mr. Maurois?

MAUROIS: No, I didn't know Proust. My wife knew him very well, but at a time when she was only a girl. . . . . She has many letters. They are very interesting because he took the same trouble to explain small details in writing to a small girl that he would in a novel.

VAN DOREN: Surely nothing was simple to him.

MAUROIS: No, nothing at all. But what *is* simple?

CAIRNS: How much of himself is in the book as a character?

MAUROIS: I think the narrator, the central narrator, is Proust, and he has put a great deal of himself into Swann too.

VAN DOREN: I have often suspected that, and it provides an opportunity to ask a certain question. This is, in my opinion, a great novel, perhaps the great novel of the twentieth century. I think it has a limitation, nevertheless, which can be understood if we remember how much effort is put by the author into the expression and analysis of taste. Thus, Swann is a man who is chiefly notable for his taste, and so is our hero. Our hero is exquisitely sensitive to right or wrong in taste; but less so, I should say, in the realm of action, of morals. If this book has a limitation, it is that its emphasis is upon taste rather than morals.

MAUROIS: I was going to say that the range of Proust is much smaller than the range of Tolstoy or Balzac, but at the same time, in his own sphere, he is just as great a master.

VAN DOREN: In his own sphere he is very great. I was only trying to say that his sphere is not as important as the sphere of Balzac.

CAIRNS: I recall an article you wrote, Mr. Maurois, about the time of Proust's death in *La Nouvelle Revue Française,* in which you compared him to the scientist, to the entomologist, and I wondered what you thought of the so-called laws that Proust generated in his novels. The laws, for example, that we cannot find happiness in another person; that it is impossible to know the external world. Do they strike you as valid generalizations?

MAUROIS: Yes. Of course, they are not exactly scientific laws; experimentation is not easy in the world of sentiment. But Proust had the scientific spirit. That we cannot know the external world is evident. . . . .

CAIRNS: He attached importance to them; but I have always

felt that the novel would not have suffered if the laws had been omitted.

VAN DOREN: The importance he attached to those laws and to his theories of fiction is something like the importance which Tolstoy attached to his theories. They are quite irrelevant to what the man was saying in each case.

MAUROIS: And what Tolstoy says about history is nearly always wrong.

TATE: Proust somehow got his imagination stimulated by Bergson, and it doesn't make any difference whether he understood Bergson.

VAN DOREN: It is personally very important for an artist to have a theory, but the theory isn't important as an ingredient in the art that he produces.

TATE: There is a question, Mr. Van Doren, that you brought up a minute ago about Henry James. Don't you think James and Proust are very much alike insofar as they both put the narrator or the "observer" inside the story as the central intelligence? They both carried that technical device very far, farther than any other novelists. I'd like to ask Mr. Maurois, if he is also an admirer of Henry James, what he thinks the relative value of these two writers is in that respect.

MAUROIS: I admire Henry James, but I think Proust is a greater writer. . . . . First of all, I think he writes better. Proust is not only a great novelist; he is a great poet. James sometimes, but very seldom. Also, I think that though Henry James was very intelligent, Proust's intelligence goes much further.

CAIRNS: Doesn't that go back to the point we made a little while ago: that Proust contributed a new sensibility to the world, something that James did not do?

TATE: He felt the world in a new way. I am inclined to think that James represents very much the same thing that Proust does, but that it isn't so highly developed. He is very much aware of the relativity of feeling and his characters are intensely aware of time. But they are constantly engaged in the moral evaluation of their own actions, and Proust's characters seem not to be evaluating their actions. As Mr. Van Doren says, they are largely concerned with sensibility and taste.

VAN DOREN: . . . . I should say that Proust's stories, because he tells many stories here, are in themselves more interesting than James's are.

TATE: Perhaps they are. I am not sure.

MAUROIS: You can remember Proust's characters much better than James's. . . . .

CAIRNS: I think James and Proust probably had the same aesthetic theory that the artist must have a new vision, that he must see reality through the conventional concept. But I think that Proust took it much further. . . . .

68. *The Artistic Vision of Proust**

R. IRONSIDE

A BELIEF in the moral function of aesthetic experience, one with which Proust's laborious study of Ruskin had made him familiar in a most passionate form, underlies the numerous reflections on the subject of art which recur throughout *A la Recherche du Temps Perdu,*[1] strengthening as the book proceeds until finally, when the principal characters of the novel are standing shrivelled on the edge of the grave, so many spent phenomena, it takes on the proportions of a faith, spreading a timely light over the whole darkened situation; it is then made clear that the delights of

* From *Horizon,* July 1941.

[1] *Remembrance of Things Past.*

aesthetic experience—and indeed, for the artist, the moral obligation to explore and preserve it, so that it is laid up as treasure, but so that he can, if he will, put his hands on it and display it formally, as in a monstrance—that these delights are what, in the last resort, prevent the solid ground failing beneath our feet, console us in the face of the vanity, proved in Proust's eyes, of human contacts. . . . . Mr. Derek Leon, in his recent critical biography of the writer, gives only a chapter to the "world of art." The more penetrating life by Pierre-Quint, published before the whole of *A la Recherche du Temps Perdu* has been issued, has a section "L'Art et le Sentiment du Divin," a more perspicacious title; but neither writer gives sufficient prominence, albeit among so much which deserves prominence, to Proust's positive belief in the saving graces of the arts. . . . .

The work of the impressionist painter, Elstir, plays a peculiarly revealing role in the growth of Marcel's emotional attitude to the arts, his reactions to it being at once a premonition of the position in which he finally found himself and a confession that there was little in the prevailing vision of the time which accorded with his deepest impulses. It would be vain to attempt to identify Elstir with any one historical person even if Proust did not warn us that his characters were confected from observations directed according to his requirements—or, as often, by happy chance—upon those whom he knew either personally or by their works. It is, however, not difficult to recognize, in particular phases of Elstir's development, allusions to artists whose works may be seen in public galleries. His earliest-known paintings are those of mythological subjects, forming part of the collection of the Duchesse de Guermantes . . . . In these pictures, the Muses, for example, were seen as beings belonging to some now fossilized species, but who, one felt, in the remote past might have been seen in the evening threading their way along some mountain path. . . . . Smart society accepted and acquired examples of this early manner. As a youth who was about to win a welcome in such society by means of the precocious intellectual brilliance of his views, Marcel was able to feel that art of this kind had been superseded by Impressionism and to turn with a more lively admiration to works of Elstir's Impressionist period. There is no inconsequence in this development of the artist's talent; Degas' earliest pictures *Sémiramide,* for instance, or *Les Malheurs de la Ville d'Orléans* are equally and similarly remote in subject matter from his mature productions. The portrait of the actress, *Miss Sacripant* (Odette de Crécy in fancy dress), is evidently later, though Elstir is able to qualify it as merely a "pochade de jeunesse";[2] the vicious and dreamy air of the sitter, "l'attrait irritant qu'elle allait offrir aux sens blasés ou dépravés de certains spectateurs,"[3] the independent and ambiguous interest of her somewhat piquant costume, the titillating quality of the technique of the picture which reminded Marcel, when he found it in Elstir's studio at Balbec, of the fur of a cat, the petals of a carnation, the feathers of a dove, these intriguing characteristics recall, as Albert Feuillerat has pointed out, certain portraits of Whistler. We are not, however, shown further examples of Elstir's work in precisely this manner, and the interest of Marcel's visit to the Balbec studio is concentrated upon the group of impressionist seascapes painted in that youthful, salubrious, poetic neighbourhood. These, one is bound to feel, are Monets; the lilac foam, the rocks seemingly of pink granite, the vapours of the shifting tide, the whole "poudroiement de soleil et de vagues"[4] could hardly be the product of another's vision. The fishing fleet of Elstir's *Port de Carquethuit* echoes the forest of masts in Monet's *Port de Honfleur* or *Port du Havre;* and that other canvas which renders, "au pied des immenses falaises, la grâce liliputienne des voiles blanches

[2] "Rough sketch I did when I was young."

[3] "The irritant attraction which she would offer to the jaded or depraved senses of some of her audience."

[4] "A powdery haze of sunlight" (page 188, *Within a Budding Grove*).

sur le miroir bleu où elles semblaient des papillons endormis"[5] must be a recollection of the same painter's series of the cliffs at Etretat. Shortly after the flight of Albertine, aspects of Marcel's vanished friend are vividly and painfully brought before him by two paintings, "où dans un paysage touffu il y a des femmes nues"[6] and in one of which "l'une des jeunes filles lève le pied.... De l'autre elle pousse à l'eau l'autre jeune fille qui gaiement résiste, la cuisse levée, son pied trempant à peine dans l'eau bleue,"[7] a scene which at once gives expression to Marcel's vision of Albertine's illicit passions and recalls the "méandre de cou de cygne"[8] of her thighs as she lay in bed beside him. The brief account we are given of these works suggests Renoir's large *Baigneuses* of 1885 and the lovely series of smaller canvasses of which it is the centrepiece. Yet this suggestion is interesting simply because it prompts us to pursue the image of Albertine and her laundress among Renoir's productions in this manner. At such a critical moment Marcel was in no fit state to ponder upon artistic quality, to form opinions upon the trend of Elstir's painting by making comparisons between the bathers and the pictures he had studied at Balbec. The former, indeed, are introduced merely to sharpen the anguish of his bereft condition. At another stage, Elstir is revealed to us as the author of a series, which we may attribute to Degas, of works devoted to what then seemed the novel theme of woman, "surprise dans l'intime de sa vie de tous les jours,"[9] pictures which discover unsuspected graces in the move-

[5] "At the foot of immense cliffs, the liliputian grace of white sails on the blue mirror on whose surface they looked like butterflies asleep" (page 192, *Within a Budding Grove*).

[6] "Showing against a leafy background nude women" (page 153, *The Sweet Cheat Gone*).

[7] "One of the girls is raising her foot, ... with her other foot she is pushing into the water the other girl, who gaily resists, her hip bent, her foot barely submerged in the blue water" (page 154, *The Sweet Cheat Gone*).

[8] Swan's neck curve (page 154, *The Sweet Cheat Gone*).

[9] . . . . "caught in familiar everyday living."

ments of women doing their hair, drying themselves, warming their feet. That there was a distinct flavour of Degas in Elstir's composite style might already have been inferred from the enthusiasm with which he described to Marcel, on the occasion of the visit to the Balbec studio, the luminous spectacle of the racecourse. Yet his interest in this motif from modern life is surpassed by his admiration of the airy splendours of a regatta, bathed in the "glauque lumière d'un hippodrome marin,"[10] as rich in the possibilities of exploitation, for a contemporary artist, as the ponderous magnificence of the nautical ceremonies of Venice for Carpaccio. This delight is, of course, Monet's; Degas' racecourses and jockeys are accessory, their role in Elstir's conversation being simply to amplify the general assertion that it is a vision of modern life which chiefly inspires the painter. The series of pictures showing women at their toilet is even less essential to Elstir's true significance in the story, serving primarily, indeed, to throw a surprising light on the capacities of Madame Verdurin, for it was she, we learn, who first suggested to Elstir this field of study and who had originally attracted his attention to many of the subjects from which he derived his happiest effects; Marcel recognized that Madame Verdurin considered herself to be a muse, but was shocked at his lack of perception on discovering that she had real grounds for this opinion. The art of Elstir is thus used, its characteristics multiplied, while it remains, in the broadest sense of the term, impressionist, to develop plots and touch up characters, without enlarging in any way our knowledge of Marcel's aesthetic response to it; it tells us, for instance, about the past of Odette de Crécy or the fashionable limits to the artistic tastes of the Guermantes. In what manner its qualities enriched Marcel's emotional life can only properly be studied with reference to the works of Elstir-Monet. Marcel's feelings about these pictures bore no relation to the attitude of mind in which con-

[10] "Greenish light of a marine race-course" (page 276, *Within a Budding Grove*).

noisseurs of impressionism so often indulge, that attitude which can regard a Renoir as a delicious morsel, or a Pissarro as if it exhaled the bouquet of some discreet but exquisite wine and that seems to shrink from the unfettered brilliance of the latest Monets, leaning upon the more obvious refinements of his early pictures. Marcel's reactions were of a more profound and even disturbing kind; Elstir certainly convinced him of those commonplaces in the criticism of impressionism, the beauties of the modern social scene, the elegance of contemporary dress and gestures, explained to him also that atmosphere and light properly apprehended can transfigure the ugliness of modern constructions so that their shapes seem quite subsidiary to the radiance they reflect. But such views could not have been immediately welcome to a devoted student of Ruskin, "ce puissant cerveau."[11] They may have indirectly provoked Marcel's delight in the Trocadéro, not, however, because he saw it catching, or refracting, or shimmering in, the light, but because it recalled the formal architecture in certain backgrounds of Mantegna; Marcel passionately loved the past, and his power of observing externals was as limited as his gift for exploring character was extensive and penetrating. He was thus ill-qualified to enjoy straightforwardly and simply the impressionist vision of the world, one which arose from the sensitivity of the artist's retina, from his acute perception of the most rapid moments of weather, the most transitory and instinctive of human movements, and was not one elaborated from the semiconscious regions of personality. Marcel's individual judgment, however, would seem to class the Balbec seascapes as the fruits of some such subjective vision. For him, they presented a succession of metaphors, as in a poem, metaphors moreover of a sibyline character, almost misrepresentations, so that at first glance the reverse of their author's intentions was conveyed to the reader. Looking at the *Port de Carquethuit* he saw the

[11] "the powerful intellect."

masts of the boats moored at the jetty as so many pinnacles built on dry land, while the churches of Criquebec seemed to emerge from the water "soufflées en albâtre ou en écume et enfermées dans la ceinture d'un arc-en-ciel versicolore,"[12] a mystic and unreal picture. Elsewhere, in the same work, a boat which should have been sailing in mid-ocean appeared to be riding through the town; another, upon a sunlit stretch of water white with foam, seemed to be rising out of a field of snow; the ocean itself was part sky, the sky part ocean. A palace mirrored in the water became, under this transmuting lens, a symmetrical object, so deceptive was the identity between it and its reflection; in a similar fashion, the spires of a riverside town seemed to hold in suspense, like pendulums, the houses clustering beneath them. It was a world of mirages which, however, as Marcel was quick to realise, were evolved from certain optical tricks recurring in Nature for those whose eyes were sufficiently "innocent" to perceive them. The absence of all apparent sequence between the causes and effects of such phenomena charmed his imagination. It was a source of delight to Marcel, conjuring up a sense of poetic correspondences, that nature and, indeed, human nature should so often prove to be the exact contrary of what it appeared to be, that the most bizarre and striking apparitions, the social conduct of Charlus, for instance, may be the result of some not uncommon natural accident. Elstir's work was, for him, composed from those rare moments "ou l'on voit la nature telle qu'elle est, poètiquement."[13] The design of the pictures, the dexterity of brushwork they revealed, the actual physical facts of the artist's translation of his vision were evidently quite subordinate considerations in Marcel's eyes; it was the reconciliation effected between the fan-

[12] "Blown in alabaster or in sea-foam, and, enclosed in the band of a parti-colored rainbow, to form an unreal, a mystical picture" (page 188, *Within a Budding Grove*).

[13] "In which we see nature as she is, with poetic vision" (page 186, *Within a Budding Grove*).

tastic and the real that gave the key to their beauty. More than that of Degas, Pissarro, or Sisley, more even than that of Renoir, the painting of Monet may be explored in this somewhat romantic manner. He was the most Turnerian of the impressionists; his art springs from a deep well of poetry, a sense of ravished amazement at the unparalleled splendours of nature so that to many eyes his snowfields glow with an iridescence, his seas shine with a multitude of lights that, like the electric visions of Turner, are a reproach to the lovely effects they imitate. Yet we must suppose that Marcel, to whom the spectacle of nature was a heraldic field the signs of which were meaningless until they recalled some moment of his history (or until their symbolism seemed actually to press for an interpretation) could not have felt that impressionism in any of its forms fulfilled the secret demands of his temperament. We may even conclude that Marcel's admiration for impressionism contained an element of artificiality. He could not doubt that the growing prestige of its adherents was deserved; he could not fail to recognize that theirs was the major contribution of the time to the evolution of painting, or indeed that such recognition would range him among an intellectual élite, even amid "les cénacles qui préparent les apothéoses."[14] He, in fact, half surrenders before Elstir, before an art which set an absolute value upon appearances, those feelings which rose at uncertain intervals from the remote corners of his mind, which filled him with a sweetness and a beatitude which in the end he comes to identify with the material out of which a work of art is constructed.

. . . . One would not . . . . identify the visionary elements in Proust with the standardized Surrealism which rigidly adheres, like Byzantine art, to a now well known set of images; it might be more precise to consider him as a protagonist of the more elastic "surnaturalisme" of Gerard de Nerval whose

[14] "the exalted councils who decree their canonization."

Sylvie he greatly admired. Yet he was certainly intimately engaged in the same spheres of the mind as those the Surrealists of today may be said to have popularized and his interpretation of appearances is often akin to theirs. To affirm, as Proust does, that by the juxtaposition of two different objects, by the establishment of a bond of union between them so that they are freed from the contingencies of time, an artist may extract their essenial significance, is to make a characteristically Surrealist claim. . . . . He loves the great painters of the past not for their draughtsmanship or colour but because the mysterious courtesans of Carpaccio or Rembrandt's Bathsheba are absolutely original figures from a world existing in their author's mind and not elsewhere, the expression of which makes possible a "communication des âmes" such as Marcel felt to have been effected as he listened to Vinteuil's quartet. Without pausing to examine in detail the *intellectual* truths which Proust evolved from his conscious memory and which are embodied in his vast story of the society and individuals amongst whom Marcel moved, we can say that Proust's observation of his characters was also touched by surrealism; they develop in a surprising and hazardous manner, are linked by fantastic coincidences, each has a hundred masks, a vital but never a logical unity; they are multiple images and are the more persuasively alive inasmuch as Proust succeeds in establishing a sort of irrational but inevitable relationship between the various inconsistent aspects they assume, a relationship which is convincing because the characters are composed without reference to other data than those provided by Proust's personal impressions; their unity is that of Proust's, of a single individual's, private vision. They can have their original being elsewhere no more than Carpaccio's courtesans, Elstir's roses or Rembrandt's old women can have taken shape outside the painters' imagination. . . . .

The figure of Elstir is clearly inadequate as the exponent of Proust's aesthetic "doctrines" as they finally emerge. We cannot doubt that he was an impressionist painter, but we can deny that the aesthetic doctrine of the impressionists accorded in any way with Proust's most earnest feelings on this subject. One is bound to regret the revelations the reader would surely have enjoyed, if the art of Elstir had been composed not of fragments chiefly from Monet and from Degas and Renoir, but, instead, from Picasso, Klee, Chagall and Ernst. His conception of the springs of beauty must be considered as nourished upon Ruskin from whose voluminous meditations, from whose enthusiasms and aversions may be extracted a pervasive opinion that art is the language of imagination, an opinion which took root in Proust's mind and which, under the light of his own imaginative experience, grew to embrace an automatic psychological symbolism (related to surrealism), by means of which imaginative truths were conveyed to him; though he by no means despised the unaided workings of the intellect, his admiration of these was qualified by his knowledge that inspiration was too spasmodic to support alone the task he had set himself. But inspiration, as he conceived it, however elusive, remained the fountain of beauty and there was a duty to pursue it far into the heart.

69. *The Waters under the Earth**

PHILO BUCK, JR.

. . . . MARCEL PROUST is not an easy writer. Concerned more with "the life of the mind" than with action, his very sentences have the sinuous, labyrinthine, and apparent aimlessness of a stream lost in a tropical morass.

* From his *Directions in Contemporary Literature,* Oxford University Press, New York, 1942.

They have nothing in common with the direct and efficient utterance of everyday time-table life. Take . . . . [the] opening sentence from his last volume: . . . . [It] does not pretend to be a description giving the recipe of a place, a panorama, in order that a conventional landscape painter might follow directions and put the scene together. Much rather it is the way the place sensuously awoke in the memory of the artist, sentient image calling up sentient image, until this whole was complete. Literally one feels, sees, tastes, and smells his way through Proust's novels. Curiously, only at rare intervals does one hear.

Reading Proust, thus, is to call into intense activity all of the varied sense responses to life. And this is a power that most find rather difficult to awaken. We want our sense responses given to us easy and ready made, and none too complicated. But here is Proust. Rosy candlelight—we let it go at that—by him is called "the twilight of a flower." Where has the magic power of the sense of smell been better displayed? To most now it is an atrophied sense with the most abjectly limited range; but once it was the rival of sight. . . . . And who of us can touch and taste silence? Milton's "smoothing the raven down of darkness till it smiled" was literary imagery of the first magnitude. Proust finds this symphony of odors "saturated with the fine bouquet of a silence so nourishing, so succulent"; and Proust is a glutton for literary imagery.

Perhaps . . . . [his] long sentences and sense impressions are difficult to read, but the experiences also were difficult for the author; they are to him the ultimate reality, "the only reality that exists for each of us, our own sensitiveness to impressions." To awaken these impressions in a reader, to call up in him the sensitive memory where these lie stored, demands a style leisurely, yet scrupulously exact, and calling for design very different from that of mere logical description.

Again, contrary to what has been written and said, Proust is not, like James Joyce or even Virginia Woolf, following the "stream of consciousness." To be sure his adventures are all of them underground adventures of the mind. None of his characters, and least of all he, Marcel, the narrator and chief character, ever does anything or earns an achievement. But he is not like Joyce, following the train that makes up the annoying, humorless, recital of significance and insignificance that is the *Ulysses*. . . . . But beyond the fact that both Joyce and Proust are concerned with the movement of the mind, there is between them all the difference in the world. It is precisely this difference between the significant and the insignificant that Proust is engaged to explore. He finds the secret in memory, but memory quite disassociated from Time, as we count its hours.[1]

But Proust's memory is a very different thing from the memory as we think of it in the memoranda of diaries or the statistical record of doings that we for convenience file away for reference. "What were you doing at twelve o'clock on the thirtieth of June, last year?" Such a question might be able to elicit a very definitely detailed answer, such as an attorney or jury might find satisfactory for an alibi. . . . . But can one call up the special sensations and images, fresh and immediate and vital, of that day in June, with its full background into which all sense details fall into perfect place? At times like

[1] It would be interesting, were it possible here, to relate this practice of Proust to the theory of Bergson on time and memory in the two books of his that preceded the appearance of Proust's sequence of novels: *Time and Free Will* and *Creative Evolution*. It is the former that is probably the more significant. For example the importance of a sentence like this to Proust's method: "Hence there are finally two different selves, one of which is, as it were, the external projection of the other, its spatial and, so to speak, social representation. We reach the former by deep introspection, which leads us to grasp our inner states as living things, constantly *becoming,* as states not amenable to measure, which permeate one another and of which the succession in duration has nothing in common with juxtaposition in homogeneous space. But the moments at which we thus grasp are rare, and that is just why we are rarely free. The greater part of the time we live outside ourselves, hardly perceiving anything of ourselves but our own ghost, a colourless shadow which pure duration projects into homogeneous space."

But the differences between Proust and Bergson are probably even more significant than their similarities. For it is not the flux, the undifferentiated movement of pure time and ultimate reality that Proust attempts to capture. For him memory does not arrest time, but abolishes it, and it is not the flux that he captures, as does Joyce in *Ulysses,* but something to him far more precious and eternally stable.

these the past lives again in the present, and the present in the past. Indeed when once past and present thus fuse, each has lost its place in the calendar, the time table has telescoped into a single entry, and for this one moment time was, is, and is no more.

It is hard to capture these moments of intense living at the same time in the past and the present. The immediate causes or stimuli that strive to call them up, though strong, may not be quite clear enough, or we not quite adept enough to follow the clue. . . . .

Proust, like all of us, sensed the difficulty of allowing these buried ghosts again to be real, and past experience to be even more vital than it was when new and fresh, because now it has been fused with the vital present. He felt its call as it strove to awaken to new consciousness and stretch to capacity its power of sensuous response. . . . . Yet when once the depths had given up part of their treasure of memory, then the power of exploring to the full its rich significance became a flight into a known and controllable region. . . . .

In these magic moments to Proust occur the revelation of true personality, the ultimate reality of self. . . . .

Great literature is full of . . . . occasions, ... "impressions" as Proust calls them, that reveal true personality to itself and to others. Perhaps of all great authors Shakespeare is the most alert to the significance of these mysterious depths from which on occasion our real selves emerge, and to the "laws" of their emergence. What a stranger the stricken Macbeth is to his wife—even more to himself; how completely Lear baffles all who have long known him; how Othello denies his early and habitual simple-mindedness and generosity. This mysterious region of the subconscious and its significance for behavior have long been known to great art.

The new psychology is not so new except in its terminology and technique, and in making its discoveries available for relieving suffering. We are learning, as Proust tells us he learned, to be a little more expert in discovering the keys that unlock the hidden trap-doors that conceal the living but yet unconscious past.

To Proust the richest store in the subconscious is memory, and through its awakening comes the discovery of the real in human personality. The present, to him, with its crowd of sensations and thoughts, is not real. It is only the superficies of life, the ripples on the surface, which seem terribly significant if one's view is only of the surface, while below are the unplumbed depths filled with mysterious and invisible and sometimes sinister life. Even a war as great as the First World War sometimes has less signicance to Proust than the glimpses he can catch as he gazes into his past.

. . . . So he set out in his series of novels on the search for the past, and only after a diligent and baffled quest did he succeed, as he describes it in the last volume of the sequence, in achieving its recapture.

Anything, even the least irrelevance, may be the occasion that will spring the lock of the trap-door. . . . .

It is the immobility of the reason, the practical sense, and clock time that make the world about us so seemingly waste, dead, and immobile. "Perhaps the immobility of the things about us is lent them by the immobility of our thought as it contemplates them." Break this immobility by awakening memory, and the world again suddenly becomes alive, alive with the past and the present vibrating in unison. In *The Guermantes' Way* he describes the process as almost the manner of a spider achieving a web. "In this manner the reaches of my memory little by little was filled with focal points which in their arrangement, in their grouping each in relation to the other, in this weaving between themselves threads more and more numerous, imitated those finished works of art, where not a single brush stroke is for itself, where each receives from the others its reason for being as it imposes its own on all." Memory thus in itself becomes a work of art, rich, organic, and complete. It reveals the reality beneath the appearance, for it transmutes the appearance as it fuses it with the treasure-house of the past.

The most interesting and significant things in Proust are his many and illuminating descriptions of how the past was recaptured. . . . .

The revelation comes with a thrill of exhilaration, like a fresh wind from the mountains when one has been living in the crowded commonplace. . . . . And he draws an enjoyment from the renewal quite different from the enjoyment of the original experience of which these memories are now the real essence. Then the mind was perhaps too fatigued, too encumbered to taste their full sensuous savor. Now they come disencumbered of all save their abiding essence, and thus flooding the mind make complete the happiness of this new and abiding moment.

Why this happiness? Because in this vivid sentient moment time has been abolished, the clock of the mind that marks the rhythm of the hours is silent, and the moment is eternal. Its qualities are independent of time as they are of formal relationship. They are as organically a whole as a flower or a perfume. Here the past and the present have fused, the individual with feet planted in the present and surrounded with its circumstance is viewing through its medium the panorama of the past, and both in the vivid moment of consciousness are indistinguishable. It is as though one were witnessing a cinema of more than one reel, where the multiple images blend so perfectly that one is unaware of their different source. More than this, during the sentient moment, as Proust lived it, even all sense of duration is suspended. Of such to him is the nature of the essence of reality, it is timeless; and it is to the study of these moments that he now devotes his released imagination.

But there is even more reason for happiness. Being timeless these moments are eternal and confer upon the beholder for the moment the experience of immortality. . . . .

But again there is nothing new or revolutionary in this discovery by Proust. Dante's vision of *The Divine Comedy* is a succession of such imaginative moments of eternal value, with a range from the depths to the heights of achievable human experience. In these, as again did Proust, he fused his own past with the past of all humanity. Only Dante does not stop to inquire, as does the experimental psychologist, just what morsel of food it was, or the odor of what flower, that sent his imagination backward until he again had the comradeship of his beloved Virgil or the ecstasy of his radiant Beatrice. All great literature in its highest moments are thus both intimately personal and confer upon the author the sense of immortality. These moments because they have thus been intensely vivid are of the nature of the eternal. And because they have been adequately set down in prose and verse, on the adequate reader they again confer the blessings of immortality; for they too defy time and seasons, immobilized as they are for all eternity.[2]

Such moments bring happiness to Proust because they are a revelation of the real personality, which otherwise is always masked under the commonplace of routine time. But is it always of the same personality? For personality is to Proust only the "conglomerate of sensations" revealed in the lightning flash of these sentient moments. But it is only of "the person we then were." . . . .

So much then for the real in personality. It is not a cha-

[2] Saint Augustine long before in his *Confessions* tells of his long study of memory and its surprising revelations. "Great is the force of memory, excessive great, O my God; a large and infinite sanctuary, who shall penetrate to its depths?" He makes the effort, like Proust, and what is his discovery? Again like Proust's, it is a joyous discovery and the fulfilment of his highest desires. "Since therefore I learned to know thee, hast thou still kept in my memory; and there do I find thee, whenever I call thee to remembrance, and delight myself in thee. These be my holy delights which thou hast bestowed upon me." There is a difference between what the two found.

meleon taking color from circumstance, but a succession of sentient moments; it is ever created anew as in memory it captures the past. It is not, as in Gide, revealed in action, but in the quality of its sensitiveness, in its passive receptivity to the ebb and flow of memory. It is these that bring the happiness that its revelation ensures; mere action or physical enjoyment on the other hand are always succeeded by disappointment, and this is the sign of their base alloy. . . . .

There is something of the attitude of the drug addict in this desire—is there not?—to reduce life to a succession of sensuously rich memories of things past. A discriminating French critic, Raymond Fernandez, has written: "Proust suffered from a complete powerlessness to achieve consciousness of life other than under conditions of purely passive receptivity." True. But is there not more that can be laid to his charge? Did he not encourage a sensitive alertness to these visions of the past to an extent that might more adequately be described as morbid? A morbid exploiting of his sensuous past. Thus he finds personality an incoherent sequence of almost dream states, and experience an incoherence of kaleidoscopic impressions. Is not this a sign of a certain type of psychic morbidity, a supersensitiveness that may be defended in a creature like a jellyfish that is always at the mercy of its environment?

It is this that makes most of the motives that govern his various characters more or less morbid. . . . .

All art is autobiography. So Marcel Proust has it in the last volume of his series. No artist can get outside of his own memories; and those of this Frenchman were not what one would call normal. There was something morbid in the life, even the external life, of this author, whose highest dread was sunlight and fresh air. Is it then any wonder that in the reality he discovers for us, and which he transfers to the canvas of his novels, there is likewise so little of the invigorating and the life-giving? For him likewise the reader of a work of art reads into it always nothing more than the reader's own autobiography—his own memories of things past. For this reason, if for no other, many a reader whose life has in it something of the sun and the outdoors, finds that Proust's reality, though ever so real, is for him also exotic and having the perfume of the hospital and death chamber. Is not the criticism then by Aldous Huxley,[3] though unfair, at least significant? . . . .

It is the death of an old order that Marcel Proust so cunningly devises and lives to the life. We perhaps too glibly use the word decadent. If it has any meaning it must associate itself with a life that has lost its motive for existence and is seeking for something spurious, the search for the sensation that accompanies action rather than for the action, the exploiting of the emotion rather than of the genuine impulse. And morbidity and illness sharpen sensations and give an added poignancy to emotion. Thus Proust's characters live on the fringes of action, in the regions of their accompanying emotions and sensations. Even an event like the World War gives only one minor character a generous impulse. It is the beauty of the aeroplanes and the searchlights that impresses Proust, that and the thrill that accompanies the detonation of bombs. His books are almost a celebration of the ecstasy of ill-health.

To those to whom an illness is ecstasy the healthy seems banal and unreal. . . . . But as a painter of this illness, though he himself was afflicted with the malady, Proust became also one of the most penetrating critics of a degenerate society of men and women like himself. Better, perhaps because he went to the roots of the disease, he has written the epic of the *mal de siècle* that came to an end with the First World War. As Gide described one of its symptoms, Proust psychoanalyzed it and recorded in seven novels the result of his investigation.

[3] In *Eyeless in Gaza.*—G. D. L.

AUTHOR INDEX